DEDICATION

To my father, Robert Alton Nelson, who believed I could accomplish anything I wanted in life.

To my grandfather, Leland Russell Smith, who spent every single day with me, working and playing, through seven consecutive summers.

And to my mule, Ingersoll, whose quick and sensible thinking and actions saved me from three life-threatening situations while I was writing this history.

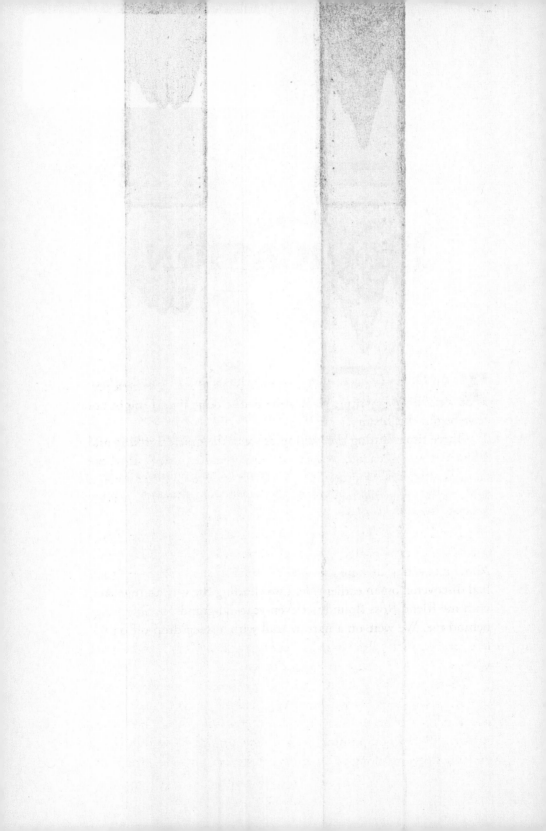

FOREWORD

About ten years ago, a Mormon bishop asked me to teach a personal history writing class. If he hadn't done that, I might not have begun this history.

Three times during the writing process, the quick thinking and actions of a big-headed, long-eared, ugly guardian angel saved me from life-threatening situations. It was almost like a sinister force of some kind was trying to prevent me from finishing this history, but it seemed my mule, Ingersoll, was always there to save me.

The first incident happened in a side canyon to Comb Wash near the Natural Bridges National Monument in Southern Utah. About a dozen of us were riding to see some ancient cliff dwellings I had discovered on an earlier ride. I was leading the way on Ingersoll, with my friend Ross Boundy's eleven-year-old grandson, Sol, riding behind me. We were on a narrow trail with a steep drop-off on the left, covered with a thick tangle of tamarisk trees. On the right was a steep, rocky ridge. The trail was perhaps a foot wide.

I'm not sure what hit my hat, but suddenly the front brim was over my eyes and I couldn't see. As I raised my hand to adjust the hat, a broken-off tree limb, about as big around as a man's arm, struck my left knee, pushing between my leg and the saddle. Since we were clipping along at about five miles per hour, it didn't take more than an instant for the limb to roll Sol and me out of the saddle. We tumbled against the steep bank and slipped under the mule's belly. I was fully aware that my right foot was slowing down my slide because it was still in the stirrup. Frantically, I was wiggling my foot, finally feeling it slip from the stirrup.

Then I turned toward Sol, who was crying. Except for having the wind knocked out of him, he seemed all right. By this time we were on our backs, my right side pressing against the back of the mule's front legs and Sol's left side against the hind legs. We rolled onto our hands and knees and tried to stand up, the steep bank forcing us to bump and push against the mule's side as we did so. Then we worked to the front, rubbing against the mule's side until we were safely in front of him. It wasn't until we started walking ahead to a wider spot in the trail that Ingersoll finally moved his feet. I don't believe he moved any of his feet, even an inch, while we were on our backs beneath him and later pushing against him to get up.

Most horses or mules in a situation like this, even the well-broken ones, will charge forward to get out of the way. Had that happened, my foot might not have slipped from the stirrup, and as the horse began to drag me, the steep bank would have rolled me under the hooves. If I didn't have my foot in the stirrup, in hopping over us, the horse could easily have kicked either or both of us in the head, or stepped on us, crushing bones and organs. None of these alternatives are good, and Ingersoll seemed to know that.

He is what some horsemen call a hot blood. That means he is full of spunk and spirit. He is always thinking and moving, sometimes too quickly for children and inexperienced riders. Hot blood is good if you want to clip along all day at five or six miles per hour without needing to kick and spur. But hot blood is usually bad when you get in a tight spot like that described above. Not with Ingersoll, however. He somehow was able to turn off the hot blood switch and stand there like Dobbin the plow horse when the situation required such behavior.

A few years later, my son Russell and his friend Matt Knight packed with me into Wyoming's Wind River Wilderness for a late summer fishing trip. We found our fish at Rainbow Lake, more than twenty miles from the trailhead, with all the rainbows, cutthroats, and brown trout we could eat, and then we headed back.

We were riding along a Forest Service trail through a pine forest. The air down where we were was warm and calm, but the tops of the trees were being thrashed by a brisk afternoon wind. I was leading the way on Henrietta, my pinto mare, with Ingersoll close behind carrying our camp outfit. Matt was further back on Huck, my gray team-roping horse. Russell was following on foot, farther back and out of sight.

All of a sudden Ingersoll's nose was in my back, his chest pushing against the mare's behind, like he was trying to hurry us faster down the trail. The trail was too narrow for him to pass and get ahead of us. This was a highly unusual thing for him to do, because Henrietta has an attitude. If other horses crowd her or invade her space, especially if they touch her, she has a tendency to kick them. Ingersoll usually respects her dominance, but not now.

Looking around, I tried to figure out what was bothering him. Up ahead, and to the left, I noticed a place where small branches and pine cones were falling from the upper forest canopy. At first I thought Ingersoll had spotted a bear high in the trees, but that was not the case. A tall pine tree, large in diameter, was falling in our direction. I could hear splintering noises from breaking limbs and roots.

Since the falling tree was in front and to the left, it seemed to me the shortest path to safety was to turn around and go back. But Ingersoll had already decided the best way to go was straight ahead. The several seconds it might take to convince him to turn back might be the difference between life and death, so I leaned forward and kicked the mare into an all-out charge. As we raced ahead, Ingersoll's head and shoulders were pressing hard against her left hip.

Fortunately, Matt had the good judgment to let Huck plunge ahead after the other horses, reaching full stride just as the green lodgepole pine tree crashed across the trail behind him. We stopped the horses and looked back. The big tree was silent now, but small branches and pine cones were still falling from the canopy. We tied up the horses and walked back. The fallen tree looked to be about sixteen inches in diameter, probably weighing several tons. It blocked the trail at the exact spot where I had first seen the pine cones falling from the sky.

As we pondered what had happened, we realized what had saved us—Ingersoll's quick decision to hurry forward and the willingness of the rest of us to do the same. A half-second delay would indeed have been the difference between life and death. As we waited for Russell, Matt pulled out his knife and carved a message on the portion of tree now blocking the trail. "Matt Knight was here, September 5, 2010, when this tree fell on the trail."

As this history was in the final stages of editing, early summer 2011, Ingersoll came to the rescue once again. We had hauled a trailer full of horses to the little town of Notom on the east side of Capitol Reef National Monument, where we were to meet a Hollywood movie packager for a day ride through a narrow canyon along Pleasant Creek through the remote south end of the park. There were no groomed trails or ranger station at the access point. I had been there twice before and had never seen another person along the trail, only wild sheep, deer, and cougar sign. Our destination was an impressive panel along a cliff face, which contained many primitive Native American drawings.

The guest didn't show, and since we had hauled the horses so far, Bryce and Jessica Mortimer and I decided to do the ride anyway.

As we were approaching the main panel of Indian writings, I saw what looked like more writings at the base of a cliff on the bench above us. A steep slope blocked our way, but it didn't look too steep for Ingersoll, so I leaned forward and urged him up the bank.

We hadn't gone far when we came to a place where his hind feet were pushing against a rock shelf. The shelf broke, allowing his hind feet to drop and sink into the soft matter below, which caused a shift to the rear of his center of gravity. We were in trouble, about to go over backward. I debated whether or not to bail out, like jumping out of a car anticipating a roll-over in a sharp curve. I removed all but my toes from the stirrups.

Ingersoll corrected the center of gravity problem by lowering his neck and thrusting his nose as far forward as possible, while at the same time lowering the front part of his body by dropping to his knees. We were not going over backward, but we were still in danger. If he tried to go right or left, we could roll down the slope, and he had been unable to find any solid footing for his hind feet.

Next, he did something I have never seen a horse or mule do in a situation like this. He decided to return to the bottom of the slope, but rather than spin around and go head first like horses and mules are inclined to do, still on his knees, he spread his hind legs wide to each side and slowly slid backward to the bottom. The ride was so smooth that I was never in danger of losing a stirrup or falling off.

As soon as we reached the bottom, I assessed the damage. The first hind foot to slide off the broken shelf had a bad cut several inches above the hoof. Blood was running over the hoof. The hair was rubbed off both front knees, plus there were numerous scrapes and bruises in other places. The shin bones on his front legs must have taken a beating, because he took turns lifting one front foot and then the other, like he was seeking relief from the pain. I rode him to a deep place in the river to let the cold water wash away the blood and dirt and relieve the pain.

Over the next few weeks we changed the dressing on the deep cut every four or five days. When it was time to remove the last and final dressing, I asked my granddaughter Savannah to do it and then was distracted by something else going on in the barnyard before I could give her instructions on how to do it. When I looked for Savannah a few minutes later, she was crouched close to the ground in front of the mule's hind feet, pushing and pulling on the dressing which was difficult to remove. She had led Ingersoll to a shady spot under a maple tree on the front lawn, dropped the lead rope on the ground, and proceeded to go to work. She had never done anything like this before, and I had not told her this mule would not hurt her. She just seemed to know that on her own, since he occasionally lifted the foot, as a person would, to make her work easier. After the dressing was removed, we applied more medicine, hoping he would be ready to ride, drive, and pack again in another week or so. By that time the book would be at the press and my work would be finished—time for a break and more horseback adventures in the wild places of Utah, Nevada, and Wyoming.

Because of my interest in Native American and African Gold Coast culture and lore, I suppose I could have called this history *Drumbeats*. Because of my feelings for the people I write about here, I could have called it *Heartbeats.*

I've known people who claim in all sincerity that they enjoy the protection of guardian angels. I am one of them. But as described above, I also seem to have the protection of a guardian mule—or jackass—so I call my history *Hoofbeats.*

—Lee Nelson
authorleenelson@gmail.com

"Words are seals of the mind, results—or, more correctly, stations—of an infinite series of experiences which reach from an unimaginable distant past into the present, and which feel their way into an equally unimaginable distant future. They are the "audible that clings to the inaudible," the forms and potentialities of thought, which grow from that which is beyond thought.

"The essential nature of words is, therefore, neither exhausted by their present meaning, nor is their importance confined to their usefulness as transmitters of thoughts and ideas, but they express at the same time qualities which are not translatable into concepts—just as a melody which, though it may be associated with a conceptual meaning, cannot be described by words or by any other medium of expression. And it is just that irrational quality that stirs up our deepest feelings, elevates our innermost being, and makes it vibrate with others."

—Tibetan Mystic Anagarika Brahmacari Govinda
Foundations of Tibetan Mysticism
York Beach, Maine: Red Wheel/Weiser, 1969
and
—Chinese philosopher Lao-tzu
(604 bc–531 bc)

PROLOGUE

The greatest thing a human soul ever does in this world is to see something and tell what it saw in a plain way. Hundreds of people can talk for one who can think, but thousands can think for one who can see. To see clearly is poetry, prophecy, and religion—all in one.

—John Ruskin
English critic, essayist, and
reformer (1819–1900)

I was speaking at a personal history conference in Mapleton, Utah, and as sometimes happens, I found myself saying something that was not in my notes. I was explaining a probable situation, a very serious and sober possibility that I had never thought about before. It went like this: If I died unexpectedly, without having written my personal history, I could see what would probably happen. Before my body had a chance to start decomposing, one of my kind and loving sisters would decide to write my story for me so that my numerous progeny would know the story of my life. Both of the sisters who might attempt such a project are intelligent, college-educated adults. Having known me all my life, either one would be able to produce a beautiful and perhaps lengthy piece of work. And

1

while they were doing it, *I would be turning in my grave.*

No matter how good and noble the intent might be, they would get it wrong. They could not help but get it wrong. They would not be able to tell my story the way I remember it, nor in the way I would want it told—not even close.

Then I wondered about all those departed souls on the other side, whose biographies have been written by well-meaning relatives who knew them even less than my sisters know me. How many of those departed souls are regretting that they didn't write something down before it was too late? How frustrated are they that the too-brief stories of their lives, often written by people who didn't know them, miss the mark by such a great distance?

Driving home from the meeting, with these sobering and disturbing thoughts still in my mind, I decided to wrap up the story of my life. I had worked on it for about ten years, and now it was time, while I was still in control, to get it published. I hadn't finished a book since retiring and signing up for social security. I was tired of resting. If I didn't die any time soon, and if I decided future happenings and events needed to be added, I could do an updated and revised edition later.

When I started writing this history, I thought I was doing it for my posterity, but the further I got into it, the more I realized I was doing it for myself too. I was wiping away cobwebs that were hiding long-forgotten events. I was discovering what I began to call the imperfect truth: events that may have seemed matter-of-fact and insignificant when they happened, but in wiping away the dust, I would find a little something—usually not very profound—that helped direct or shape my future and determine what I eventually became.

My life made more sense to me as I wrote about it. I began to see pattern and purpose instead of accidents and dead ends. As I wrote about regrets and mistakes, the kinds of things you wish you could turn the clock back and do over, I began to see some of these events as wonderful learning opportunities preparing me for future events.

Shortly before I started writing my history, Ed Morin, a Mormon bishop, asked me to teach a personal history-writing course in Sunday School. I told him this could not be a class where I just talked about personal history and told funny stories. My students would be required to do the work; to write their life stories while attending the class, and they would have to be willing from time to time to read portions of their stories in class. This would be a class with homework, and those who wouldn't do the work couldn't come.

The wise bishop knew that some of the people, those who needed the class most, would balk at the requirement to read personal items out loud in front of a group. He decided to meet with prospective students individually and ask for personal commitments to attend the class and do the work for a certain period of time, like twelve weeks. And so it began.

Writing personal history is not like writing an algebra textbook or an article about the ideology of Karl Marx. Writing a personal history is nothing more, or less, than telling the stories of your life; some are short and funny and some are longer and more serious. Sometimes you explain at the end of a story what you learned, and sometimes you don't. Everyone can do this; it's easier than you think.

I tell my classes that writing a personal history is the easiest kind of writing a person can do, because you have already done the research by living your life. When you start writing, the hardest part is already behind you.

Sometimes the female students, or stay-at-home housewives, would say their lives were not interesting enough to justify a personal history. At first this worried me. Perhaps they were right. But as students began reading their stories in class, I became convinced that none of my students were boring people, especially the stay-at-home housewives who were raising children and providing service in the community.

One day a woman who had lived in Mapleton her entire life read a story about having warts on her face when she was a teenager and was beginning to think about boys and dating. As I remember her story, she described the warts and how embarrassed she was when anybody noticed them. Medical products and treatments didn't seem to help.

Some local sisters from the Church gathered at her home to discuss the warts. They offered a sincere prayer that the warts would go away. Then they collected money, which they put in a jar so the girl could receive a quarter every time one of the warts disappeared. Over several months, one by one, the warts disappeared, and each time that happened, the girl removed a quarter from the jar. She was so grateful to the women who had saved her from an unpleasant situation.

I remember another neighbor reading a story about her father arriving home with a trunk full of groceries for a family picnic. The girl was ten years old at the time and asked permission to carry in the watermelon all by herself. Her father handed it to her. As she followed the cement sidewalk around the side of the house, she tripped and dropped the watermelon, which splattered on the cement at her feet.

Fearing she had ruined the day for the entire family, and thinking her parents would be angry or at least disappointed, she ran to the tree house in the backyard to hide. It wasn't long until her father showed up, a happy smile on his face, inviting his daughter to come in the house with him to get spoons and forks so the children could gather around the broken watermelon and eat it before the ants discovered it.

I've never met this man, but from one simple story, I like and respect him. I feel like I know him. In telling a story from childhood, the woman had revealed the character of a good father.

I was surprised when long-time neighbor Lorna asked to join the class. She said she couldn't write, had never been to college, and insisted that her children would never want to read anything she wrote. I wasn't sure why she wanted to be in the class. Every once in a while I would ask her if she was working on something. After a number of weeks, she confessed that she was writing but didn't have anything to bring to class.

Then one Sunday I noticed at the beginning of class that she was holding a folded paper in her hand. I asked if she had something to read. She said she did, but she wanted me to read it for her.

It was a story about Lorna and her husband, Dan, going to a square dancing event in Savannah, Georgia, and when the dancing was over, joining other dancers to go on a bus tour of Savannah.

"Oh no," I thought. "This isn't a story, but a travelogue. No wonder she thinks her children don't want to read what she writes."

As I began to read, however, I noticed how careful she was in describing the weather. She commented on how no clouds were in the clear, blue sky, and how it was so hot that Dan rolled down the car windows partway so the car would not become an oven while they were gone on the tour. Then she described how a new tour bus left from the starting place every hour, stopping at the same places, making it possible for the tourists not to have to hurry back to the bus if they found a place of particular interest. Since a new bus came along every hour, they could always catch the next one later.

It occurred to me that there might be a method in so much detail. Perhaps she was setting up the reader for something important that would happen later. She was doing what every good storyteller or fiction writer does all the time.

Lorna described getting off the bus at a newly remodeled Catholic cathedral and going inside to see all the wonderful improvements. As they passed a table where a woman selling souvenirs was talking on the phone, Lorna couldn't help but overhear some of the conversation. The woman was angry about something and was swearing into the phone.

Lorna told Dan and some of the other dancers that she wanted to talk to the woman at the table about the offensive language. Dan and the other dancers told her not to do it, that it would be embarrassing, and there might be an argument that would reflect poorly on the Mormons from Utah. They hurried Lorna off on the group tour.

A half hour later as they were leaving the building, Lorna noticed that the woman at the souvenir table was alone. Using the excuse that she was going back to get a souvenir, Lorna carefully approached the woman and asked if the Catholic Church had a policy or rule against its members using the Lord's name in vain.

"Of course, we do," the woman said.

Lorna shared with her the words she had heard in the cathedral within the last hour. The woman denied that any such words had been spoken there. Nobody in the cathedral would talk like that.

"It was you," Lorna said. "I overheard you talking on that telephone."

The woman denied saying those things.

"I would never say anything like that in my church," Lorna continued. "I'd be afraid that the Lord would strike me down with lightning."

By this time both women were talking too loud. Someone from the church came over to see what was wrong. Lorna's friends returned to rescue her.

A little while later, the bus dropped the square dancers off at a restaurant near the edge of town. While they were eating, the sky blackened with clouds, they could hear thunder, and it began to rain. After eating, everyone gathered under an awning to wait for the next bus.

The bus didn't arrive at the scheduled time. The dancers looked at their watches and were thankful they were protected from the rain as they continued to wait.

Finally the bus showed up—an hour late. The driver was sorry for the delay. He explained that there was a huge traffic jam downtown. Police cars and fire trucks were blocking the streets around the newly remodeled cathedral that had been struck by lightning.

I didn't gather the above stories from papers and notes in my files. I wrote them down from memory, from hearing them, or from reading them in my class years ago. Stories can be remembered for a lifetime and beyond, while most of the other stuff we hear and say is soon forgotten. Stories can have layers of meaning. A college professor might hear something quite different than what a five-year-old hears when listening to the same story. There is magic in stories. Jesus used stories all the time, frequently leaving the interpretation to the reader. Why not follow His example?

While teaching the class, it didn't take me long to realize that everyone had interesting stories to tell; stories their grandchildren would want to hear. I also realized that with a little coaching, everyone could learn to write his or her life story. I told students to write like they talked; to pretend they were standing in the backyard, telling a story to a neighbor over the back fence, and to write it down just like they could imagine telling it to that neighbor. I told them their writing would be easier to understand if they didn't use big words that few people understood. I instructed them to avoid adjectives and abstract words whenever possible, and to keep nouns in front of verbs unless there was a good reason to do otherwise. I advised them to pretend their audience consisted of seventh graders so that everyone would be able to understand what they wrote, and to write stories instead of essays, at least most of the time.

I told them there's nothing better than a story to hold the attention and interest of readers. If they wrote down enough stories and sorted them into approximate chronological order, they would have the story of their life to publish in a book.

I soon learned to check the left rear pocket of my suit to make sure I had a clean handkerchief when I left the house to go to class. It seemed almost every week someone read a sad story, causing the rest of us to reach for handkerchiefs and tissue paper. And if someone read a funny story, it wasn't uncommon for a teacher from another class to knock on our door to ask us to quiet down so we wouldn't disturb the other classes.

Sometimes a student would say that she read a story to her sister, and her sister remembered it differently. They couldn't agree on the facts. I'd respond by saying that I'd be amazed if two people who shared the same experience forty years ago—or even two years ago—could write the same story about the same experience that was seen through different eyes. History is written by the people who win the wars. If the losers wrote the history, it would be different. Different people remember different facts. If the sister didn't agree with the way my student wrote the story, then the sister ought to write her own story and leave my student alone. If the sister said that the student could not have been nine years old when something happened in Oregon because the family didn't move to Oregon until the sister was ten, then the mistake can be corrected if the sister ends up being right.

Sometimes I have to remind students that even though writing a personal history is an imperfect process, it is wrong to fictionalize or to just make stuff up. If you say you made the cheerleading team in high school when you didn't, that's a lie. Don't do it. There will always be some factual mistakes in writing from memory, but you'd better be honest about what happened, how you felt, and what you think you learned. Sometimes, in writing down my boyhood adventures, I simply couldn't remember my age at the time, but I tell the story anyway because many of the other facts and details are as clear in my mind as something that happened yesterday.

I tell students that a personal history won't always contain the perfect truth, but there's something higher called the imperfect truth, where thoughts and feelings get all mixed up with the facts to create a beautiful and sometimes profound piece of writing.

My memory is hazy when I try to remember when I was three and four years old. Vaguely I remember finding a mousetrap on my grandparent's back porch, in a pantry by the back door. I cannot remember the perfect truth about what happened that day, but I know the imperfect truth. Although I cannot remember exactly what either of my grandparents said when I brought it into the kitchen to play with it, I know what they would have said.

My grandmother would have told me to put it down; that mice, which are dirty and carry germs, had touched it. But worst of all, if I touched the cheese, the wire clamp would slam shut on my little fingers and make me cry.

My grandfather, on the other hand, would tell me that the mice living in the house were clean so I didn't have to worry about germs. This was a good trap for me to play with because it was a slow trap. When I tried to set it, it would not hurt my fingers.

I don't know how many times I hurt my fingers trying to set slow mouse traps before I finally learned to set them right. I don't have a story about learning to set mouse traps in my history because I was too young and simply cannot remember enough details for a good story.

Four or five years later, I had an adventure with mousetraps that could have been included in this history because my memory of the details would allow me to tell mostly the perfect truth. The story reveals a budding mindset for taking risk, a trait that caused some agony in my life while rewarding me with an occasional victory.

It happened after my parents moved to California, probably when I was nine or ten years old. My friend Syd and I had ridden our bikes to a nearby hardware store. We found a large barrel full of brand new mouse or rattraps. They looked larger than the ones I had played with at my grandfather's house, but they were built exactly the same, with flat wood bottoms and copper-colored spring clamps that would slam shut on a mouse or rat when it nibbled on the cheese.

Syd had never set a trap before, so I showed him how. In a few minutes he could do it as well as I could. We noticed an interesting phenomenon. It was easy to see that a trap was set if we set it and placed it on a nearby shelf. However, if we set a trap and placed it on the big pile of new traps in the barrel, all you saw was a heaping tangle of wood bases and springs. It was almost impossible to tell which traps in the pile were set and which ones were not.

After looking around to make sure none of the store clerks were watching, we started setting traps and placing them carefully on the trap pile. When we had a dozen or fifteen traps in place, we sauntered out of the store and got on our bikes, wondering all the way home how many hardware customers would have sore fingers by the end of the day.

Later my grandfather taught me to how to use and set claw traps, the kind used by early mountain men to catch beaver. He offered me a bounty of fifty cents for every muskrat I could catch and kill. Muskrats were digging tunnels around head gates and through ditch banks, causing the loss of precious irrigation water. My job was to save the water by getting rid of the pesky muskrats. Unfortunately, I discovered that by putting bait in the traps I could catch other things too, like feral cats and birds. My grandfather put a quick stop to that when he found out.

I didn't include any trapping stories in my history, probably because I already had too many prank and mischief stories, like some of the men in my classes who seemed to have an endless supply of them as if that's all they did. After a while such stories aren't amusing anymore. I urged these students to write about the first funeral they attended, how the family survived a farm foreclosure, or about a child's struggle with cancer.

Just before this book went to press, I removed two rather long hunting stories, not because they were not interesting, but because I had too many hunting stories already. I enjoy several weekend hunting trips in September and October, and that's about it. Too many of these kinds of stories might give the reader the impression that that part of my life is more important than it really is. I have stories about growing up, school, basic training in the Marine Corps, books and reading, missionary and church service, falling in love, raising children, running businesses, doing research and writing articles and books, and cooking and food. I even have a story about when I spoke to a hall full of murderers and bank robbers at the Utah State prison.

It is the nature and disposition of almost every novice personal history writer to believe that if they go to the trouble and effort to write something down, it has enormous value and can never be changed or thrown away. Such writers have not discovered the delete button on their keyboard.

Every professional writer I know has the ability to look at his or her work objectively and, once in a while, block out a paragraph, story, or chapter, hit the delete button, and send that boring, unnecessary, or inappropriate block of copy off into cyberspace—lost and gone forever. I tell my students not to worry about deleting things in the beginning, but after they have composed fifty or a hundred stories, as I have done here, they will have a feel about which ones must stay, which ones might be marginal, and which ones deserve the firing squad.

My wife and I like to watch classic movies from time to time. Sometimes we experience a pleasant surprise. Some of the dialogue is too profound, some of the scenes are too funny, or characters are speaking lines of pure poetry. The movie is too good to be something a Hollywood screenwriter wrote in a week, a month, or even a year. That's when we realize that the movie we are watching started out as a stage play.

Does this mean stage play writers are better than screenplay writers? No. It means the process or path followed by a stage play in nearing perfection is different than the path followed by a screenplay or a novel in reaching the public.

Most new plays stay in the theater a week or two, but some may last a year or more. That's when someone decides to take it to London or New York. Some new plays in these cities last only a week or two, but a few grow legs, with audience support lasting for months or even years. That's when someone in Hollywood says, "Hey, let's make a movie."

Because the stage play makes use of live actors and live audiences, change is inevitable. The writer with the script may be sitting in the wings, backstage, watching the performance for the thirty-fifth time. Suddenly a section of dialogue sounds forced or unnatural, and it is perfectly clear in the writer's mind how it should be fixed, so he pencils in the changes on the script. After three hundred performances, perhaps he has penciled in a hundred changes. And every time the stage play script is reprinted, the new changes are incorporated. Sometimes it is the actors, not the writer, who initiate change. After playing a role fifty times, one night the hero says a line differently, and the audience explodes with laughter. Someone writes down that new line on the script so it will be part of the play from this point forward.

I can see William Shakespeare, after finishing the rough draft of *Hamlet* or *Romeo and Juliet,* wanting to hurry forward with production. After all, not only was he the writer but also the producer. He owned the theater and collected the money too. Perhaps he needed extra money to pay off his tab at the local pub.

Today we don't know what the first draft looked like, but we know what the final draft looked like after three or four hundred performances. William sat back stage, making notes, changing this or that, and maybe even added a little bathroom humor when he became bored with the three-hundredth performance. When people say that Shakespeare is the best writer who ever lived, they neglect to say that he was probably the best rewriter and editor too. Like wine, his plays became better with age.

The book *Outliers*, by Malcolm Gladwell, describes the preparation that The Beatles, a teenage singing group, experienced before coming to America for their first appearance on the Ed Sullivan Show. At the time, most of us had the wrong idea about who these boys really were. We thought they were some freethinking teenagers who were too lazy to go to school, who worked up a few songs that they practiced on a homemade stage in somebody's garage. Not so. Before coming to America, the Beatles had performed over three hundred times at clubs in Hamburg, Germany. The boys didn't speak German, and the audiences for the most part didn't speak English. If the boys couldn't entertain these audiences for six or eight hours at a time, they risked getting fired. By the time The Beatles came to America, they were polished and seasoned professional entertainers. The music they brought with them had been honed to perfection in front of difficult audiences. It is no surprise that these brilliant and hardworking boys won us over so quickly.

After ten years of writing, I finally finished the first draft of this history. A week later I was working on the second draft, which I sent to some friends and relatives for review. A week later I was into the third draft, and then the fourth. I am adding a section to the prologue as part of the fifth draft. I figure with two or three more drafts, I'll be ready to go to press. That's what professional writers do. Anyone who is serious about producing an excellent personal history, one that has a chance to endure through generations of time, will do the same.

In my classes I tell students about Joseph Campbell, the professor from Mary Lawrence College in New York, who spent a lifetime studying the classic myths and legends of the world, the stories that never die, even after hundreds of years.

He found common elements in the great stories: a reluctant hero or heroine in an ordinary world, who embarks on an adventure or journey, meets obstacles of increasing difficulty while having adventures and struggles, and eventually enters what Campbell calls the belly of the whale or the ultimate ordeal. The sympathetic hero or heroine eventually finds his way home to the ordinary world and brings along some kind of prize or reward. Of course, the ordinary world is not the same at the end of the story because the hero or heroine has changed.

Campbell found common characters in the great stories. In addition to heroes and heroines, there were companions, mentors, threshold guardians, heralds, shape shifters, spirit guides, and formidable adversaries.

At the end of his book, *Hero with a Thousand Faces,* Joseph Campbell asks the big question. Why do all the great stories have basically the same plot elements? Why do the great stories have the same types of characters? Why are the stories that lack these elements soon forgotten?

Campbell's answer is profound. He could find only one answer to the above questions. The elements in the great stories, the stories that never die, are the same elements we see in our own lives. The great stories parallel the lives of human beings. All of us are reluctant heroes or heroines engaged in life's journey. All of us have mentors who help along the way and spirit guides who give us direction. All of us are confronted by threshold guardians who try to turn us away from what we want or need to achieve. In the words of Joseph Campbell, the hero has three choices when confronted by a threshold guardian: he can win him over, he can sneak by, or he can kill him. We are puzzled by shape shifters, who may appear to be friends but indeed are enemies, or appear to be enemies but in the end are our best friends.

Each of us somewhere along the way enters the belly of the whale or must endure the ultimate ordeal, sometimes more than once. No one escapes this life unscathed. If we see someone who has not entered the belly of the whale, either we don't know him very well, or his time has not yet come.

At the end of the hero's journey, when we return with the prize, we find the ordinary world different, because we are different, a result of the journey we have traveled.

Chris Vogler, a student of Joseph Campbell, did a popular version of Campbell's work, called *The Writer's Journey.* I encourage my students to study this book and look for the same plot elements and character types in their own lives. I promise the students that if they look hard enough they will indeed find the plot elements and character types that are found in all the great stories. As they include these elements in their own personal histories, they will have a great story too, one that will endure for a long, long time.

It seems whenever I start a new group of students, at least one approaches me, sometimes after class, and says there are things in her life that she would prefer not to put in a history for the children and grandchildren to read. This never surprises me, because I have learned that everyone has memories they'd like to forget, things they'd prefer the grandchildren didn't know. I believe there are some experiences in almost every life that are simply too personal and private to share with just anyone who may choose to read your story.

Sometimes a student will ask me to explain the difference between a journal and a personal history. Mark Twain once said that if you wrote down everything in your journal, everything that happened in your life every day, you'd have over three thousand pages, or ten books instead of one. If you did that, there would be passages that would bore readers to tears, items that would embarrass you and others, items that would be hurtful to the ones you love, and as already mentioned, items too personal and private to be shared while you are alive.

You might mention in your journal that you had bacon and eggs for breakfast, mowed the lawn until the mower ran out of gas, and went to the BYU football game with the University of Utah where BYU lost seventeen to thirteen. Then you came home and picked apples until dark. Even though you might record such events in a journal, you'd never write something like this in a personal history.

Instead of including everything, good or bad, the personal history writer is selective. He includes only the best stories. Some stories are interesting, and some are less interesting, but they all show what your life was about. Instead of ten books in your history, you produce one very good one, because you can pick and choose what to put in and what to leave out.

I tell the students that when they have finished their stories, they should resist the temptation to make one or two thick and beautiful binder scrapbooks, including photos, diplomas, awards, passports, and anything else they can dig up, and then give copies of this beautiful piece of work to one or two children, risking the loss of these remarkable tomes to water, fire, or careless handling later on.

I urge the shotgun approach to publishing a personal history, which is producing a hundred or more perfect bound copies like this one—a printed story with some photos on the cover, a bound book that is inexpensive to print. Give multiple copies to children, grandchildren, and friends. In a hundred years, if someone remembers there is a book about your life but nobody seems to have a copy, they can do a used book search on Amazon or another used bookseller's website and probably find a copy that can be reproduced, ensuring that your story will be available to your posterity for another hundred years.

A word of caution. When you finish the first draft, you will be so excited about your story that you may decide to run off copies to hand out to a few select family members and friends so they can give you feedback to help make corrections before going to press.

It's likely that these special few won't be nearly as excited about your history as you are. Don't be surprised if one or more of them tell you they are too busy to read it but that they'll get to it as soon as possible. If this happens, don't toss your story in the trash.

I know from experience that many good books become available in the marketplace with little fanfare and excitement. After a few weeks or months, someone will pick it up and start reading it, and if this reader finds it entertaining or worthwhile, he will recommend it to other friends and family members, who in turn will do the same. In the book business this process is called *word of mouth exposure*. All the good and great books find their audiences through word of mouth.

Once in a while the word of mouth spreads like a benevolent cancer, creating a bestseller, and if it continues hundreds of years, through generations, the book is called a classic. Even if no one else seems excited the day you finish the first draft, it is still possible for your work to become a classic, at least among your posterity.

Be patient. Remember my story about the family of turtles who enter a café for some ice cream. It starts to rain outside, so the father turtle tells the little boy turtle to hurry out to the ditch where they live and fetch the umbrella. The mother and father go ahead and order the ice cream. A week later when the boy hasn't returned, the mother and father are still sitting at the counter. The father turns to the mother and says, "Maybe we should eat the boy's ice cream before it dries up."

From behind the door the boy yells, "If you do that I won't fetch the umbrella."

If you think you are too busy or not sufficiently skilled to write a personal history, you can hire me to do it for you. My fee is sixty thousand dollars, because it will probably take two years for me to write it. I will let you in on a little secret. There is no secret. I would simply do what is described above. It's not that hard, but it does take time and attention, usually over several years. It might go faster if I do it for you, but it might be better if you do it yourself. After all, you are the one who did the research.

If you are under fifty, you still have time to think about it and perhaps start a file to fill with story ideas. If you are over fifty, I hope you feel an urgency to get going at once while there is still time to make your story the best it can be.

As you read my history, keep a pen or pencil handy, because my stories will trigger memories of events in your life. Jot down notes to help you remember events and happenings that you'll want to write about. Make notes in the margin so you will not forget. Later, you can transcribe your notations to a notebook where you can expand and add detail. When you finish, you will have a beginning outline for your own history.

As you begin to outline and take notes, remember that in addition to your posterity, you are also doing this for yourself to help make better sense of the life you have lived. If your posterity will read it, so will others. Keep your audience in mind as you do the work. Don't listen to those who may try to discourage you.

Elisha Warner (1889–1979), publisher of Utah's *Payson Chronicle* and *Spanish Fork Press*, said the following:

> I have always believed that every person should write the story of his life. He should not leave the matter to others. He is the best informed on the details of his existence, the motives which actuated him to do certain things, the hopes which spurred him to activity, the reasoning which led to his conclusions. No other can understand fully the goals toward which he aimed, or explain the reasons why his shafts sometimes fell short. No other can operate without cutting too deeply and producing painful complications, or too superficially and failing to accomplish the desired result.

CHAPTER I

Nothing in the world can take the place of persistence. Talent will not; nothing is more common than unsuccessful men with talent. Genius will not; unrewarded genius is almost a proverb. Education will not; the world is full of educated derelicts. Persistence and determination alone are omnipotent. The slogan "Press on" has solved and always will solve the problems of the human race.

—CALVIN COOLIDGE
30th president of the United States
(1872 –1933)

The world was at war on October 18, 1942, the day I was born. Three million German soldiers were marching to Moscow, finding little resistance from the Russian army that seemed mostly unprepared for the German invasion. Almost without effort Germany had conquered Poland, France, the Netherlands, Belgium, Holland, Denmark, Czechoslovakia, and Yugoslavia and was dropping bombs and rockets on London.

I wouldn't meet Arthur Naujoks, one of the Wehrmact's forward artillery observers, until many years later. On the Russian front, his job was to sneak out during the night, climb a hill or building behind Russian lines so that the next morning he could observe and report where the huge German artillery shells were exploding.

Many years later, Arthur and I used his research on the Third Reich to coauthor a book called *The Last Great Secret of the Third Reich*.

On the day I was born, Erwin Rommel was having his way with British forces in North Africa. I was nearly a month old when George Patton began Rommel's route after landing U.S. forces at Casa Blanca.

In October, 1942, German U-boats were sinking allied merchant ships with impunity around the world. The Wehrmacht was undefeated, and it appeared it wouldn't be long until about half the world would be speaking German. The American bombers had not yet begun to bomb the German cities where nineteen years later I would serve as a Mormon missionary.

Less than a year before my birth, Japan had destroyed much of the American fleet at Pearl Harbor while wrapping up its invasion of China, the largest country in the world. On the day I was born, thousands of U.S. Marines were in a life and death struggle on Guadalcanal. After landing on the sandy beaches, the Marines watched helplessly as Japanese warships sunk the Marines' support and supply ships.

Private Winesap was at the front of the struggle, fighting desperately while witnessing the deaths of some of his best friends. Eighteen years later he was my drill sergeant when I began basic training at the Marine Corps base in Quantico, Virginia.

At the time of my birth, future U.S. president Harry S. Truman was making the news, saying there was finally some good news coming from the war. The Germans were fighting the Russians. Many hoped there would be plenty of killing on both sides.

My father, Robert Alton Nelson, was still undrafted by the U.S. Army. He was attending the Utah State Agricultural College, later called Utah State University, in Logan, Utah. My maternal grandfather, Leland R. Smith, was raising and training mules, which would join a herd of about seventy thousand mules, later used to pack and drive and ride when U.S. forces invaded the mountains of southern Italy and the Philippine jungles.

On the day of my birth, Utah men, who were not cruising overseas to kill "Japs" and "Krauts," were marching into the Utah mountains to kill deer. My father and grandfather were among those men. On the third Saturday in October, the hunt began. School was usually cancelled the Friday before the opening, so children could go into the mountains to shed animal blood with their fathers.

Upon returning home to Bountiful, Utah, my father and grandfather were discussing who had bagged four-point, three-point, and two-point bucks, when my grandmother announced that she had bagged a one-point buck. It was her clever way of announcing that the first male grandchild was born.

My father was working on a master's degree in economics. He worked part time in a beer brewery, measured snowpack for a government weather agency, and read papers for his professors. He also liked to fish for brown trout in the Logan River. I was his second child.

I don't remember any of this, but I do remember some of the stories told about me when I was little, like when a police officer came to the door looking for Leland Nelson. A window in the neighboring house had been broken, and the neighborhood children told the investigating officer that Leland Nelson had done it. My mother led him to my bedroom where he could see me in my crib, taking a nap. I was only two years old. It was later discovered that other children lifted me up to the window and told me to smack it with a toy telephone, which I did. The policeman decided not to arrest me.

When my father joined the Army to become a chaplain, my mother moved to Bountiful to be closer to my grandparents. I remember a dark oval-shaped rag rug on a hardwood floor in the entry hall. I remember my father coming home from basic training in an Army uniform, and how hard my mother hugged and kissed him.

I remember when I was three, my mother sent me to the store, a block or two up the same side of the street, for a loaf of sliced bread. I had trouble carrying it home and broke it in half, which resulted in losing several slices.

When the war ended, my father obtained work with the Utah

Department of Education and purchased a little house on Sylvan Avenue in Salt Lake City. In a few years my parents had two more children, Susan and then Margaret. When Mother was pregnant with Margaret, she said I told her she looked like a horse.

My sisters were some of my best friends through most of my adult life. Saundra was my consultant when I didn't know how to cook something. Susan was my most avid book fan. And Margaret produced amazing wedding receptions.

My parents would put the children to bed early, about 7 p.m., and Saundra, the oldest, would read to the rest of us. My favorite books were in a series called *The Boxcar Children*. I remember how the stories would frighten me and then make me laugh, and how I would beg Saundra to keep reading when she wanted to stop and go to sleep. Her reading started a fire in me, a passion for books and stories; a love that never died. My favorite radio programs were Sky King and the Lone Ranger.

I remember pulling my red wagon around the backyard during the fall deer hunt, looking up at the mountains, trying to see my father who had gone hunting, wishing desperately that I could go with him. I remember lighting matches behind the neighbor's back fence, and a tin rake cutting a nasty hole in my upper lip, which resulted in three stitches at the hospital.

Even though my father had not fought in the war, he brought home with him a remarkable souvenir—a black-handled sheath knife with a bright red swastika on it. The inscription on the blade read *Blut und Ehre* (blood and honor). The knife was beautiful and very sharp.

One day it occurred to me that it might be my ticket to some unprecedented blessings. I sneaked it out of the drawer and strapped it to my waist. With two or three of my friends following close behind, I climbed onto the big vegetable bus that came down our street two or three times a week.

We were not interested in the beautifully displayed vegetables along both sides of the interior of the bus, only the ice cream chest at the front. I pulled the knife out of the sheath, pointed it at the bus driver, and demanded he give each of us an ice cream bar. Instead of giving in to my demands, he said that if we did not leave his bus that instant he would give us spankings we would never forget. I shoved the knife back in its sheath as we scampered to safety.

One fall afternoon three or four of us wandered into the basement of my friend's home where his mother was making grape juice. Big soggy bundles of grape pulp wrapped in cheesecloth were hanging from a long clothesline, dripping delicious purple nectar into a row of pans on tables below the clothesline.

I crawled onto a table, put my mouth to one of the cheesecloth bags, and demonstrated to my friends how the calves at my grandfather's farm sucked on their mothers to get warm milk. The other children joined me, and we had a great time playing "baby calf" until the lady of the house discovered us and sent us home. Needless to say, our faces were purple with guilt for several days.

I remember at age four riding in the back seat of my parent's car from Salt Lake City out to West Bountiful where my grandparents lived. We drove by the University of Utah and the state capitol building, along the side of the mountain down to Beck's Hot Springs, and then north on State Street to Bountiful. I remember Saundra pointing out the little round-pillared enclosure on top of the big dome of the capitol building. She told me God lived there. I believed that for several years.

On one particular trip, I remember my parents being excited about a surprise that awaited us. Before leaving home, they made sure I dressed in my cowboy outfit, which included leather chaps, boots, spurs, vest, wrist cuffs, holsters, pistols, a silver sheriff's badge, and a little cowboy hat. They said Aunt Romaine and Uncle Van were coming too and bringing Karen, my favorite cousin.

I suppose it was hard for the children to share my parent's excitement until we saw the four beautiful ponies my grandfather had tied to the fence in the big corral. My grandfather, whom we called Poppy, had fashioned a riding course. It was sort of an oval on the south side of the big corral. Mangers, barrels, ropes, and the south fence set the boundaries. The idea was that ponies inside the riding oval couldn't get out of control or go where they weren't supposed to, and it wasn't large enough for them to run away—something Poppy always worried about with children and horses. Each horse had a little saddle on its back.

I don't know how long we rode the ponies, but when the adults said it was time to go in the house for lunch, Karen and I didn't want to leave. We just couldn't get enough of those ponies.

The four ponies didn't stay around long. I suppose Poppy decided four was too many. He sold all except little Boots, who soon became the property of Karen and me. We would catch her and take her out on the lawn, where we would brush and wash her and feed her carrots and sugar cubes. I remember her stepping on our bare feet many times. It usually didn't hurt, unless she did it while we were on the cement sidewalk.

It was hard for us to put on the little saddle, so we mostly rode bareback. We couldn't get on by ourselves, so we took turns boosting each other on. Boots was "corral balky," which meant she was always trying to go back to the corral when we were riding her. In the beginning, we weren't good enough riders to make her go where we wanted, so we led her up the street, sometimes as far as the neighbor's house. Then we'd get boosted on, grab the thick mane, and hang on for dear life as she scampered back to the corral gate.

The single most memorable event between Boots and me was on Christmas day that year. We had spent the night at Poppy's. Santa Claus had come Christmas morning. He was wearing an Army hat and his cheery Santa voice sounded an awful lot like Uncle Van.

About eight inches of new snow was on the ground when we woke up that morning, but all I wanted to do was go outside and ride Boots. I had brought all my cowboy stuff and was more interested in riding than playing with the new toys.

Finally, Poppy caught Boots, saddled her up, and put me on her so I could ride around the yard. By this time I could handle her a lot better. He went back in the house, leaving me by myself with the pony.

The next thing I remember was a limb from a peach tree pushing against my chest and forcing me out of the saddle. I don't know how my little cowboy boot got caught in the covered stirrup, but it did. Boots stampeded, dragging me behind her as she raced around the corner of the house and back to the corral. Fortunately, those inside heard my cries and hurried to the rescue.

When Pop finally cornered Boots and removed my foot from the stirrup, I was unharmed, but still screaming in terror. The new snow was a gentle buffer, and I didn't have a single scratch or bruise, but all I wanted was to get away from that stupid horse and go in the house.

My mother had a different idea, however. She feared I might lose my love for horses and riding if I stopped now with the memory of the runaway fresh in my mind. After making sure I was all right, she picked me up and put me back on the pony. I cried in protest, but she made me do it. She stood watching as I rode around, making sure I didn't get off. After a while she allowed me to go in the house. I have always wondered if I might have lost my interest in horses and riding if she had not done that. Horses eventually became a big part of my life, and certainly had an impact on the kinds of books I later wrote.

During the late forties and early fifties, Pop sometimes bought a pen full of pigs to feed for slaughter. A local potato processing plant sold him hundred-pound bags of cull potatoes for ten cents each. He sometimes took me with him to feed the pigs. He emptied the heavy bags into a huge iron vat and covered the potatoes with water. The vat was elevated off the ground by big cement blocks. He would shove a worn-out airplane tire from the Salt Lake airport under the vat, splash diesel fuel over it, and then set it on fire. The burning tire would make a lot of black smoke, burning all night, eventually bringing the potato water to a boil.

In the morning Pop would shovel the cooked potatoes into a trough for the hungry pigs. Sometimes he would stop shoveling and peel an extra nice potato for me to eat. The potatoes cooked at home never tasted that good.

Horses were shipped on the railroad, and when the men at the Salt Lake stockyards found one that had been injured, they called my grandfather to come and get it. They charged him ten dollars. He would unload the horse at the pigpen, shoot it, skin the hind legs, and then pull the hide off with the tractor. Then he dragged the red and raw carcass into the pigpen where the hogs would clean it up in a day, leaving nothing but bones. Pop would sell the hide to a tannery for five dollars.

When Pop was busy cooking potatoes or killing a horse, he would hand me a hot shot or battery-powered electric prod with instructions to shock any pig that came near. He believed that if the pigs would eat a raw horse, they would eat a little boy too. I'm sure my mother and grandmother would have been very upset if they had seen me, three or four years old, wandering through a herd of a hundred hungry pigs, all by myself, ready to shock any wet, grunting nose within reach of my electric prod. Pop would check the batteries from time to time to make sure there were plenty of volts and amps to keep the pigs away.

Later, when Pop no longer raised pigs, he bought the cull potatoes for his cattle. The cattle, with multiple stomachs and the ability to chew cud, had better digestive systems than pigs, so the potatoes didn't have to be cooked for them. We just dumped the raw potatoes out on the ground.

My parents learned of a doctor in Tooele or Grantsville who was having a special on tonsillectomies. They decided to save money and do all four children at one time. I remember becoming very sleepy when the nurse held a big wad of cotton over my nose and mouth and poured ether onto it. When I came to, my sisters and I took turns vomiting black blood into a kidney-shaped pan. We continued throwing up as we drove home.

Because my birthday was in October, I was still four when the day came for my friends to begin Kindergarten. The school officials wanted me to wait one more year, but my parents were insistent that I begin school now, so that's what happened. I don't think I was ready. I remember wetting my pants in class and trying to convince the teacher that the puddle on the floor was spilled milk. Still, she sent me home to change.

All through school, until about the ninth grade, it seems I was the littlest or next to the littlest boy in the class. I had a hard time competing with the bigger boys in football and baseball and felt inferior in many ways because I was so little. My parents told me I couldn't compete with the other boys because of a bout with rheumatic fever when I was a child, but I don't remember any of that. As a result I spent less time in sports and more time reading books and riding horses. I never seemed to have a lot of friends, but I always had enough good ones.

Eventually Karen and I outgrew Boots. When we were seven, Poppy introduced us to Mr. Carrot, a full-sized palomino gelding.

After getting my foot caught in the stirrup that memorable Christmas day, Pop encouraged us to ride bareback, like Indians.

The problem with riding Mr. Carrot bareback was that he was so big that it was impossible for us to get on by ourselves, so Pop trained him to do a special trick for us. We would climb up on a fence—any fence—and then slap Mr. Carrot on the neck with the reins. This was his signal to crowd up close to the fence, making it easy for anyone who could climb a fence to slip onto his back.

One time I asked Pop how he trained Mr. Carrot to side up to fences and gates for us. Pop said he climbed up on the sturdy fence by the bull pen and started slapping Mr. Carrot on the side of his neck, with the reins, not real hard, but hard enough that the horse didn't like it. Mr. Carrot would start moving around, hoping to get away from the reins. If he moved farther away from the fence, the slapping continued. If he moved closer, even just a step or two, the slapping ceased. After two or three sessions, Mr. Carrot figured out that if he wanted the slapping to stop, all he had to do was push his ribs up against the fence. It was a lesson he never forgot.

Mr. Carrot had another unusual characteristic, one that Karen and I hated but Poppy liked. Most of the time when we tried to gallop him, without warning, he would suddenly stop and put his nose between his front legs, causing us to tumble down his neck and over his head. In time we learned never to gallop him, unless there was a saddle to help us hang on.

We put hundreds of miles on that old horse, riding him through the pastures, up and down the street, around the block, and down to the pond. I remember many lazy summer afternoons, stretched out in the shade on the lawn or in a meadow, listening to Mr. Carrot crop and chew grass as I looked up at the clouds, wondering about things, sometimes with Karen and sometimes by myself. Karen and I discussed the price for which we would be willing to sell Mr. Carrot. It was always more than a million dollars.

Other horses came and went, like Ichabod, a lazy little dun horse that would walk with his nose nearly touching the ground when he was tired. He wasn't much of a horse, and Poppy cut his tail in a "bob" like they used to trim the tails of mules. I was embarrassed to ride him up the street. He didn't last long—only one summer.

When I was seven, my father landed a job with United States Steel in San Francisco. We moved to a new home in Concord, California. I remember driving over the Sierra Nevada Mountains, along Highway 40 before the interstate highway was built, singing "California here I come, right back were I started from. . . ." There was snow on both sides of the road, and when we drove out of the snow, heading out of the mountains, I thought the snow line was the California border.

We lived at 142 Roslyn Drive in Concord. It was a new subdivision house, painted light green. My parents paid $7,200 for it. They received a G.I. loan since my dad had been in the Army. The grass in the backyard was extra thick and green over the septic tank. If you were in the backyard when someone flushed the toilet, you could see water bubbling out of the ground.

On Sunday evenings we drove over to San Leandro where my Uncle Tom Clark and Aunt Janet lived. They had a new black and white television set. As we drove to their house we would count antennas to see how many other people had televisions. I remember being excited when we saw four antennas in a row. Our favorite shows were Red Skelton and Ed Sullivan.

I remember my sister Saundra telling me that Uncle Tom said I was lazy. I felt very bad. It didn't occur to me that it would be hard for an adult to draw a conclusion like that about a nine-year-old child who only visited his house on Sunday nights to watch television. Maybe that's why I have a lazy streak even today.

I remember Aunt Janet taking me to a movie in Oakland one day. I think my parents were away on a business trip. I became ill and threw up in the gutter. I remember how nice Aunt Janet was to me and how much I loved her. She died during an experimental brain surgery a few years later. My grandparents were bitter about doctors and hospitals for the remainder of their lives. Every year on the anniversary of Janet's death, my grandmother would write a letter to Janet's former doctor, telling him he was going to Hell.

On one of our first Christmases in California, my grandparents came to visit. My grandfather gave me a BB gun. My parents didn't seem too happy, but they let me keep it. Soon I was the best marksman in the neighborhood, and no bird was safe.

I remember some mean kids teasing my friend and me one day and me driving them off at gunpoint. As they pedaled away on their bikes, I shot both of their behinds, multiple times, making them cry. The targets were easy to hit, and since their backs were toward me, I knew I couldn't hurt them really bad, like putting out an eye. Still, their mothers called the police, and when the officers showed up at my house, all they seemed to want to say was that I might have put an eye out. They simply couldn't grasp my reasoning that it is impossible to put an eye out when shooting someone in the behind.

I remember having an interesting dream the Christmas my grandparents came to visit. In the dream there was a huge cougar in the tree outside my grandparent's kitchen window. It was growling and snarling and switching its tail. I was not afraid and was walking around the base of the tree trying to shoo it out of the tree with a garden rake.

Then suddenly I woke up, finding myself in my bed in Concord, but I could still hear the cougar, growling and snarling, just like in the dream. The house was pitch black. I couldn't see a thing, but I could hear the growl of a big cat. There was a cougar in the house, and it was going to kill someone. Now I was scared—really scared.

As I lay there in my bed, full of fear, I began to reason, to calculate the probability of a giant cat finding its way into our house. Impossible. There had to be another source for the growling and snarling sounds. The sound was not coming from the television or radio.

Slowly I figured out that my grandparents were snoring. I had never slept near a snoring person before. They were in the next room and the door was open. As I continued to listen, I found a pattern and rhythm in the growling noises. Yes, it was snoring, not a big cat. Happily relieved, I went back to sleep.

As a child I had frequent nightmares. One time I remember dreaming I was being chased by monsters or evil people. Everything was going wrong. I was about to be caught and killed or eaten. I was terrified. I remember thinking, *This is too awful to be really happening. I must be dreaming. If I don't want them to catch me, all I have to do is wake up.* So that's exactly what I did. I didn't have many nightmares after that.

One year my father's brother Uncle Herm, his wife Helen, and their five children moved to Concord. It seemed we were always at their house—or they at our house—on holidays, especially Thanksgiving and Christmas. I remember when Uncle Herm got a second television so he could watch two football games at the same time.

It seemed every Christmas Aunt Helen outdid herself by piling more tinsel on the tree. I didn't know there was that much tinsel in the world, but every year there was more on her tree until we could barely see the sagging branches. I tried to get my mother to put more tinsel on our tree, but she wouldn't do it.

The two older boys, Ron and Bill, were good football players, and I did my best to keep up with them. The third son, Phil, was more like me, always checking out books at the library. He later became a doctor.

One time my father bought me a springer spaniel named Poncho, a cute little black and white puppy. He was bred to hunt birds, and it was only proper that his tail be cut off. My father's thinking was, why spend all that money for a vet to cut it off, when it would be so easy to do it himself?

One Saturday morning he got out his hunting knife, the one with the German swastika on the handle, and started sharpening it. He told the children to catch the dog and bring it to the patio. When he was ready to do the deed, he went outside to find four sobbing children, hugging and holding a very happy, tail-wagging puppy. My father lost his resolve, and Poncho spent the remainder of his life with a long tail.

A few years later we had a tiny Mexican Chihuahua named Tinkerbelle. Most Chihuahuas are skinny, but not Tinkerbelle. She was spayed, and eating was her favorite pastime. She looked more like a little brown pig than a dog. I found I could take little pieces of meat from the dinner table and get her to do about anything.

In time I trained her to shake hands, sit up, and roll over; not just one time, but clear across the room if I kept moving my fingers in a circular motion. She could play dead with her eyes wide open, and best of all, run to the far side of the room, rear up, and walk to me on two hind legs. When we had company, my parents would have me fetch the dog to do tricks.

I was so excited when I saw the announcement in the newspaper that a new pet store, for its grand opening, was going to give a bike to the kid whose dog could do the best or most tricks. I knew Tinkerbelle and I could win. I spent every day after school that week helping Tinkerbelle review her tricks. Her favorite food seemed to be smoked ham, so I had a pocket full of ham pieces when I took her up to the grand opening of the pet store the next Saturday.

As the other dogs started doing tricks, my confidence grew. One would sit up. Another would shake hands. Another would lie down on command. One boy put a piece of food on his dog's nose. The dog wiggled his nose so the food fell off. He caught and ate the food before it hit the ground. Big deal. Tinkerbelle could do so much more.

When it was my turn, I held out a piece of ham and told Tinkerbelle to sit up, her easiest trick. She just sat there and shivered like she was freezing to death. I brought out a bigger piece of ham and ordered her to shake hands. She sat and shivered. I told her to roll over. She sat and shivered. She would not do any of her tricks. The boy who put food on his dog's nose won the bike.

I never had much to do with Tinkerbelle after that. I didn't teach her any more tricks, and wouldn't make her do tricks for company anymore. I realized she did tricks for food, not to please me. She didn't love me, because if she had cared anything at all for me, she would have won the bike for me. I didn't want anything more to do with her. Later in life I had dogs who would risk their lives for a pat on the head.

I remember my father taking me hunting at a pheasant farm. About a hundred men with guns lined up in a long row, each man about fifty feet from the next, along the edge of a thousand-acre field where hundreds of pheasants had been turned loose. I don't know how much he paid for this highly organized hunting opportunity. I was too little to do the shooting, so I followed closely behind with the expectation that I would get to carry dead birds.

Almost before we got started, a bird flew between my father and the sixteen-year-old boy who was hunting to the right of us. The boy missed the pheasant, but his load of shot hit my father square in the chest, like a sledgehammer, knocking him flat on his back. I thought he was dead. Fortunately, it was a very cold morning. The lead shot did not penetrate my father's heavy coat and thick shirts, though several of the BB's hit his face, penetrating the skin. We went to a medical clinic where a doctor removed the shot from his face. My father never went hunting again.

One summer we went on vacation to Yellowstone National Park. Those were the days when you saw lots of bears—literally hundreds of them. I remember my mother sitting in the passenger seat of our car, a beef roast on her lap, cutting off little pieces and slipping them out her window, which was rolled down about an inch, to the waiting bears. I remember staying in a cabin and being afraid to go to the outhouse at night because I could hear bears rummaging through the garbage cans.

To get to Yellowstone, we had to go through Wyoming, where I discovered that firecrackers were legal and could be purchased in about any store. When we returned to California, my little suitcase contained an abundant number of firecrackers that I had spent all my money on. I had a hunch that I could turn a profit by selling those firecrackers, which cost half a cent each in Wyoming, for a nickel in California. My hunch proved correct, and soon I was the richest boy in my neighborhood.

When a friend told me he was going with his family on a vacation to Mexico, I gave him a twenty-dollar bill, with instructions to pick me up some cherry bombs. Pretty soon, boys were standing in line to pay me twenty-five cents for cherry bombs that I had paid four cents for. I didn't get very rich, however, because I used up a lot of the inventory myself.

My friend Syd Smith and I were on our way to becoming grade-school demolitions experts, because we found many creative things to do with the firecrackers and cherry bombs. At first we would just wander around the neighborhood at night, tossing a cherry bomb under the partially raised garage door where a mean dog was kept, or placing one on the sill below an open window at a girlfriend's house.

In time our mischief became increasingly risky, because people would call the police, forcing us to invent a delayed ignition system for our pyrotechnics.

We would remove the flash powder from legal fountain-type fireworks and pour a little pile of the powder where we wanted our explosion to take place. Then we would put down three or four firecrackers or a cherry bomb next to the powder, with the fuses inserted into the little pile of flash powder. Next we would light the end of a piece of white kite string and stick the unlit end into the pile of powder. With a little experimentation we knew how long the string needed to be to produce a ten, twenty, or thirty-minute delay. One Saturday night we lit ten equal-length strings at the same time, hurried around the neighborhood to seven or eight different locations, and set the strings in piles of flash powder, cherry bombs, and firecrackers. Then we went home, keeping one of the burning strings so we would know when we were about five minutes away from blastoff. That's when we called the police to report that a lot of firecrackers were going off in our neighborhood. When the police arrived, the explosions began. We watched out the front window, hearing the explosions, and seeing two police cars race back and forth, trying to find the guilty parties.

One night at a church youth activity, we climbed onto the roof of the church and placed our glowing strings with flash powder and firecrackers at three or four different locations in the rain gutter around the top of the building. Because the gutter was made of metal, we assumed there would be no chance of starting a fire. About five minutes from ignition, we went inside, found the bishop, and began asking him questions about our deacons' basketball program. While we were talking we could hear our firecrackers going off.

When we were finished, the bishop put his arm around me and said he owed me an apology. He said he thought I was the one who had been bringing firecrackers to church, but now he knew he was wrong, because someone else was setting them off while he was talking to me. I graciously accepted his apology.

One day we found a three-foot section of one-inch steel pipe, threaded at both ends. We screwed a cap on one end and a sleeve on the other. We found that by placing a firecracker inside the sleeve and rolling a marble over the fuse, we had a neat little cannon, one that would bury marbles into the wall of the elementary school behind Syd's house. They didn't bounce off, but actually embedded themselves in the wall.

I wasn't a very good student in elementary and intermediate school. I had what I thought was a bad habit of daydreaming. I would look out the window and have wonderful adventures in my mind. Teachers would sometimes scold me or make me stay after class, which would make me feel guilty for daydreaming. They tried to convince me that I had a very bad and lazy habit.

When I wasn't daydreaming in school, my nose was usually buried in a book from the library, one that had nothing to do with the class I was attending. It wasn't unusual for me to check out five or six books a week and read them all, mostly fiction, but nonfiction too. I think I read every novel in the Loma Vista intermediate school library.

My parents subscribed to *Time* and *Life* magazines, and I remember my father telling me that if I read every issue of *Time*, in about ten years that would be as good as a college education.

I believed everything I read in that magazine, until one week there was an article about the Mormon Church. The article was condescending, cynical, disrespectful, and very inaccurate. I was just a kid, but I went to church. I knew what went on there, and it was nothing like what was described in the article. I quit reading *Time* magazine, concluding that the writers were more interested in being clever than in being fair and accurate.

One winter afternoon I was at Syd's house with a couple of other friends. We were learning to play poker, trying to win each other's pennies. The potential for bluffing was as much fun as drawing winning hands. Syd's father noticed what we were doing and decided to teach us a lesson. He asked if he could play too. We told him he could, as long as he brought his own pennies.

It wasn't long until he had taken all our money and ruined our afternoon of fun. I'm sure he felt very smug at having taught us a lesson on the evils of gambling.

By this time I had exhausted the school library and was making regular visits to the Concord City Library. The following Monday I asked the librarian if there was such a thing as a book on how to play poker. She asked if I'd ever heard the saying "According to Hoyle."

She led me to a bookshelf and showed me Hoyle's book on poker. I checked it out.

The book presented the mathematical probabilities of drawing the many different poker hands—when to draw, when to raise, and when to fold. It explained the psychology of bluffing. When you won a hand by bluffing, forcing everyone else to fold, you never showed them your cards. They had to pay to see.

I read the book two or three times, made lots of notes, and let Syd in on the many secrets and strategies I was learning. The next Saturday, when we knew his father would be home, we laid our money and cards on the table and somehow enticed Syd's father to teach us another lesson on the evils of gambling. This time we took all his pocket change, forcing him to leave the game. He never bothered our poker games again.

During our school years we had a tradition of having a big poker game every New Year's Eve. We would set a time limit, 7:00 p.m. until 7:00 a.m.; twelve hours—no more, no less. No girls allowed, and no fathers either, just other boys our own age. Each boy who wanted to get in the game had to bring at least five dollars in pennies. Hoyle said the ideal number of people for a good game was seven, so we tried to have that many. Sometimes new boys would get mad when they lost money, and there would be wrestling matches on the front lawn, but nobody went to sleep, and no boy left early—unless he lost all of his money. Nobody complained if someone wanted to quit early and go home broke, but let a boy be seven or eight dollars ahead and try to leave, that was grounds for fighting. That's why we set a time limit, 7 p.m. to 7 a.m., and nobody who was ahead could leave before morning.

Like boys everywhere, we loved to build forts. One time we dug a huge hole in a friend's backyard. We covered it with planks and scrap plywood and shoveled a huge pile of dirt on top. We had a trapdoor with a short tunnel leading into our secret den. We built a little fireplace in one of the walls, had candles for light, and a pantry full of drinks and snacks.

As we were finishing it up, with just two of us inside, the other boys decided to play a trick on us by stacking some cement blocks on top of the trapdoor, trapping us inside. Then they went to the front yard to play football in the street.

No big deal for my friend and me. We had light, food, and drink. We figured we could survive in there for days if necessary, and in fact, we kind of wanted to do that.

After a while we began to feel cold, down in the damp earth like that. No problem. I built a little fire in the fireplace. Almost instantly we were warm, but just as fast, the oxygen in the air was used up. We couldn't breathe as the den filled with smoke because we had neglected to engineer a chimney to vent our fireplace. We began to yell and pound on the ceiling and the underside of the trapdoor, but the other boys were in the street and couldn't hear us. I knew if help didn't come quickly we would die.

It was my cousin Bill Nelson, the one who loved playing football the most, who received the strongest feeling that he ought to check on us, so he did. As he sauntered around the side of the house he noticed tendrils of smoke seeping from the dirt. He raced to the trapdoor, shoved away the blocks, and pulled it open, releasing billows of smoke and two coughing boys. We scrambled out into the clean air, rolled on our backs, and just drank it in for about ten minutes. We thanked Bill for saving our lives. I don't know if he ever realized what he had done for us. He acted like it was no big deal for him, but it was for us.

In northern California it seemed that most years the rainy season began in December. One time Syd and I had ridden our bikes to a sandstone quarry. We liked to go there and explore the many steep cliffs. We played too long one day, and it was already getting dark when we started for home. It had been raining a lot that week, and it looked like more rain was coming. In an effort to get home faster, we decided to ride our bikes through a huge walnut orchard.

The path we were following, which was sort of a jeep trail, got muddier and muddier the further we went. Pedaling got harder and harder as our tires became heavy with the sticky mud. Eventually the pedals and sprockets were so clogged with mud that we could no longer make them move, and it seemed our wheels were buried in foot-deep muck. We couldn't pull our bikes out and didn't know what to do. We didn't have a lot of time since it would soon be dark. We were cold and wet.

I suppose we could have just walked home and come back to get our bikes another day, but somehow that didn't seem to be an option. We used our bikes every day. We had to get them out, but we didn't know how to do it.

With all our firecrackers, pranks, poker games, and the trouble we got into at school, we weren't the most religious boys around, though I was active in the local Mormon ward. I suggested to Syd that we say a prayer. I didn't know what else to do, and he didn't object. We bowed our heads. (We didn't kneel because we were already ankle deep in mud.) I said a very humble prayer asking the Lord to help get us out of this muddy mess.

When we finished praying, we just stood there looking at our bikes wondering what to do. Then, in the distance, we heard a motor. It was getting closer. Pretty soon we could see the headlights of what appeared to be an army Jeep. The owner of the orchard was driving it. We thought we were in trouble. Maybe we would go to jail for trespassing. There was no way to escape without losing our bikes.

To our surprise, the man was friendly and very nice as he got out of his vehicle and came up to us. He was wearing rubber boots. He pointed to his house on a nearby hill and said he had been looking out his front window, watching our struggles with our bikes in the mud. He decided to come and help. He didn't say anything about seeing us pray.

The man had a long rope, which he tied to the front bumper of his Jeep, and one at a time he pulled our bikes out of the mud. We thanked him from the bottom of our hearts and headed for home.

Mike Thompson was the bully of my fifth grade school class. You had to get out of the way if he wanted to be first in line at lunch or first out the door at recess. Mike wasn't any taller than most of the kids in class, but he was heavier and stronger, maybe two hundred pounds or so, I thought. Those lower than Mike on the pecking order, including me, had better watch out and keep out of his way. He had blue eyes, rosy cheeks, and blond hair trimmed short in the popular flattop style.

I was sitting behind Mike the day our teacher, Mrs. Mosher, handed out watercoloring materials, which included paper, paint, brushes, and cans of water for rinsing the brushes when we changed colors. After a while Mike seemed to become bored with the painting, because every time he rinsed his brush he turned around and flicked colored water on me, sprinkling my face with a few annoying drops.

I asked him to stop, but he was having too much fun. Pretty soon he stopped painting altogether and went to work full time sprinkling me with paint water. The more I protested, the more he seemed to enjoy it. Occasionally he would pretend to be painting, so Mrs. Mosher would not catch on to what he was doing.

Finally, I'd had enough. I suppose I could have raised my hand and told Mrs. Mosher what was happening, but that seemed like a cowardly thing to do, besides I was not the kind of kid who would rat on anybody, not even my enemies.

The next time Mike sprinkled water on me, I picked up my coffee can full of colored paint water, reached forward, and poured it over Mike's pretty head, the dirty water running down his face and neck, over his clean white shirt and onto the floor.

Both of us flew out from under our desktops; me stepping back, raising my hands and forearms to protect myself, and Mike rolling forward like a bowling ball, his pudgy fists thrusting back and forth like little sledgehammers. He blackened my eye, bruised my ribs, and when he punched me in the stomach, my wind was gone. I couldn't breathe. I couldn't have called for help had I wanted to. Lamely I tried to hit him back but couldn't seem to land a solid blow.

Mrs. Mosher raced to the scene, pulling Mike away from me and sending him to the principal's office. She held me up until my breathing returned. Actually I felt pretty good, having learned a very interesting lesson, that black eyes and bruised ribs aren't nearly as painful as a fearful heart.

The transition from sixth grade at El Monte Elementary to seventh grade at Loma Vista Intermediate was dramatic. Not only was the intermediate school much larger, with hundreds more students, but its geographical area also included downtown Concord and Pacheco. I now shared my classrooms with many students of other races. Some were Japanese and Chinese, but most were Hispanic or Mexican students.

The problem wasn't the differences in eyes, lips, and skin color. It was the fact that some of my new classmates belonged to gangs, and there were rumors of gang members stealing lunch money from white kids from the suburbs.

Mostly we called the gang members hard guys or greasers, because many of them had long, greasy sideburns that were combed straight back on both sides. Usually they wore white tee shirts. Sometimes, because they weren't allowed to bring cigarettes to school, they had empty cigarette packs rolled up in their sleeves. New Levi jeans were worn without belts, as low on the behind as possible without falling down. The too-long pant legs were folded up on the inside. New Levis were never washed, eventually being able to stand up by themselves in a corner.

The greasers wore huge horseshoe taps nailed loosely to the heels of their shoes, which made clanking sounds when the boys walked.

At first I couldn't figure out why the greasers seemed so much bigger and stronger than the rest of us. Some of them needed to shave, and many of them looked like high school kids who had been lifting weights. Later I figured out that some of the greasers were simply older than the rest of us, having been sent back to junior high school because they were not able or willing to handle high school academic courses.

One day a classmate, Bobby Deltasondro, showed me his switchblade knife. It was so cool. He'd push a little button, and like magic a six-inch blade suddenly appeared. He told me all the greasers carried switchblades, so if they demanded my lunch money, I had better give it to them if I didn't want to get stabbed.

A few days later, while browsing through a comic book at the grocery store, I discovered an advertisement for mail order switchblade knives. I ordered two and gave one to Syd.

I took my new knife to school, but I didn't feel any safer. I knew if a bigger boy demanded my lunch money I'd just hand it over. There was no way I wanted to get in a knife fight with a guy twice as big as me. I decided I needed better protection than what a knife could offer.

I read the newspaper every day when I got home from school. One day I read an article explaining how the Oakland police were concerned about the increasing number of zip guns being carried by teenage inner city gang members. The article didn't explain what a zip gun was, but I finally figured out it was simply a homemade gun. I didn't know it was possible to make a gun at home. Wow!

I asked some of my friends at school what they knew about making zip guns. They didn't know anything, except one of them thought you needed a welding license from the union to do something like that. Another thought you had to have a machine shop, and another boy said they poured molten steel into molds to make gun barrels, and you needed a foundry to do that. They said it couldn't be done, not by a boy in junior high school.

After school I went to the Concord library to see if there was a book on making guns at home. There wasn't any such thing. For a week or two, in and out of school, I tried to figure out how to make a gun, but without success.

Then one Saturday morning I rummaged through my dresser drawers where I found a couple of .22 bullets I had brought back from my grandfather's ranch in Utah. I headed down to the hardware store.

Snooping around in the plumbing aisle, I found an eight-inch section of galvanized pipe, threaded at both ends, with just the right-sized bore for a .22 bullet. The front of the cartridge slipped easily into the pipe, but the wider flange at the rear was too wide to enter the bore. I had found a gun barrel.

Next I found a one-inch sleeve with female threads, just the right size to screw onto the threaded end of the pipe. Now my gun had a chamber.

In a bin right next to the one where I found my gun barrel, I located a 2½-inch threaded pipe, the same width as the barrel, that I could screw into the rear of the sleeve until it reached the back of the cartridge, holding it firmly in place.

I had fired .22 rifles at my grandfather's enough to know the cartridges were rim fired, meaning the firing pin struck them on the outer edge instead of in the middle like in larger hunting rifles and shotguns.

I figured that if I could thrust something as simple as a nail through the shorter pipe, with a force that was not centered, causing the nail to strike the edge instead of the center of the bullet, it would fire.

I bought the two pieces of pipe and the threaded sleeve. The following Monday, I took the sleeve into the metal shop where the teacher helped me solder a finishing nail in a perpendicular position across the top of the sleeve. When the teacher asked what I was making, I remember telling him I was working on an invention. He didn't bother me with any more questions.

Upon arriving home, I laid a 16-penny nail with a wide head on the sidewalk and began tapping the head with a hammer until both sides were turned back into a U shape, like the notch on an arrow.

Finally, I was ready to see if my gun would fire. Inserting a bullet into the long pipe, I screwed the sleeve with the crosspiece over the rear of the cartridge. Then I screwed in the short pipe until it was firm against the back of the cartridge.

Last, I attached a rubber band to the crosspiece on the sleeve and inserted the U-headed nail, point first, into the rear of the short pipe, slipping the other end of the rubber band into the U at the end of the nail. The gun was ready to fire.

I pointed it at our redwood fence that surrounded the patio in the backyard and pulled back the nail. Then, closing my eyes, I released the nail, allowing its pointed end to slam forward into the back of the bullet.

Nothing happened. Just a clicking sound. I was so disappointed. I removed the bullet to see if I could figure out what went wrong. I could see a tiny little dent where the front of the nail had struck the edge of the cartridge. I needed more thrust from the firing pin, so I added another rubber band. Again, only a click.

Finally, with the power of four rubber bands, the bullet fired. The slug made a hole through the redwood fence. The report was much louder than expected.

I went to the store and bought some more bullets. Since my mother was home, and knowing she wouldn't approve of target practice with real bullets, I went over to Syd's. His mother was a schoolteacher and didn't get home until later.

We learned very quickly that my little gun didn't fire every time. We found some thick, heavy rubber bands that seemed to work better.

We also found that an eight-inch galvanized pipe is not suited for accuracy. The bullets were creating twelve-inch random patterns at a distance of only six or eight feet, and slugs were bouncing all over the place if we shot at a cement wall. Concluding there was no way to make the gun more accurate, and for the sake of safety, I went back to the store and bought a box of long rifle bird shot, essentially turning my little handgun into a tiny shotgun. I suppose it seemed to make a lot more noise than a regular .22 rifle because the barrel was so short.

I took my gun to school, knowing I'd get into a lot of trouble if I got caught. I knew I could fool the teachers by taking it apart and putting different parts in different pockets. Nothing I had looked like a gun.

I carried the pieces with me to school for several weeks, wondering how fast I could get everything screwed together and loaded if someone demanded my lunch money. But nobody ever did.

My gun was insurance or protection, a weapon of last resort, that's all. I didn't want to shoot anyone, not even a greaser. I didn't want to get kicked out of school. I wanted the greasers to be afraid of me, or at least respect me so they would not try to take my money.

One day after school I invited some kids to come down to Cowell Creek next to the school to see my new gun. I showed them what it would do, making hash out of some crawdads resting in the shallow places. I figured that with some of the kids knowing about my gun, the news would spread to the greasers, and they would decide not to bother me. It didn't occur to me that news of my gun might spread in a different direction.

A day or two later, a teacher stopped me on the playground. He said word had reached the school office that I was bringing a gun to school. He asked me to empty my pockets. I pulled the pipe and some money out of my left pocket and then removed the short pipe, sleeve, yo-yo, marbles, and rubber bands from my right pocket. I pulled the bent nail firing-pin nail out of one of my back pockets. I was careful not to pull out any bullets. He shrugged his shoulders and walked away.

Nobody ever tried to take my lunch money, and after awhile I stopped taking the gun parts to school. I never showed the gun to my parents. I was certain they would take it away and make me promise not to make another.

I regret, in the worst way, from the bottom of my heart, not taking my homemade gun to Utah on the next summer vacation and showing it to my grandfather. He would have been so proud of me. I can see it now, him offering five dollars to buy it from me. I would hesitate, saying that amount would hardly cover the cost of the parts. Then he would offer ten dollars and I would hand him the gun. He wouldn't just show it to his friends. He would load and fire it too, telling the story of his smart little grandson inventing a gun that fired real cartridges so the big kids at school wouldn't steal his lunch money.

Mr. Wolverton was a huge bear of a man. Maybe in his younger years he looked like a defensive end on a football team, but when I knew him he was shaped like a pear because much of his weight had shifted to the middle. His black hair was cut short and flat on top. His eyebrows were thick and bushy, and his face seemed a little too flat in front. His eyes were dark and friendly. He was my seventh grade math teacher.

Mr. Wolverton must have liked his job, but I didn't notice things like that back then. He gave us regular homework and frequent tests. He was determined to teach us math. He was good at it and was seldom distracted. He was one of the few teachers who didn't seem to mind if I read outside books in class, as long as I did the homework and passed the tests.

I don't know what prompted him to get off the subject one winter afternoon, but he did, and that is the lecture I remember most. In fact, that is the only lecture from junior high to stick with me throughout my life. I don't remember his exact words, but I remember perfectly the content of what he said.

He began the lecture by saying he looked forward to seeing our fresh and eager faces each day. He said if any one of us didn't come to school on a given day, he missed us. He said that if any of us came up for adoption, we could move in with him, his wife, and children.

I didn't have any reason to doubt his sincerity. Then he got real serious.

He said the school administration had hired him to teach math, and he regretted he was not allowed to do more than that. He said he had a special lesson he would like to teach all the boys in his classes, but if he taught that lesson, he would be fired.

He asked if any of us would like to guess what that special lesson might be. Not a single hand went up.

He said in order to teach this special lesson he needed a single room with no windows, no furniture, and a big lock on the inside of the door, and he was the only one with a key to the lock.

He said he would invite the boys to join him in the room, one at a time. Once a boy was inside, Mr. Wolverton said he would lock the door and then tell the boy the teacher's intent, that in a few minutes he was going to give the boy a severe beating. The teacher fully intended to blacken the student's eyes, smash his nose, pull his hair, bruise his ribs, and kick his stomach—the works.

After making this surprise announcement, Mr. Wolverton said he would then give the boy a chance to talk him out of it. The boy might argue that he had done nothing to deserve a beating. He might threaten a lawsuit from parents, or warn the teacher that turnabout was fair play, that if the teacher proceeded with the beating, he might find sugar in the gas tank of his car, or a poisoned pet dog.

When the student had said everything he wanted to say to persuade the teacher to change his mind, Mr. Wolverton would then proceed with the beating. And he would give every boy in the class this same experience.

By this time hands were going up.

"Why do you want to hurt us?"

"Why don't you want to do it to the girls?"

"It isn't fair."

Mr. Wolverton didn't explain and didn't answer our questions. He said that some of us might understand someday why he would want to do such a thing. Then he smiled and went back to teaching math.

But I wasn't listening to the math instruction. I was tying to figure out why such a smart and kind man would want to beat us up. I could maybe see him wanting to beat me up, because I wasn't applying myself in his class, but why would he want to hurt the boys who were always raising their hands, the ones who got perfect or near-perfect scores on the tests? I was puzzled.

I wasn't happy in junior high school where I was one of the littlest kids in class. I thought I would be a lot happier once I got into high school. By then I would have gone through a growth spurt and be as big as most of the other boys. High school kids drove cars, even to school. You could leave school property to have lunch in town. The wrestling team had a weight class for little guys like me. The cute girls from junior high school were becoming attractive young women. Yes, I thought life would be better once I got to high school. Some of my friends thought they would finally be happy when they were out of school and had a good job. Most of the girls thought that when they got married they would live happily ever after, like in the fairy tales.

It seemed Mr. Wolverton wanted to teach us that life never got easy, even after high school, and life wasn't fair either. Life was messy and was supposed to be that way. If you wanted to be happy, you just learned to be happy, even when easy and fair never came.

Later in life, when I had children of my own, I found myself telling them that life isn't easy and life isn't fair. I didn't lock them in a room and beat them up, but I told them what I had learned from Mr. Wolverton.

We have judges, policemen, and courts to make life as fair as possible. Still, we might see a young mother of three fighting a losing battle with cancer. We might know a cocky and lazy young man with no education or skills who inherits ten million dollars. We might have a son who works harder than all his friends to prepare for football camp, only to be the first one cut by the coach.

We do so much to make our lives easy and comfortable, but still life is difficult. Once we accept the fact that life is difficult and expect it, then the fact that life is difficult no longer matters. We can roll up our sleeves and tackle whatever it is we have to do, and it's easier to be happy.

Maybe there were other lessons Mr. Wolverton had in mind, but these are the ones I gleaned from his lecture. I have wondered if I might have learned them earlier if he had indeed taken us into the locked room and given us beatings.

In the eighth grade my bad habits in school began to catch up with me. There were some Ds and an F on my report card. I just couldn't stop daydreaming, and when I got into a good book, I couldn't put it down, even in class.

The stories would paint pictures in my mind; pictures so vivid and real that if I closed the book the pictures didn't go away. I'd just get on my horse and ride into the picture, my own adventures unfolding, sometimes all day long, in episodes, as I wandered from class to class totally oblivious to what my teachers were trying to accomplish. I'm sure Ruth Ann Sweetzer, Barbara Roe, and Mrs. Perry would have been amazed if they knew how many times they were rescued and saved by the skinny little kid who always had a book in his hand.

One day the counselor told me I was not going to graduate from intermediate school, that I would have to repeat eighth grade. Some of my best friends were in the grade below me, so I wasn't terribly opposed to the idea of being held back. But it was a different story with my parents. My mother marched into the school office ready to do battle until they decided to graduate me.

I remember one day that my history teacher, Marion St. John, asked me to stay after class. I assumed I was in some kind of trouble. I sometimes sold firecrackers in the hall outside his class. I brought my homemade gun to his class, had a little cannon that could blast holes through school walls, and had been luring boys into poker games to take their money.

Mr. St. John was not one of the popular teachers. He was a small balding man who didn't play sports. My classmates thought he was too soft spoken and hard to listen to. Before he became a teacher, he was a Catholic priest and a missionary to the Navajo Indians. I remember him describing floating eyeballs and pieces of brain in mutton stew served up by his Indian friends. I liked him, but it seemed I was always reading something other than the textbook in his class.

To my surprise I was not in trouble. He talked to me like he was a friend who liked me. This surprised me. He said he was aware of my bad grades and the intentions of the administration to hold me back a year. He said he observed my reading habit too, how I checked out a pile of books from the library each week and seemed to read them all. He said he could tell from the way I answered questions that I was learning a lot from all my reading.

He said he thought I was in the process of getting a better education than any student in the school. I just wasn't doing it the conventional way. He said I should not let the adults with the power take that out of me. Sure, I needed to start paying attention in class and do the work assigned by my teachers, but in no way should I let them talk me out of my outside reading.

He said he was putting in a good word for me, so I graduated from the eighth grade without being held back.

Later, when I started writing novels, I realized all that practice at daydreaming in grade school was not a wasted effort. Now I sit in front of a computer, scenes and stories unfolding in my mind as I pound away on the keyboard. A publisher puts my words in books and sends me a royalty check each month. Now I get paid to be a dreamer.

I came to realize too that my reading addiction was an essential part of my development process. I do not know a good writer who is not an avid reader. All the good writers read a lot. I see people who do not read other authors' works trying to write novels, and they almost always fail. I find it amazing that among all the adult teachers and administrators who monitored my progress in grade school, only Marion St. John seemed to appreciate and understand the value in my reading habit. He was the only one who encouraged me to keep doing it, even when my schoolwork suffered because of it. I feel a deep and profound gratitude for this quiet man.

My first taste of good grades started when I was a freshman in high school. I don't know how it happened, but I ended up in an algebra class comprised mostly of junior and senior football players. Half of them were bigger than my father, and I couldn't tip the scale at a hundred and five pounds.

I feared that if I got out of line one of them would beat me up. I sat straight in my chair, looking forward, never raising my hand, never looking at anybody, and never opening my mouth. I was guarded, feeling like I had to be careful.

A few weeks into the term, near the end of a class period, the teacher put a simple problem on the board, and none of the students could solve it. The teacher seemed irritated that no one in the class could do the problem. One after another, the big guys sauntered to the front of the room and failed to get it right. I closed my eyes and prayed that the teacher would not call on me.

Finally, the teacher announced that no one was leaving the class until someone solved the problem. Then he asked me if I would come to the blackboard and attempt to do it. I swallowed hard, wondering if the chalk would slip out of my sweaty fingers. I hoped I wouldn't trip and make a fool out of myself on the way to the front of the room.

I wasn't worried about the problem. It was simple. I just couldn't figure out why my handsome, muscle-bound classmates, the ones the girls swooned over, couldn't do the work.

When I arrived at the board, I wrote down the two or three steps one had to go through to arrive at the answer. Then I wrote down the answer. I didn't have to look at the teacher to know I had done it correctly.

After that, some of the football players began to notice me and even call me by name. When the teacher gave us time to work on problems, some of them would come over to my desk and ask me to help them. I loved algebra and stopped bringing outside reading to class. I remember the teacher having me do problem after problem at the blackboard during parent-teacher night. For the first time in the history of my public school education, I received an A. After algebra, my favorite class was physics.

When counselors talked to us about career ambitions, I gradually settled on the idea that I would like to be an engineer, probably a civil engineer, building dams in Brazil or Pakistan and roads in the arctic. I didn't think the love of reading and the daydreaming would ever leave me, but I would make my living building things, using my interest in math and science.

CHAPTER II

How long can men thrive between walls of brick, walking on asphalt pavements, breathing the fumes of coal and of oil, growing, working, dying, with hardly a thought of wind, and sky, and fields of grain, seeing only machine-made beauty, the mineral-like quality of life. This is our modern danger—one of the waxen wings of flight. It may cause our civilization to fall unless we act quickly to counteract it, unless we realize that human character is more important than efficiency, that education consists of more than the mere accumulation of knowledge.

—CHARLES LINDBERGH
American aviator, author, inventor,
explorer, and social activist
(1902–1974)

When I was nine, as soon as school was out, my grandfather invited me to come to Utah to spend the summer on his 160-acre farm in West Bountiful.

I remember walking home from school, passing some stores in Concord, and seeing what I thought was a fancy pair of cowboy boots in the window of a shoe store. They were just what I needed to go to Utah and be a cowboy for the summer. The price was about thirteen dollars. The end of school was still a month away, so I went to work earning money for the boots—mowing lawns, selling a few more firecrackers, and initiating a few friendly neighborhood poker games.

On the Saturday before I was to go to Utah, I counted my money and had just enough to buy the boots. My intent was to go to the store the following Monday, right after school, and make the purchase.

When I went to church that Sunday, the teacher gave a lesson on tithing. I don't remember anything she said, only the feeling that the right thing to do was to pay tithing on the money I had earned. I remember slowly counting it out that afternoon between Sunday School and sacrament meeting. If I paid the tithing, I wouldn't have enough left to buy the boots. There wasn't enough time before my departure to earn more money. It probably occurred to me that my parents would make up the deficiency if I asked them to, but since I had tried so hard to make all the money myself, I viewed a donation from my parents as a failure. Finally, I gathered up the tithing portion of the money, took it with me to sacrament meeting, and gave it to the bishop. I decided not to buy the boots if I couldn't do it with my own money.

The next day, on my way home from school, I went by the store to take one last look at the boots I could no longer afford. They were on sale! The store owner had marked down the price to nine dollars. I had plenty of money to buy them. I hurried home to get my money, believing that the Lord had blessed me for paying my tithing.

That summer was the first of many spent in Utah with my grandparents. From the time I was nine, until I turned sixteen, I went to Utah the week school ended for the summer and returned the week school began in the fall.

Sometimes I went in the family car since vacations were sometimes planned around my schedule. Several times I flew on commercial airplanes. Sometimes I traveled with family friends, like the time a distant cousin, Ralph Lubeck, took me to Utah. He was teaching in California, and at the end of school was returning to Utah to meet his fiancée, Marge, and get married.

I remember Ralph's old white coupe and how we frequently had to stop at roadside ditches to put water in the radiator. Whenever we stopped for gas or food, I begged for the opportunity to put my money into the one-armed bandits that were everywhere. He reminded me that one had to be twenty-one to do that and that I must wait. I continued to beg for the chance to lay my hands on some of that easy money. I assured him I would be discrete and no one would catch me doing it.

Finally, Ralph gave in. Besides, he had decided it was time I learned a lesson on the evils of gambling. He said I could put a quarter into one of the machines. No dimes or nickels, but a whole quarter. He wanted the lesson to be painful.

So I plunked a quarter into the nearest machine and pulled down the handle. I watched in fascination at the spinning cylinders. The first one stopped at a cluster of cherries. The second one stopped—another cluster of cherries. The third one finally stopped, showing even more cherries. Eighteen quarters tumbled into the tray. So much for my lesson on the evils of gambling. When we arrived at my grandparents' farm, my pockets were bulging with quarters.

I stayed in what my grandfather fondly called the guest bedroom, which was a converted coal storage room off the back porch. The thick adobe walls kept it cool, even on days when it was over a hundred degrees outside. The room was small—barely big enough for a double bed, a chest of drawers, and a gun rack. Pop had papered the walls with pictures from huge calendars, the kind they used to give away at hardware and feed stores. For hours I would lay on my back looking at grazing cattle, drinking horses, and Indians from C. M. Russell paintings. I doubt if there's a bedroom in a king's palace anywhere in the world that I would have preferred over that tiny, colorful room.

Life on the farm soon fell into a normal routine. We would get up between six and seven to do chores, which consisted of feeding cows, horses, and chickens, and changing the irrigation water. We would come in at eight for a breakfast of bacon, fried eggs, hot cakes, fried potatoes with thinly sliced zucchini and onions, and Tang breakfast drink. Hot or cold, cereal was never served there—never.

After breakfast we did our work for the day: putting up hay, cleaning ditches, moving cattle to different pastures, mending mangers and fences, hauling junk to the dump, or planting, watering, and weeding the huge vegetable garden.

At noon we would have dinner, which consisted of roasts and steaks or chicken or lamb, with vegetables from the garden, including green onions, cucumbers, potatoes, green beans, corn, carrots, beets, turnips, tomatoes, and squash. There was a big row of raspberries and thirteen varieties of peach trees providing fruit for desserts. When we had sliced tomatoes, Pop always covered his with white sugar.

We never missed saying a blessing on the food, but when Pop said it, I could not understand what he was saying. It was always the same length, with a familiar rhythm and cadence, but none of the words made any sense to me. I knew he did not know a foreign language, and the few times when I asked him what he said in his blessings, he would pinch me, or change the subject. But his prayers never changed, and to this day I have no idea what he was saying, other than it probably had something to do with offering thanks and blessing the food.

The noon meals were never hurried. Stories were always plentiful to go along with the food. Because we would frequently enjoy the same food, the same stories were repeated many times over the years.

I remember Pop telling how he courted my grandmother. They did it with horse and buggy, before cars were available. He said when you took a new girl for a ride and wanted her to put her arms around you, all you had to do was whip your horse into a dead run. The driver held the reins, but the passenger didn't have anything to hold onto but the driver. The girl would have to throw her arms around you if she didn't want to bounce out.

On one of the first buggy rides when Pop had a chance to be alone with my grandmother, a neighbor boy on horseback joined them. He rode alongside, chatting and teasing, refusing to leave the couple alone. Pop remembered a trick his father had taught him. Carefully and nonchalantly, he maneuvered the buggy until the right wheel was directly behind the hind legs of the saddle horse the boy was riding. At just the right moment, Pop applied the whip to his buggy horse, causing it to lurch forward, forcing the right wheel between the hind legs of the saddle horse, tipping it over on its side and unseating the rider.

On another occasion, Pop stopped by Olivia's to make sure she was going to the dance with him the following night. She said she was not and that she had agreed to go to the dance with one of Pop's friends, whose name I cannot remember.

The next morning, Pop asked the same friend to ride in the buggy with him to the resort at Black Rock or Salt Air at the south end of the Great Salt Lake where Pop had to pick up a horse. Pop said he would be back in time for the dance. The boy welcomed the chance to visit the resort.

Upon arrival at the resort, Pop let the boy out, agreeing to meet in an hour for the drive back to Woods Cross. Of course, Pop returned home immediately, without his passenger, who had no way of finding another ride that would get him home in time for the dance.

That evening it was Pop, not the other boy, who showed up at Olivia's house to take her to the dance. At first she refused to believe the other boy wasn't coming. They waited an hour. The boy never showed up, so she finally went to the dance with Leland. He later boasted that they were married on December 21, the longest night of the year.

After the noon meal, Pop usually took a nap, while I saddled my horse and went for a ride. Eventually I found friends up and down the street I could visit and play with. Some had horses too.

Sometimes I would ride over the railroad tracks and through the pastures to the pond Pop had dug during the 1950s to store irrigation water for the fields closest to the Great Salt Lake. The pond covered about a third of an acre and was surrounded by weeping willow trees. At first we could fish in it for carp, then blue gill, and then small-mouth bass. There were lots of leopard frogs in the grass along the edge of the pond. When we could catch a lot of them, we'd fry up the legs for breakfast after soaking them in salt water all night. Sometimes we'd find a mother duck with babies swimming among the willow branches. On hot days, my cousin Karen and I would ride our horses in the pond. There was only one spot where it was deep enough for a smaller horse to actually swim.

Just before dark, muskrats would come out of their dens and swim through the water looking for food or to play. Pop encouraged me to hunt them, because sometimes they'd go up the irrigation ditches and do a lot of damage digging holes around the dams. Sometimes, just before dark, I'd jump on my horse, bareback, with the reins in my left hand and a loaded shotgun in my right and gallop over the railroad tracks and through the meadows to the pond. Pop didn't mind me doing that, and my grandmother never said anything, but I doubt I would want my children carrying a loaded shotgun on a galloping horse.

One time I was riding by myself down to the pond on a very hot day. About a quarter mile away I began hearing laughing. Then I could see four or five bikes leaned up against the gate to the lower dirt road. I slowed the horse to a walk and approached cautiously.

The uninvited guests were teenage girls, two or three years older than me. They were playing in the water and swimming around, and they were not wearing any clothes. Their clothes were on the ground near the bicycles.

When they finally saw me, one or two of them became angry and started yelling at me. They said if I didn't turn my horse around and go back the way I came, and do it this instant, they would pull me off my horse and beat the tar out of me. I felt embarrassed and intimidated. Following orders, I turned my horse around and headed back to the house. If they had just asked me to leave, I would have done so, because the situation was embarrassing and uncomfortable. But because they threatened to jerk me off my horse and beat the tar out of me, I wanted to fight back.

It wasn't long until I was kicking myself for being such an unthinking coward. What would those girls have done if I had told them I couldn't leave until I had fed the alligator? Or, if they didn't believe that, I could have galloped over to the gate, grabbed most of their clothes, and jumped back on the horse before they could have stopped me. Then I would be the one barking the orders. But I was too slow to think about any of that while they were yelling at me.

Later in life, when I was writing novels, sometimes I would get a new idea for a scene I had written weeks or months earlier. I would go back and change the scene to incorporate the new idea, happy that I had been able to make my story even better. Maybe this is why good novels seem better and more interesting than real life. A good novelist can go back again and again, changing the events of his story, making them better and better. Oh, how I wish we could do that in real life. I don't understand some writers' claim that they never edit or rewrite, that what they write is always best the first time. I love the movie *Groundhog Day*, where the selfish, egotistical hero, Bill Murray, has to repeat the same day over and over, perhaps hundreds of times, until he finally gets it right. That's what good novelists and public speakers do all the time.

Some days Karen would come to play. We had so much fun together. We hoped the summers would never end. Her long dark hair was always braided in pigtails. Her tanned face was round, and her dark brown eyes were alert and intense. She was four months younger than me and fiercely independent. Though she was smaller than me, she could run faster and ride better. When we wanted to do different things, or when we both wanted to sit in the chair to the right of Pop at dinner, she was the one who usually got what she wanted.

Our time together was mostly spent riding the horses, sometimes riding as far north as Kaysville along the dirt roads through the Farmington Bay Bird Refuge, or south as far as the Salt Lake stockyards. Usually we rode bareback. It was three miles around the block, and sometimes we would do that three or four times in one day. On occasion we would set up a pole on bales of hay and jump our horses. Karen's mare, Pedal Pushers, could go the highest. We would do this bareback, a rope tied around the horses' necks so they wouldn't jump out from under us.

After a while my horse figured out that if he stopped real quick, right in front of the jump, I would fall off. He started doing it on a regular basis. We told Pop. As usual, he knew exactly how to correct such a problem. He tied a long rope to the horse's head and started running it in circles, making it go over the jump. When the horse tried to stop in front of the jump, it felt the sting of his long whip, again and again. After a while the horse learned not to stop in front of the jump. He never did it again.

On the really hot days, sometimes we would gallop around the pastures, squirting each other with water guns, or go for a ride in the pond. Sometimes we dragged the hose from the garden over to the sand pile under a big weeping willow tree by the milk house where we would make ponds. The hose would be in the highest pond, the water flowing through sections of pipe to lower ponds. Sometimes there would be seven or eight ponds, the water flowing smoothly from one to another. When the ponds were finished, we made Spanish galleons from big zucchini squashes, and Indian canoes from pea pods. We got really dirty crawling around in the wet sand, but my grandparents never complained. Sometimes we would climb high in the big sycamore between the sidewalk and the street, dropping cherries and apricots on passing cars.

One time, when I had learned from a neighborhood boy how to hypnotize a chicken by holding it on the ground and drawing a line in the dirt out from its eye, we decided to play a joke on Pop. While he was taking his afternoon nap, we hypnotized five or six hens in the driveway between the house and the barnyard and ran into the house yelling a dog was killing the chickens. Pop grabbed his shotgun and ran outside. When he saw the chickens lying motionless on their sides, he knew the problem was serious. But he couldn't find the dog. Pretty soon the chickens started to get up and walk away. Karen and I laughed at how clever we had been to play such a joke on him.

Sometimes Pop would kill a chicken for our dinner. We loved to watch, first as he cut the head off with a hatchet, and then how the blood would squirt all over the place. Once or twice a chicken got out of his hand and would run around with no head. We thought that was so neat.

Pop never bothered plucking feathers off the chickens. He just skinned them, giving the warm, limber, and sometimes-bloody skins with the feathers still on them to us to wear as Indian hats, which we were delighted to do. My grandmother didn't like him doing this. She was afraid we would get lice, but as far as I know, we never did.

Sometimes when something funny happened, Karen would look at me, or me at her, and we'd start giggling—softly at first, and then louder. The problem was that once we began, it was nearly impossible to stop. We usually did it in places we weren't supposed to be doing it, such as in church or at the dinner table, where after asking us to stop three or four times, Pop would send us outside.

Not long after Ralph brought me to Utah to spend that first summer when I was nine, we were all invited to his wedding in Salt Lake City. Neither Ralph, nor his future wife, Marge, belonged to the Mormon Church, so the wedding was held in their Episcopal Church.

When it was time to be seated, Karen and I somehow got separated from our parents and were sitting with some other children in the first or second row, several rows out of reach of our parents. Ralph and Marge had a lot of friends, and as I remember, the chapel was full.

All was fine until the minister or priest walked up the isle. He was wearing a sparkling white robe with gold trim that to us looked very much like a dress, and we had never seen a man in a dress before.

Karen and I didn't dare look at each other, knowing we were involved in a very serious event and that this was not the place to find mirth. When the priest reached the front of the church, he turned to face the audience. He was wearing a gold hat—not exactly a crown like we had seen on kings in books and movies, but a strange hat with the gold front part appearing to be about two feet high. He had such a serious look on his face. It was the funniest thing either one of us had ever seen.

We just had to look at each other. I don't remember who giggled first, but soon both of us were doing it, knowing full well we deserved to die for such an offense. But bring on the gallows, we simply couldn't stop. Tears were running down our cheeks, and every adult in the room was scowling at us. The brave priest, bless his heart, went ahead with the ceremony as if nothing was wrong.

When it was all over and Ralph had kissed his beautiful bride, we went outside to receive our beatings, but nothing like that happened. I remember our parents telling us how disappointed they were, and as I think about it, I can't remember Karen and I both being invited to the same wedding ever again.

I clearly remember being ten years old and standing face to face with Karen on the west side of the hay barn, next to the wire gate. I could see the light in her face and the fire in her eyes as we made plans for our future together. We decided to get married as soon as we were old enough. I would earn the money, and she would tend the children and animals. Every evening we would ride our horses. The children would ride too. It was perfect. We would be husband and wife. We were engaged!

We thought we were the happiest kids on the planet, but then we made a terrible mistake, something ten-year-olds in love should never do. We ran to the house and told our parents and grandparents what we intended to do. I suppose we thought they would be as excited about the good news as we were, that our mothers would want to hurry to town to order the wedding invitations. Such was not the case.

They told us cousins couldn't get married—not ever. It was against the law. We demanded to know who would pass a stupid law like that. They couldn't tell us. They tried to explain that our children might have six toes on each foot and wear diapers until they were twelve, but we didn't believe them.

We were surprised and devastated, but the discussion was not over. They told us that since we were talking about marriage and having children, we would not be allowed to sleep in the same bed anymore. When Karen stayed over, she would have to sleep upstairs instead of with me in the back porch room with the calendar wallpapering.

We were furious. We demanded to know why they were so mean—so unfair. What had we done that they would want to punish us in this manner? What did they think we were going to do, besides scratch each other's backs and giggle until midnight? Our questions were not answered to our satisfaction. We did not like the explanation that if we didn't understand it now, someday we would. But the decision remained in place. After that we never slept in the same bed again, and we gradually abandoned our plans to be married. We remained good friends throughout our adult lives. Sometimes years would pass without seeing each other, and I feel bad about that because we had been such good friends as children and shared so many wonderful memories. Later in life, when I saw Karen as a mother with babies, or a grandmother with streaks of gray in her hair, I could still see the light in her face and the fire in her eyes as we stood face to face by the wire gate figuring out a lifetime of raising children and riding horses.

I suppose true love, even if you're only ten, never dies.

Karen married Jan Price and moved to his farm at McCammon, Idaho. I liked to go up there where I would ride horses, hunt, or take the children swimming at Soda Hot Springs. If we stopped at a gas station for cold drinks, Jan always had his money out first. If we went to dinner or a movie, it was almost a fight to convince Jan it was my turn to pay. One time when he bought a new shotgun, he gave me his old one. Whenever I think about Jan, I find myself wanting to be more like him—more generous.

On those summer evenings at Pop and Nana's house, our supper consisted of bread and milk, cheese, boiled eggs, tomatoes sprinkled with sugar, green onions, and whatever else was ready in the orchard or garden. Sometimes we would go to the drive-in theater with a picnic supper. The admission was ten cents a person. Sometimes we took our picnic up Farmington or Weber canyons where Pop and I fished.

On Wednesdays, we hitched on the stock trailer and went to the Producer's Livestock auction in Salt Lake. Pop had an arrangement with the dairy farmers in Farmington and Centerville to haul their cull cows to the auction for fifteen dollars a head. These were usually old cows declining in milk production, with injuries of one kind or another or swollen milk bags.

We went to the auction even if we didn't have a cow to take. Pop was always bidding on various horses and cows when he thought the price was right. When he bought a horse, we trimmed hocks and mane to clean it up. I would ride it for a week or two, and then we'd take it back to the sale, hoping to turn a profit.

While at the auction, we'd usually take a break and go to the coffee shop in the Producer's Livestock office building. Our favorite dessert was cherry pie, which we would smother in sugar and pour coffee cream over the top. On the really hot days, we stopped at the A&W on the way home for a frosty mug of root beer.

Since Pop was always buying and selling horses, he would coach me on the ancient art of horse trading. Certain rules applied. Whether buying or selling, you always tried to get the other fellow to mention the price first. Then the dickering began. If you were selling and wanted to get as much as possible, you talked about the good features. If you were buying and wanted to pay as little as possible, you talked about the negative features, and you could always find some. In those days there were very few horses with papers, so age was always a concern when one of the parties didn't know how to read the horse's teeth.

One afternoon, Pop purchased a horse from a man who had sold him horses before. When the deal was done, Pop was surprised at how little he had to pay for the horse.

"John," he said to the seller. "You sold him too cheap. Now the deal is done, and you have my money, tell me what is wrong with him."

John just laughed and said, "You can't bridle him." There were no hard feelings. That's the way the horse-trading business was done. We put the horse in a chute, tied his head down, and bridled him a hundred times, two or three days in a row, until he stopped fighting it. Then we sold him for a nice profit.

Pop had a way with horses. He was stern, even mean in the eyes of Karen and me, but his methods worked. One time I was having a hard time catching Donkey Jack, a big donkey we liked to ride. He would come to me when I had a bucket of grain in my hand, but as soon as I picked up the halter to catch him, he ran away. I tried holding the halter behind my back, or dropping it on the ground until he was happily munching the grain, but I could not succeed in catching him. Finally, I went to Pop for help. He got Donkey Jack to come to the bucket of grain and then gently wrapped his right arm around the donkey's neck, nodding for me to bring up the halter. When I was about five feet away, Donkey Jack tried to pull away, and Pop refused to release his hold. Donkey Jack was the stronger of the two and went bucking across the field, but Pop didn't let go. While the donkey was running and bucking, Pop was doing something with his left hand, but I could make no sense of it.

Finally the donkey came to a halt. Pop still had his right arm wrapped tightly around the neck. He called for me to bring the halter again. When I arrived I could see what the left hand had been doing. Pop had reached in the donkey's mouth, grabbed the tongue, and twisted it into a bulging knot. Blood was oozing from the twists and creases because the donkey had tried to bite down on the hand and tongue, but Pop had not let go of the neck or the tongue. Donkey Jack gave us no more trouble as we slipped on the halter.

From a previous owner, Donkey Jack had learned to drink beer out of a paper cup. This was a great entertainment item for guests. Pop would pour beer into a cup until it was about half full and hold it out to the donkey. Using his teeth, the jackass would grab the cup by the rim, lift it high in the air, and suck in the beer as it spilled over his front teeth. When the beer was gone Donkey Jack would drop the cup on the ground and shake his head. I'm sure Pop had to answer some awkward questions from his Mormon friends at the grocery store when they saw him buying beer for his pet donkey.

On another occasion, I persuaded Pop to train one of our horses to pull a two-wheeled cart I found hanging in the back of one of the barns. We put the harness on the horse and drove him around a bit before hitching him to the cart. We led him and the cart to the edge of the big field west of the house. I held the horse's head while Pop got into the cart. Then he held the reins while I hurried back and got into the cart beside him.

With the long reins, Pop patted the horse and clicked his tongue. Nothing. The horse refused to move forward. More clicking and rein slapping only made the horse more tense. His ears were back, his nostrils flared, and his flanks quivering.

Pop stopped slapping the horse and quietly handed me the reins. He whispered to me that the horse might be getting ready to explode into a bucking rampage. Quickly, Pop slipped out of the cart and hurried forward until he had taken hold of the horse's bridle. He bent over, scooped up a handful of dirt, and gently shoved it into the horse's mouth. Immediately the horse began opening and closing his mouth while attempting to push out the dirt with his tongue. Pop hurried back and joined me in the cart. He took the reins and clicked his tongue. This time the horse moved forward, walking and trotting, still trying to get rid of the dirt in its mouth.

Pop never explained the psychology involved in his technique. I guess it had something to do with getting the horse's attention away from the cart. The dirt in its mouth did that.

On another occasion, Pop agreed to board a thoroughbred

stallion for a friend who was going on vacation. We put the horse in a large stall inside what used to be the milking barn. My job was to feed the horse every day and make sure his water trough was full.

On about the third day, I told Pop the horse was losing weight. All it did was trot back and forth in the stall for hours every day, seldom, if ever, stopping to eat and rest. Pop went to the barn with me to see for himself.

After watching the horse for a few minutes, Pop went into what we called the grain room and brought out a short-handled scoop shovel. He let himself into the stall with the horse. Holding the shovel in both hands, Pop moved quietly toward the horse. At first it moved away from him, but finally it let him get close.

Suddenly Pop was swinging the shovel like Babe Ruth at bat, it sounding like a gun shot when the broad pan slapped the horse on the side of the neck. The horse was so stunned he almost fell over backward. *Wham*, Pop hit him again. This time the horse scrambled to put as much distance between it and Pop as possible. Pop returned the shovel to the grain room and left the barn.

I hung around to see what the horse would do. He went over to the manger and started eating. To this day I cannot explain how slapping a horse with a scoop shovel got it to relax and eat. I only know that I was there, watched the whole thing, and saw the results.

Pop was born in 1892, before Utah became a state and before people traveled in cars. He belonged to a generation that depended on horses and mules for travel and for earning a livelihood. I have often wondered how much more he knew about horses; things that are lost to my generation.

His father, William Henry Jex Smith, had a freighting business, hauling goods from Missouri to Utah before the railroad came, and after that, hauling freight and supplies from the railheads in Salt Lake and Ogden to the mines in Montana.

Pop told me that when his father was a young man he spent an entire summer hauling Mormon converts to Utah from Nebraska for the Church. At the end of the summer, he went to Brigham Young and asked him if he could have some hay to get his mules and horses through the winter since he had been hauling for the Church instead of earning money that summer. Brigham Young told him, as the story goes, that he should consider his services a donation to the Church. Young did not give him any hay. After that, William Henry avoided Brigham Young and the Church.

One time, a teamster, who had been working for William for many years hauling supplies to the mines in Montana, decided to quit. William took the man aside, saying something like:

"You have been stealing whiskey from me, and I have not been able to catch you. Now that you are leaving, tell me how you did it. No hard feelings; I'd just like to know."

The man walked over to a wagon that contained a barrel of Utah spirits—or Valley Tan, as everyone called it. Using a coal chisel and hammer, he began tapping against one of the iron rings. As the iron moved, the man showed William a little hole with a piece of cork in it. Using his pocketknife, he removed the cork and sucked on the hole until he'd taken several swallows of his favorite drink. He replaced the cork and tapped the iron hoop back in place to hide the hole. William thanked the man for revealing his secret.

Pop said his father would never hire a man who parted his hair in the middle or smoked cigarettes. Pipe and cigar smoking were permitted, as well as chewing, but he didn't like cigarette smoking and would not allow it. He fired any man who drank out of a stream or ditch, probably because of the abundant bacteria contamination and the potential of getting sick. They had to boil drinking water, usually flavoring it with coffee or tea. They could drink beer or whiskey from a jug, but any man who dropped to his knees or belly to drink from a stream lost his job.

The family moved from Centerville to the farm in West Bountiful when Pop was eight. They had a dairy with horse-drawn wagons hauling the milk and buttermilk to Salt Lake City every day. They milked draft horses to provide mare's milk to women whose babies were allergic to cows' milk. The signs on the wagons said *Jake Smith's Celebrated Buttermilk, Best in the World*. Pop thought his father's dairy was the first to deliver buttermilk in Salt Lake City.

Pop said at one time they hired a man who was superstitious and was afraid of the dark. He sometimes talked about how it frightened him to go into the dark barn before daylight to begin harnessing the horses for the milk wagons. Pop was only about ten when one morning he hid in the hay storage portion of the barn behind the wall where the harnesses hung. Part of one of the boards was broken away. When the superstitious man reached up to take down the first harness, Pop reached through the hole and grabbed the man's stomach. The man didn't scream or slap at Pop's hand. He just collapsed on the floor.

Pop said he got in trouble when he traded his saddle horse for a bicycle. All the boys were riding bikes, and Pop wanted one too. His father told him he would never amount to anything if he continued making such foolish trades.

When Pop was about fifteen, his father and oldest brother, also named William, went to Twin Falls, Idaho, to homestead some free land made available when the Snake River was dammed up to provide irrigation water to the new farms. Pop's mother refused to go with them. There were seven children still at home, with Pop second to the youngest. The burden of running the farm fell squarely on Pop's shoulders. He quit school in the fifth grade to work full time on the farm. There was a seven-thousand-dollar mortgage, which he eventually paid off.

When I knew Pop, he was defensive about his lack of education. He liked to make fun of professors and doctors who did stupid things. He didn't trust doctors and lawyers. He also liked to make fun of star athletes who didn't know how to work like real men.

One time he discovered a survey crew on his property, staking out a course for a proposed power line. When he asked the young surveyors what they were doing, they had some fun with the old farmer. They told him they were marking locations for oil wells— or was it a big gold mine or the new uranium discovery they were staking out?

Quietly, Pop turned and left. At the end of the day, when the surveyors were loading their equipment into their truck, Pop came walking up with an armload of stakes, all the ones that had been placed on his land.

"If you fellers can't decide what it is you are surveying, I don't want you doing it on my land." Then he tossed the stakes over the fence.

One time, when we were driving through one of the lower fields,

Pop spotted the unmarked car of the local game warden parked on the lower road. Pop stopped the truck, pulled the .22 rifle out from behind the seat, and started shooting out the window toward a pile of horse manure about a hundred feet away, hoping the game warden would see him. Then he had me get out of the truck, grab a gunnysack from behind the seat, run over to the pile of manure, shove it into the bag, and run back to the truck. When I accomplished this, we turned around and hurried up through the fields to the house.

When we arrived, the game warden was parked in the driveway waiting for us. We gave him the bag of manure, and he drove off in a huff.

Pop had only one dog during those summers I spent in Utah, but he had lots of dog stories, and we had some dog adventures. Sometimes Pop would tell me about a German shepherd he once owned. The dog's name was Nick.

One time Pop was in one of the lower hay fields repairing a piece of equipment when he remembered something he was supposed to do at the house. As he started back, he told Nick to stay and guard the tools.

After Pop finished his business at home, something else came up requiring him to go to town. Then it was dark and time for supper.

The next morning, when he went out to do the chores, he noticed the dog was missing. He called Nick's name. Pop went down by the barns and looked around—no dog. He was afraid a car or train had hit Nick.

After breakfast when Pop went back down to the lower field to finish repairing the equipment, he found Nick, waiting and guarding the tools. The dog had stayed there nearly twenty-four hours with nothing to eat or drink. Pop said he cried when he put his arms around Nick and thanked him for being such a loyal friend.

One Wednesday morning, when we arrived at the Church farm in Farmington to pick up a cow to take to the auction, no one was there to help us catch and load the cow. The two watchdogs, which were Doberman pinschers, were turned out. They were growling and snarling outside our truck doors when we came to a halt. No way was I getting out of the truck.

Pop called me a sissy for being afraid of a dog. He got out of the truck and walked around to my side. The dogs backed away, sensing he was not afraid of them, but they were still growling and barking.

Pop assured me that I would be fine if I stayed at his side. Reluctantly, I slid out of the truck and walked beside him toward the barn to search for the cow. The dogs were right behind us, still growling. I kept looking around at them, certain we were going to be attacked at any moment. Pop seemed to ignore them completely, acting like he didn't even know they were there.

With our backs turned, the dogs gathered courage and began inching closer and closer. I figured Pop might be able to handle one of the dogs, but the other one would catch and kill me for sure.

Suddenly, without warning, Pop reached back with both hands and simultaneously grabbed each dog by the nose—one with his left hand and one with his right. The dogs howled in surprise and tried to attack, but Pop only tightened his grip. In a few seconds the growling stopped and both dogs were whining in pain. Pop kicked each one in the belly and then let go of their noses. With tails between their legs, they ran back to their pen, and we found our cow.

Pop told me one time that when he was at the barbershop in Bountiful, the men there started talking about a mean, wild dog that wandered up and down Main Street. Pop doubted any dog was as mean and wild as the men said, and soon he had a ten-dollar bet with several of them who didn't believe he could call the dog to him and pet it.

Pop said he had to go home for a minute but would be right back and prove once and for all how gentle that dog could be. Instead of going home, he went to a neighbor's house where there was a female dog in heat. Pop held the dog's collar while rubbing his boot and pant leg against her behind, smearing the menstrual blood on his boot and trousers. He drove back to Bountiful, walked up and down Main Street, and sat down on the bench in front of the barbershop.

It wasn't long until the dog that everyone thought was so mean and wild was licking Pop's boots and sniffing his pant legs while letting Pop pet its head. Pop happily collected on his ten-dollar bets.

Pop was active in the local Lion's Club. He loved to organize and cook the big meals for hundreds of people, and the fall turkey shoot was a big event. One time Pop called four or five Leland Smiths in the Salt Lake phone book and brought them with him to the monthly meeting, getting a big laugh when he introduced each one of them as Leland Smith.

One time Pop caught the neighbor's tomcat. With his gloves on so it couldn't scratch him, he shoved it headfirst into his boot and had me hold the boot while he castrated the cat with his pocketknife. He said if men who committed sex crimes were treated this way there wouldn't be so many sex crimes. When he was finished, the cat ran home and never came back.

Sometimes when a pheasant wandered into the yard, we would eat what Pop called "stubble duck," or "pheasant under glass," out of season. I remember sitting on lawn chairs, behind the house, in the shade of the evening, shooting at seagulls as they returned to their nests in the marshes by the Great Salt Lake. He said there was a fifty-dollar fine for shooting the state bird, but since there were millions of them, there was no harm if you didn't get caught.

Once the local Church leaders asked Pop to help raise money for an addition on the West Bountiful chapel. Pop found a place in Nevada that rented him a pickup full of one-armed bandits, or slot machines, which he set up in the church parking lot during an outdoor dinner and fund-raising party. Plenty of money was taken in, but they never asked Pop to help with fund-raising again.

One time when we were in the grocery store, he pointed out a pious and good sister from one of the local wards. She hadn't seen us yet. He told me he was going to start a conversation with her, and while he was doing that, I was to find a carton of cigarettes and a tin of coffee and sneak up behind her. When she had her back to the shopping cart, I was to quietly place these items into it and disappear.

I did what he told me to do, but I didn't entirely disappear. I watched from a distance as Pop suddenly stopped talking in the middle of a sentence and stared with shock into her cart. That's when the good sister first noticed the cigarettes and coffee, taboo items in our Mormon culture. She was talking a mile a minute, trying to convince Pop that she would never put things like that in her cart. We laughed all the way home.

One time the joke was on him, and he didn't think it was very funny. My grandmother was in her eighties and had a massive stroke.

She was unconscious on the kitchen floor, and mouth-to-mouth did not revive her. He called 911. He was frantic.

When the paramedics arrived, he told them he had already given her *artificial insemination,* meaning, of course, *artificial respiration,* but that isn't what he said. The ambulance crew knew there was nothing funny about an old woman having a stroke, but they couldn't stop laughing as they hurried my grandmother into the ambulance. Pop never said anything about this, but one of the paramedics told my aunt and was very apologetic about the laughing.

Pop had a friend, Doc Roberts, a retired medical doctor who had lost his wife. He would join us for the noon meal from time to time. During the summer when I was eleven, after we had finished dinner, Doc noticed I had been playing the IQ game that had been a bestseller the previous Christmas. My parents had one at home in California too, and I had probably played it a thousand times since Christmas.

The plastic game board had thirty-three holes in it, shaped in the form of a cross. You played it by yourself, the outcome indicating your IQ or intelligence level. The setup included two blue pegs and thirty red pegs, which you placed in the holes, leaving the middle hole empty. A move consisted of jumping one peg over a peg beside it, as long as there was an empty hole on the opposite side for it to go into. After the jump, you removed the peg that had been jumped over, much like in checkers. The object was to keep jumping and removing pegs until no more moves could be made.

As I remember it, the directions on the box explained that if you could do it with as few as six pegs remaining, you were smart enough to go to college. With four pegs remaining, you should consider graduate school. With only two pegs remaining, you were among the smartest people in America. With only one peg remaining, you were as smart as Albert Einstein. With one peg in the middle, it said "Einstein, move over." With one blue peg in the middle, you were so much smarter than anyone else that you might want to consider donating your brain to scientific research.

Doc Roberts asked me how well I could play the game.

"Usually six, but sometimes four or five," I bragged. The game said I was smart enough to go to college or graduate school. The doctor was not impressed.

"Who wrote the directions on the box?" he asked.

"I dunno," I said sheepishly. "It doesn't say who wrote them."

"Did God do it?" he asked.

"No."

"Then who?"

"I dunno."

"My guess is a bunch of advertising guys in New York did it because they want to sell a bunch of plastic game boards and pegs," he said.

I didn't know what to say.

"What gives them the right to write a bunch of stuff on a box telling an eleven-year-old boy in Utah that he's not smart enough to do it with one left in the middle? They don't know anything about you and never will. The sad thing is that you believe them."

I was beginning to think I wasn't smart enough to go to college after all.

"Do you believe me?" he asked, sounding a bit angry.

"I dunno."

"Watch this," he said, motioning for me to hand him the game.

After making sure there were pegs in all the holes except the middle one, I handed him the game board. He looked at me and smiled. Then he started jumping and removing pegs, slow enough that I could see clearly what he was doing. He didn't stop and ponder any of his moves.

In about a minute he was finished, one red peg left in the middle. I couldn't believe it. My grandparents, who had been quietly watching this entire episode between me and Doc Roberts, began laughing, probably thinking how cool it was that their friend and neighbor was as smart as Albert Einstein. I was so excited I could no longer sit in my chair. I stood up, demanding he do it again.

He refused.

When he got up to leave, he gave me a clue, telling me not to make random moves when playing the game, but to look for a pattern or system of jumps that was orderly and logical. I said I didn't know how to do that. He told me to try, and if I couldn't figure it out, he'd show me again sometime. Then he left.

I gathered up the board and pegs and headed into the dining room where I could be alone to concentrate as I toyed and experimented with the system or pattern idea. A half hour later I returned to the kitchen to show my grandparents how I could play the IQ game with one blue peg left in the middle every time. It appeared to me that the game producers had convinced the world that this could not be done, but Doc Roberts had proved them wrong.

My grandmother, Nana, was the reader in the family. When we went up the canyons to fish in the evening, she would stay in the car, reading a novel. Sometimes when she finished something she thought I might like, she gave it to me to read. My favorite, one I remember after so many years, was *The Rose of Tibet*, by Lionel Davidson, about two explorers wandering the mountains of Tibet.

I never dreamed that someday I would be riding horses through that part of the world, gathering research for my books. When I read Tarzan books by Edgar Rice Burroughs, I never dreamed that someday I would be studying the rivers, mountains, and history of West Africa for my own books. When I read *Call of the Wild* and *White Fang* by Jack London, I never dreamed that someday I would fly over White Horse and Dawson Creek as I followed the Yukon River in a small plane on my way to Anchorage, Alaska. I could not have imagined that someday I would study the same prospecting books used by the Spanish as they sailed to the New World to look for treasure. I didn't know I would carry a gold pan on my pack mule as I explored and prospected the backcountry of Utah, Idaho, Montana, and Nevada. I never dreamed as I read *Soul on Ice,* a national bestseller by Eldridge Cleaver, a notorious member of the Black Panther gang, that someday I would interview him in his apartment in Berkeley and ask him questions about his gunfights with the Oakland police, his escape to Algeria and subsequent return, and his finding religion—the only true religion—that practiced by the Mormons. I'm sure that reading *To Kill a Mocking Bird* by Harper Lee and *The Adventures of Huckleberry Finn* by Mark Twain helped make it possible for me to weep with joy when the Church resumed giving priesthood to black people in 1978.

One evening, during one of those summers in Utah, the conversation around the supper table turned serious. Pop told about the hobo he found sleeping in the hay one time in the shed west of the railroad tracks. It was winter, early in the morning, and Pop told the man he could stay as long as he wished. During and after the Great Depression, a lot of men rode the rails, so this was not an unusual occurrence.

Pop went back to the house for breakfast but could not stop thinking about the hobo. After breakfast, Pop piled a plate high with leftovers—eggs, bacon, fried potatoes, pancakes and syrup—and took the plate to the man in the shed. Pop said the man stayed for several days, during which time Pop brought him more food.

They met on the railroad tracks the day the man left. As Pop said good-bye, the man reached out and placed his hands on Pop's head. The first reaction was to pull away, but he didn't as the man blessed him that he and his family would never want for the things of this world. Pop said there were tears in both of their eyes as the man turned and left. And, of course, the blessing was fulfilled. There was always plenty of food at the Smith house for family and guests, and guests there were many.

CHAPTER III

If you can't count it, you can't manage it . . . when performance
is measured and reported, performance improves.

—CHUCK COONRADT
Founder and CEO of
The Game of Work

When I turned sixteen, the carefree summers in Utah came to
an abrupt halt. My father decided it was time for me to get
a real job. He told me one evening to go down to the local Safeway
grocery store and fill out an application.

I didn't think there was any chance of them giving me a job. The
store was union and paid much better than the other jobs usually
available to teenagers. Some of my friends had applied there without
success. I didn't believe they would hire a skinny kid like me,
barely sixteen years old and no previous job experience. My friends
agreed—it couldn't be done.

What I didn't know was that my father knew the manager of the
store. My father was president of the Kiwanis Club and on the city
council. Later he became mayor. I don't know what strings he pulled,
but when I finally went down and filled out the application, I was
hired immediately as a carry-out boy.

I wasn't allowed to stock shelves, operate cash registers, or even bag groceries. All I could do was carry out groceries, bring in carts, sweep floors, and wash windows. I was earning $1.33 an hour—not bad in 1958—but my feet got really tired. I stuck with it. I was the youngest and littlest person on the payroll, and I tried not to get into trouble.

My father was from Utah where he learned the old-fashioned work ethic. He told me I should do more than expected and give the company more time than they paid for. So I arrived ten or fifteen minutes early and went right to work while other workers were waiting for the clock to reach the top of the hour. At the end of my shift, if there were still carts that needed to be brought in, or if the floor needed sweeping one more time, I would stay to do it, working an extra ten or fifteen minutes without being paid for it.

Several times the older clerks warned me that I would get in trouble with the union if I persisted in giving free time to the company. The Retail Clerks Union was strong, but not as strong as the Teamsters Union. I remember one of the bread truck drivers telling me one day that he would not be coming the next day because it was his birthday, and union drivers got their birthdays off with pay. Even at sixteen I thought that was an abuse of union power. On the farm we never stopped doing chores or work because it was someone's birthday.

One day everything changed. The assistant manager asked me to follow him to the back room, to the messy back corner where they rolled the huge wooden bins full of empty pop bottles. In those days customers brought their empty soda bottles back to the store to redeem deposits. All the bottles were made of glass. Quart bottles were worth a nickel, and the smaller twelve- or sixteen-ounce bottles were worth two or three cents. When the customers brought in the bottles, they were deposited in huge four-by-eight plywood bins on rollers, four feet high in the front and six feet high in the back. Three or four bins would fill up on a typical Saturday, and maybe a dozen during the week.

Before the bottles could be returned to the various vendors, they had to be sorted by kind and size in wooden cases, and the cases were stacked neatly against the wall. There were probably fifty different kinds of redeemable bottles, making the work confusing and frustrating at times. Clerks who sorted the bottles typically had a hard time remembering where this or that rare or unusual bottle was supposed to go. Pepsi, Coke, and 7-Up were easy to remember because there were so many of them. The cases of empty bottles were stacked eight feet tall, and if the stacks weren't perfectly straight, they sometimes fell over, which resulted in the falling bottles hitting the cement floor like hand grenades, spraying broken glass in every direction.

When two people tried to sort bottles together, they got in each other's way, so it was a lonely, one-man job in the darkest, dingiest back corner of the store. Working bottles was the most hated job in the store. Nobody wanted to do it. It was a messy, sticky business, and someone was always cutting a hand or finger on broken glass.

The assistant manager explained the process. He told me how the other clerks hated to work bottles, and since I was the newest employee, at the bottom of the pecking order, I was going to do it.

He showed me where the empty cases were stored, which bottles could be combined in the same cases, and which had to be kept separate. Then he showed me where the full cases needed to be stacked.

Just when I thought I knew all there was to know about the new task and was ready to go to work, the manager said, "It takes most clerks one hour to empty a bin. You won't be able to do it any faster than that. I hope you aren't very much slower than that."

He looked at his watch. I looked at mine.

"Let me know when you finish the first bin." He turned and walked away.

Suddenly my work took on a new meaning. Working the bottles was not just a dirty job that needed to be done. My performance would be measured against the one-hour standard set by my peers. The manager was keeping score on me. I was keeping score on myself.

I looked at the bins of bottles with new interest. Compared to my favorite sport, basketball, the manager had put me into a competitive situation and turned on the scoreboard. I flew at the bottles.

An hour and ten minutes later I finished the first bin, frustrated at my clumsiness, but confident that if I persisted I could beat the magic sixty-minute barrier, the accepted standard in my new working world.

I became the regular bottle worker, and a record was kept on how long it took me to work each bin of bottles. A month later I worked three bins of bottles in one hour—three times the accepted rate set by my fellow workers. The manager was pleased. The other workers talked about it. I believed I was possibly the fastest bottle worker in the entire Safeway chain. Maybe the other workers knew more than me about checking, stocking shelves, cutting meat, or trimming lettuce, but I knew more about working bottles than anyone and could do my job about three times as fast as anyone else in the store.

I suppose I learned some lessons. It's hard to know if you are winning or losing at what you do if you don't keep score. You can't manage it if you can't count it. When performance is measured, performance improves. Ralph Waldo Emerson said, "That which we persist in doing becomes easy to do; not because the nature of the task has changed, but because our ability to do it has increased." Everything is hard before it is easy.

One of the other clerks told me to slow down and spend an hour with each bin. Otherwise, because I was the fastest, I would be stuck in this job the rest of my life. That wasn't the case.

The manager of the night stocking crew heard about the kid with the fast hands and arranged for me to be assigned to him as soon as school was out for the summer. The night shift worked from 11 p.m. until 8 a.m., and my hourly wage was increased from $1.33 to $2.42 an hour. I had graduated from carry-out boy and bottle worker.

Bill Cunningham, the manager of the night crew, was a naturally competitive individual, both on and off the job. Every task was a race to see who was the best and fastest.

My eyes could hardly follow Bill's price marker as it flew over the cans. He could throw six soup cans at a time onto the shelf, three in each hand, the labels all facing forward when the cans came to rest. On Tuesday nights when we washed and waxed the floors, Bill's mop was the fastest. He learned that in the Navy.

Bill challenged me to try to keep up with him, which in the beginning appeared an impossible task. But I tried, and every week got a little closer. It seemed every task was timed and measured,

73

including the tearing up of boxes for the incinerator. Speed and accuracy were the game, and we kept score. Some of the other night crew members didn't like to race with Bill and me. They accused us of being too gung ho. They seemed to prefer watching the clock instead of beating it.

Nothing felt better than to walk out of the store into the morning sunshine, my body winding down after a night of running full speed in an effort to keep up with or beat Bill. And when Bill would say in parting, "Big load coming in today; wear your running shoes tonight," it was magic to my ears. I felt like an athlete getting ready for a big game.

When fall and school came, they made me a bagger, and I learned to throw groceries in the sack so fast that the customers could hardly see what was happening—the eggs, bread, bananas, tomatoes, and avocados always ending up on top.

When the store asked if I had any friends who wanted to work, I got them to hire Syd Smith, my best friend, neighbor, and poker buddy. I told Syd the key to success was working fast and running everywhere, like playing fast-break basketball—the more hustle the better. The second day Syd wheeled a dolly loaded with bottled soda stacked five feet high too fast around a corner. It tipped over, sending broken glass and soda everywhere. It took the two of us an hour to clean up the mess. The manager told him to slow down.

Since that time I've come to realize that faster is better only some of the time, like working bottles and bagging groceries, weeding the garden, picking fruit, memorizing scriptures, or racing horses. With other things, slower is better, like stalking a big buck, cooking a pot roast, driving in a snow storm, kissing my wife, or walking into a pasture to catch a spirited young horse.

Writing is a profession that requires both speed and care. Sometimes I'll spend half an hour on a single sentence, changing it a dozen times to get it just right. When writing a radio commercial, I might rewrite it ten or fifteen times until every word works just right. When I write a scene in a story that is pivotal, important, or sensational, a scene I know will cause the word-of-mouth phenomena among readers, I may spend a few hours on two or three paragraphs and come back for fine-tuning again and again. But then there are days when I will write twenty pages or four thousand words. Some years I may finish half a book, while others I may finish two volumes from start to finish. I think I've learned not to confuse speed of motion with quality. The process is only as valuable as the result achieved.

CHAPTER IV

You cannot teach a man anything; you can only help him find it within himself.

—GALILEO GALILEI
Italian physicist and astronomer
(1564–1642)

I had one big regret in high school. It was during my junior year—a single event that occurred one spring day as most of the students were enjoying the second half of the lunch hour outside in the quad, the main place for students to hang out between classes, a patio-like area in the middle of the campus, surrounded by buildings with lots of places to sit.

There was a handicapped girl attending our school. Her eyes were crossed, she had braces on her legs, was uncoordinated, and her speech was slurred. She couldn't do the schoolwork very well, but apparently her parents felt she should have the experience of going to a normal school with normal students.

I don't remember how it started, but one of the boys on the basketball team—a handsome, popular fellow with wavy black hair—said something to tease the handicapped girl. She responded by trying to hit him with her purse. It hung on a long leather strap, and she had learned to swing it in a wide arc. Of course, the boy was able to dodge the flying purse. Some of the nearby students thought this was funny and laughed.

The boy taunted the girl some more in an effort to get her to swing the purse at him again. She complied. Again the students laughed. The taunting continued, and soon she was awkwardly chasing him about the quad, the boy easily avoiding the flying purse as he danced in front of her. By this time the girl was angry and in tears, frantic in her efforts to punish him for teasing her.

It seemed the entire student body was watching and laughing. I knew, like every other high school student in the world, how cruel children can be to each other, so the boy's actions didn't really surprise me. I had seen him taunt other students.

The thing that surprised me most was how my classmates seemed to be enjoying what was happening. Years earlier I had watched some boys throw baby kittens into a gunny sack with some rocks and then toss it into a pond. They laughed and threw rocks at it as it bubbled to the bottom. Instead of laughing with them, I felt sick to my stomach. Now I had that same feeling, but my fellow students seemed to be enjoying what was unfolding at our school. I didn't understand.

Before I could figure it out, the action moved in my direction. The boy was dancing backward through the open space directly in front of me, the girl with the leg braces still chasing him, desperately trying to hit him with her purse.

It would be real easy to stick my foot out and trip him. Then everyone would laugh at him. He would get up and come after me—a fistfight for sure. He would then be taunting me, saying how the handicapped girl was my girlfriend. He would probably win the fight. But would he? He was the bully. I was defending a child who couldn't defend herself. I was right, he was wrong. I couldn't lose, even if he bloodied my nose and blackened my eyes. If I took a stand against what was happening, perhaps the rest of the students would realize the wrongness of it and join me in opposing a popular student. Yes, I would trip him.

By the time I figured all this out, the boy was no longer where I could trip him. My analysis had taken too much time. I was too slow—too late. A teacher was coming to rescue the girl. I had missed an opportunity to do a good thing, and I felt so frustrated at my slow thought process. That girl never came to school again.

I suppose some opportunities in life are like harvesting sweet, ripe cherries. If you hesitate, the birds will eat them up and you will be too late.

Because of this incident and others like it over the years, I think I am better able to appreciate it when others express a spontaneous ability to do good, like in 2003, when I turned on the television to watch an NBA playoff game between the Portland Trail Blazers and the Dallas Mavericks.

Dallas had the better record. It had already won the first two games in the seven-game series and was expected to win the third. The coach for Portland, Maurice Cheeks, a handsome black man and a former player, was in his first or second year as head coach. Though his team had made the playoffs, he was embroiled in controversy. Infighting among his players had been highly publicized, and the press was wondering if Cheeks had the ability to make it as a coach. Portland was on a ten-game losing streak, with another loss expected that night before twenty thousand fans and a national television audience. It is an understatement to say that the Portland coach was under a lot of pressure.

Minutes before the game started, a blond thirteen-year-old girl from a nearby junior high school walked to the middle of the playing floor to sing the National Anthem. I doubt that Cheeks was even listening as she began to sing. But suddenly she stopped. The audience was silent, restless. The girl had forgotten the words. She looked down at her feet, then up at the ceiling. She seemed to be biting her lip. Her father, who had come with her, sat in horror in the first row, staring at his daughter as if he were watching a deer in the headlights.

Everyone felt bad for the girl, but nobody did anything—except Maurice Cheeks, the coach with a hundred other things on his mind. He hurried to the middle of the floor, a bright smile on his face. He put his arm around the girl and started to sing. She tried to join him, gradually remembering the words. It was soon apparent that Cheeks couldn't remember the words either, but he was trying. The audience joined in to help finish the song. When the singing ended, Cheeks gave the girl a warm, fatherly hug. She had a bright smile on her face as she left the floor. The coach had turned an embarrassment of monumental proportions into a happy experience for this beautiful young woman.

As far as I am concerned, Cheeks deserves the coach of the year award, the coach of the century, the MVP, and admission to the hall of fame. Who even cares that Portland lost the game that night and extended its losing streak to eleven? The real hero in Portland that evening was Maurice Cheeks.

It is interesting that Portland went on to win the next three games in a row against the highly favored Mavericks. Perhaps something in the team chemistry had changed. Perhaps the incident with the girl gave the players a different opinion of their coach. Perhaps the Lord was blessing Cheeks for his spontaneous goodness.

One Monday at the beginning of English class during my senior year, the teacher was late, and I remember remarking to Steve, my friend, who sat across the isle, that it was unfair that the teacher always gave him A grades on his essays and me Cs.

"I am a better writer," he said simply. He really believed that.

"I don't think so," I said. "I've read some of your essays, and they are no better than mine. The teacher likes you. You kiss up in class by raising your hand a lot, so she gives you better grades."

As we continued our little debate, I suddenly had an idea for an experiment that could settle our difference of opinion. We had essays on our desks that we had written over the weekend. We would be handing them in for grading as soon as the teacher arrived. I suggested that we switch names on the essays. I would put my name on his paper, and he would put his on mine. We'd turn them in that way and see who got the A and who got the C.

"My paper, even with your name on it, will still get an A," he insisted.

"No, the paper with your name on it, the one I wrote, will get the A," I argued.

So we did it, eagerly anticipating the day when the graded papers would be returned.

When it finally happened, he was the one who was surprised,

not me. My paper with his name on it got the A. And his paper with my name on it got the C. After that I did as little as possible in that class, seeing no sense in trying to improve my performance when the teacher had already made up her mind that I was not capable of writing a decent essay.

Later I realized that this English teacher was one of the classic archetypes described by Joseph Campbell. She was a threshold guardian, or someone who was trying to block my path. She was trying to convince me that I had no talent for writing and that my destiny was anywhere but the writing profession. She did a good job of it. I didn't like her English class, but she could not extinguish my love for books.

CHAPTER V

All progress has resulted from people who took unpopular positions. All change is the result of a change in the contemporary state of mind. Don't be afraid of being out of tune with your environment, and above all pray to God that you are not afraid to live, to live hard and fast. To my way of thinking it is not the years in your life but the life in your years that count in the long run. You'll have more fun, you'll do more and you'll get more, you'll give more satisfaction the more you know, the more you have worked, and the more you have lived. For yours is a great adventure at a stirring time in the annals of men.

—ADLAI STEVENSON
American politician
and 31st governor of Illinois

One evening at the dinner table, shortly after graduation from high school, I announced I had joined the United States Marine Corps. I experienced a growth spurt and had finally caught up with my classmates. I had been on the wrestling team, taken a boxing class in college, and could shoot the head off a magpie at a hundred yards.

My parents were stunned by my announcement. They had

visions of me quitting school so I could be shot to pieces on a battlefield in Korea or some other distant place. I tried to explain that I had joined the Platoon Leaders' Class, which required that I attend basic training for two summers during college and then receive a commission on graduation from college. My intent after that was to go to flight school where I would learn to fly jet fighters or helicopters.

A few weeks later, I flew back to Quantico, Virginia, for the first basic training session that was to last six weeks. I remember joining up with some other recruits at the designated place in the Washington DC airport.

We were having a modestly good time getting acquainted when the sergeant in charge of taking us to the base finally arrived. He was a short, thin man wearing a neatly pressed uniform and brightly polished black combat boots. The word *Winesap* was stenciled over one of his shirt pockets. I later learned he was fighting the Japanese at Guadalcanal the day I was born.

I expected a warm greeting and a handshake. How wrong I was. This soldier was nothing like the recruiter back in California who had talked me into joining. He began yelling and screaming at us, ordering us into a formation of straight lines, where he criticized the way our hair was cut, how we wore our clothes, and the disgusting lack of shine on our shoes. A crowd gathered to watch our harassment— businessmen, old people, women, and children.

Then, in front of all those people, he called us numb nuts. I had never heard that term, not even in the junior high or high school locker rooms. I assumed from the tone of his voice that the term was derogatory or demeaning, but I didn't know what it meant. The term was colorful, making me want to laugh. Some of the female spectators seemed embarrassed, like he had said something nasty. I wanted to raise my hand and ask him what numb nuts meant, how *Webster* would define the term, but a little voice inside warned me not to do it. I was glad my cousin Karen wasn't present. The demeanor and words of my new sergeant would have triggered a giggling spree that we could not have controlled.

The sergeant herded us into a waiting bus. When we arrived at the base, even before the bus came to a stop, a sergeant was pounding on it with a wooden fence post. Officers and sergeants converged from every quarter, yelling and screaming at us. None of them seemed able to talk in a civilized tone.

We were called every foul name I had ever heard, along with some new ones. I couldn't figure out why the United State Marine Corps equated filthiness with manliness. There were no F words in the Marine Corps hymn. I could see no honor or *Espirit de Corps* in the gutter language that surrounded me. It didn't make any sense. The boys in junior high who talked like this weren't people I wanted to follow into battle.

We were herded into a big hall with piles of military clothing stacked on tables and were ordered to take off all our clothes and get into uniform. One Mormon boy who was wearing Mormon garments took a lot of abuse, but all the yelling and teasing didn't seem to bother him. He was older than the rest of us, a returned missionary.

Anyone who made the mistake of calling trousers pants was punished severely. Girls wore pants; men wore trousers. Smiling or laughing invited abuse, which included a severe and profane scolding, followed by pushups and laps around the building. I put on my best poker face and tried to maintain it at all times.

If the sergeants and officers thought a recruit was particularly sensitive to being yelled at, they singled him out, sometimes four or five of them yelling at him at one time. One boy simply couldn't button up his trousers and shirt while they were yelling at him. Instead of backing off, they just tried to make it worse for him. They let us know if we didn't like what was happening, we could quit and go home. Some did.

After we were in uniform, they herded us into the barbershop. I think "sheering shed" would describe the place more accurately. The barbers, guys in white T-shirts, with hairy chests and arms, would politely ask some of the recruits with longer hair how they wanted it trimmed, but all the haircuts were the same. A big electric horse clipper hit you in the side of the head, and in about a minute all your hair was gone. The barbers were so rough that everyone leaving the room had blood trickling down the side or front of his face.

Our barrack was a corrugated steel Quonset hut bolted on a

cement floor, with a row of bunk beds along each wall. Each platoon had its own hut. Each of us was assigned two sheets, a pillow, and a wool blanket. We were told we would be very sorry if we didn't make our beds before leaving in the morning. I picked an upper bunk.

Lights went out about eleven that first night. There was no conversation. We slept like dead men. At first I didn't know where I was when the lights flashed on at three in the morning. The yelling started all over again,

"Get up! Get up, you dirty ——— !"

I rolled out of bed at attention, landing on the cement floor, straight and stiff, my knees locked. It hurt so bad I thought I might faint.

Ten minutes later we headed out on a three-mile run, in formation. Some of the boys who were not in shape had to drop out, a few of them throwing up. About half the recruits were college football players and in pretty good shape. I was surprised I could keep up with them.

When we arrived back at the barracks our bedding was scattered all over the place, some of it outside in the dirt. Sergeant Winesap reminded us that we had been instructed to make our beds before leaving in the morning, and that's why our stuff was on the ground.

But we had made our beds, every one of us. The sergeant said beds weren't made unless they were made right. We gathered around so he could show us how a Marine bed was made. First he wrapped the bottom sheet around the mattress, the folds at each corner at a forty-five-degree angle. Then he tucked in the bottom part of the blanket and top sheet, the folds at the corners also at forty-five degrees. He pulled the blanket and top sheet to the head of the bed and folded them back, leaving exactly twelve inches from the head of the mattress to the fold. He assured us that if the distance to our folds was eleven or thirteen inches, we would find our bedding in the weeds behind the hut. The length of the fold from that point was exactly six inches to where the sheet and blanket were folded under. Again no allowance was made for variation. He said if we wanted to get the twelve and six-inch folds correct we needed to use a ruler when making our beds, at least in the beginning.

Last, he showed how to stretch the blanket across the mattress while tucking in the sides. He said the top surface had to be flat, even though there was sag in the mattress and springs. When he was finished, he held out a quarter and dropped it on the middle of the bed. It bounced. He said that was the final test for a correctly made bed. If a quarter didn't bounce, we'd likely find our bedding outside in the dirt.

Then he added another twist. He said if one of the beds did not pass inspection, none of them would, and we would all be in trouble. He wanted us checking on each other, sharing rulers, and so on. I suppose he was teaching us that a chain is no stronger than the weakest link.

If there was anything good about those first difficult weeks of basic training, it was the mess hall. They yelled at us the first day, but after that we were left by ourselves to feast like dogs. For breakfast there were fried and scrambled eggs; hot cakes; hash browns; country gravy; ham, bacon, and sausage; two or three kinds of juice; toast and rolls; butter, jams, and jellies; coffee, tea, and hot chocolate; five or six kinds of cold cereal; and two kinds of hot cereal with milk or cream and white and brown sugar. They gave us metal trays as big as desktops, so there was plenty of room for everything we could possibly want.

The main meals included roast beef, chicken-fried steak, roast chicken, and pork chops; mashed potatoes, French fries, and baked potatoes; three or four kinds of steamed vegetables; green salad and Jell-O salads; cheeses and luncheon meats; bread and rolls; ice cream, cake, pie, and puddings; and lemonade, fruit punch, and any kind of soda.

The lack of sleep, midnight runs, strenuous physical activity, and constant emotional pressure caused most of the recruits to lose weight even with all the good food, but I stuffed myself at every meal. With no limit on calories and protein, I managed to maintain status quo at about 150 pounds.

We were one of the last groups of recruits to be assigned the M-1 rifle, the one used in World War II and Korea. It weighed nine and a half pounds and was fairly tricky to take apart and clean. We took our heavy weapons everywhere we went, and I soon learned that while sitting on a bench on a troop truck or in a darkened classroom where they were showing a film, I could slip the end of the barrel through the buttonhole in my collar, so it would prop me up while I leaned forward for a quick nap. If a rifle didn't pass inspection, sometimes a recruit would be required to sleep with it, the idea being it wouldn't get so dirty under the covers.

We were nearing the end of basic training when the lieutenant gathered us around one morning to make assignments to prepare for a special meeting that afternoon in a nearby assembly hall. Some were assigned to arrange tables, others to set up chairs, and someone else was supposed to make sure the public address system was working.

Then the lieutenant looked at me and ordered me to make sure there was a blackboard with chalk and eraser next to the podium. We'd had meetings in this hall before, and I knew there was no blackboard there, so I raised my hand.

"Where can I find a blackboard?" I asked when he looked at me.

"I don't know," he said. "That's your problem." He turned and walked away.

I asked some of my friends what I should do. None of us had ever seen a blackboard on the base—not ever. We were not free to leave the base. One of my friends said that because I had not been in any kind of trouble for a couple of weeks, the lieutenant had ordered me to do something that couldn't be done so they could punish me with more pushups, cleaning toilets, and midnight guard duty.

A little later I remembered that there was a small administration building by the front gate. None of us had ever been in it, because we were told it was off-limits to enlisted personnel. Maybe I could find a blackboard there.

My ticket for admission was a long-handled mop. I figured that if anyone asked me why I was entering the building, I'd just show them the mop, like I was going to clean up some spilled beverage.

No one stopped me at the door. It was lunchtime, and most of the offices were empty. I marched from floor to floor, trying to appear business-like, like I knew exactly where I was going.

At one end of the second floor, I found a conference room joining a general's office. I opened the door and looked in, finally finding my blackboard, one that was mounted on tiny wheels. The secretary in the front of the general's office showed no interest in what I was doing. I figured if I asked her for permission to use the blackboard, she'd probably say no. I couldn't chance that, so I quietly polished the floor with my mop until she left her desk to go to a part of the office where she could not see me.

I hurried into the conference room and wheeled the blackboard into the hall, making sure it had chalk and eraser in the tray as I moved confidently toward the stairwell, fearing at any second a voice behind me would order me to stop. None did. When I reached the outside door I enlisted the aid of another recruit to help me carry it to our conference hall.

When the lieutenant entered the hall to start the meeting, he walked over to my seat and asked me where I had found the blackboard. I told him I was not at liberty to answer his question. Instead of pushing harder for an answer or scolding me, he gave me a sly wink, like he was happy with what I had accomplished.

When the meeting was over, one of my friends helped me return the blackboard to the conference room. Feeling a little smug, as we were leaving, I stepped into the doorway to the general's office and asked the secretary to thank the general for letting us use his blackboard. She said she would.

At the end of basic training, for the first time we were permitted to sing the Marine Corps hymn. Now they called us men instead of boys. We had a graduation ceremony with a brass band and patriotic speeches.

I remember looking over at my lieutenant, whom I guessed was one of the meanest people I had ever known. He was sitting with his family—a wife and two little girls who were crawling all over him, grabbing his hair, and trying to unbutton his shirt. I kept watching, thinking any second he would start slapping them and yelling at them. I could hardly believe they were not afraid of him. With his family, he looked just like any ordinary guy. Amazing.

They ushered us into a hall for our graduation party. We were all seated, by platoon, at long tables. The back doors swung open, and handcarts stacked high with canned beer and soda were rolled in and passed out. There was plenty for everyone.

We were having a great time until Sergeant Winesap jumped up on the stage to make a speech. He turned on the microphone. His speech was slurred from the beer he had already consumed.

He said he had noticed that some of the men were not drinking beer. Marines were men, and men drank beer. He ordered everyone who had not been drinking beer to do so now. Some of the other sergeants and officers jumped up to make sure the men in their platoons did as ordered too. It soon became obvious that some of the men in the room, including me, were disobeying the order.

We were singled out one at a time and forced to drink. They started at the back, officers and sergeants gathering around the selected individual, barking their commands to drink, increasing the pressure until the man finally obeyed. One at a time the men who had not been drinking gave in to the pressure.

I was near the front, and knew my turn was coming. My friends sitting by me watched as I rinsed out an empty beer can and poured 7-Up into it. When the sergeants and officers gathered around me, ordering me to drink, I gulped down my 7-Up. They seemed pleased and moved on. I had outsmarted them. I thought I was very clever, and none of my companions exposed my secret.

Finally, our drunken leaders were gathered around the last man whom they thought had not tasted beer, up in the right front corner of the room. Everyone was watching, and many were cheering as the sergeants and officers yelled at this handsome blond boy from Minnesota. He was not a Mormon, but his reasons for not drinking were religious, same as mine. He was one of the top recruits, smart and athletic. He didn't swear. Yet he seemed strong and tough, like he could handle pressure.

No matter what they said to this young man or how loud they yelled, he refused to take a drink. He insisted they had no right to make him do this.

No one was having fun anymore. Some of the sergeants and officers were getting angry with the recruit for trying to ruin the party for everyone else. They began pouring beer over his head, drenching him to the skin. Still he refused. They couldn't make him do it. If they pointed guns at him, I knew he would still refuse. He reminded me of how I thought Joseph Smith would have acted, standing up to his enemies at Liberty Jail.

By this time I decided I had been wrong drinking 7-Up like it was beer. Technically, I had not broken the health laws of my church, but only a few of my fellow Marines knew that. I had not stood up for what I believed was right. I had been smart like a fox but not valiant in defending my beliefs. I wanted to yell to the officers and sergeants, "Hey, you dummies, there was 7-Up in my can. You didn't make me drink beer either."

But it was too late. A higher-ranking officer, who was sober, entered the hall and ended our party. I felt bad over a missed opportunity, the kind where you never get a second chance to do it right, like in high school when I decided too late to trip the boy who was teasing the handicapped girl.

I hurried up to the young man in the front and shook his beer-soaked hand. He did not glory in his victory but remained quiet and subdued. I felt so much respect for him, and hoped I could be more like him in the future.

CHAPTER VI

History teaches us that men and nations behave wisely once they have exhausted all other alternatives.

—ABBA EBAN
Israeli diplomat and politician
(1915–2002)

Following basic training, because of high math scores on the SAT exam, I managed to get into the University of California at Berkeley. It was 1961, the beginning of the free speech movement. Some kind of protest or rally was going on every day. Some students smoked in class, more a demonstration of independence than a need for tobacco. Some teachers routinely used the F word in their lectures. Long hair and sandals were commonplace, even among the professors. My parents called people who had this look *beatniks*.

All the undergraduate classes were graded on the curve, and it was common knowledge that half the freshman class would flunk out each year. The pressure was intense. The bell tower was the favorite spot for suicide leaps. There were so many that one day some fraternity boys painted red target circles on the cement at the base of the tower so those jumping would have something to aim at. These were probably the same students who put "Please don't feed the sharks" signs on nearby beaches after a student was dragged out to sea by a big fish.

I remember looking through the course catalogue on registration day like it was a menu at a grand buffet in Las Vegas. Without the benefit of a counselor, I just signed up for what I wanted to learn. My class schedule included physics, calculus, philosophy, boxing, German, and the required course in freshman English.

Actually, for the first time in my life, I was looking forward to English. I managed to get in a section taught by a well-known professor who had published several books on the Donner Party, a band of pioneers in 1846 who were stranded in the deep snows of the Sierra Nevada Mountains. Some of them resorted to cannibalism to survive, eating those who had succumbed to starvation and sickness. Forty-eight of the eighty-seven members of the party survived to reach California. I had read this professor's books and could hardly wait to meet him in person and sit at his feet for a semester.

The excitement ended when my first essay was returned. I had stayed up all night writing it, wanting to impress my famous teacher. Unlike high school, where written assignments were returned with all kinds of marks by teachers who wanted to point out your mistakes, my first college essay was returned without a single mark on it, except the letter grade at the top of the first page—a big, red F.

I made an appointment to see the professor. It was like going to the doctor as I waited for what seemed an hour before he could see me. When I entered his office, the aging professor was behind his desk, leaning back in his chair, and smoking a pipe. He did not stand to greet me, nor did he shake my hand. I took a seat.

"What can I do for you, Mr. Nelson?"

"I received an F on my essay," I said. "There are no marks on the paper to tell me what I did wrong. I don't know how to do it better. I need your help." I showed him my essay and the big, red F.

He leaned back in his chair again and glanced through my essay. From the look on his face, I guessed he was not the one who had given me the bad grade. Then he said, "Mr. Nelson, all I can tell you is that you must write better. I believe someone else is waiting to see me." A pretty girl with long, black hair was waiting outside, and he obviously wanted to talk to her more than he did me.

I was dismissed, receiving absolutely no help at all. I decided two things as I retreated out of his building. One, I would never read another one of this man's books; and two, I would do everything humanly possible to pass this class so I would never have to take another English class as long as I lived.

Joseph Campbell would have called this professor a threshold guardian, because whether he knew it or not, he was pushing me away from a life of writing and books, like the high school English teacher in the class where Steve and I switched names on papers. As I left the professor's office, I hoped I would never have to write another essay as long as I lived. If at that moment someone had told me that someday I would publish forty or fifty books, I would have laughed at such foolishness.

I ran into another threshold guardian in my philosophy class. The young professor had a harelip and a chip on his shoulder. He argued persuasively that no one could *know* there was a god. He enjoyed making those students who claimed to believe in God look foolish. Fortunately, like my English teacher, he preferred interaction with attractive young women, so he always seemed to call on them to defend their religious beliefs. Of course, he always had the last word as he tried to make their beliefs look foolish.

"If there is a life after death, why hasn't anyone ever come back to tell about it?" he asked one day. I did not know how to respond to this, and neither did any of the other students.

But I know how to respond to that question today, having studied the out-of-body phenomenon and having published four books containing stories of near-death experiences.

The answer to the professor's question is that millions have come back to tell about it. Anybody who asks that question today is naive or doesn't read much. After Raymond Moody's book, *Life after Life*, became an international bestseller in the 1980s, Gallup did a poll concluding that as many as six million Americans have had some kind of out-of-body experience. I don't know how anyone with an open mind can read the hundreds of books on the subject today and still believe the human spirit is snuffed out at death.

After observing the atheistic attitudes of my philosophy professor and the apathy and laziness of my English professor, I was more determined than ever to have a future based on the exact sciences such as math and physics, where problems have one correct answer that all the intelligent people in the world can agree on. But life has a way of turning the tables on us.

A year later I was in southern Germany on a mission for the LDS Church. I was struggling with my philosophy professor's arguments that humans could not *know* the things of God, so while my companions were bearing fervent testimony that they *knew* this or that was true, I would say that I *believed with all my heart* that this or that was true.

I was getting up at five thirty in the morning, every morning, doing fifty pushups, memorizing lessons and scriptures, and mastering a foreign language while spending the greater part of every day calling on people who did not want to learn about my religion. At no other period in my life have I worked so hard or exercised so much discipline. On top of all this, I was praying seven or eight times a day and fasting for twenty-four-hour periods at least once a week and sometimes twice a week. Good things were happening to me, but I'm not sure I realized it at the time.

The standard missionary discussions at that time comprised about sixty single-spaced pages in small type in the lesson plan book. Of course, all of it was in German. It took me about six weeks to learn the fifteen-minute introductory screening discussion in German.

At first I didn't know most of the words and didn't understand a lot of the sentences, so it was pretty much rote memorization with little understanding involved.

After the screening discussion was committed to memory, I went on to the first discussion, which took about an hour to present to investigators, and that took me five weeks to memorize. I carried the lesson pages in my shirt pocket, referring to them continually as we walked, rode busses, or ate lunch or dinner.

It took about four weeks to memorize the second discussion, and three weeks for the third. It was getting easier, and I was beginning to understand what I was saying. By the time I got to the sixth discussion, I was able to memorize the whole thing in four days. While all this was going on, I had lists of vocabulary words and scriptures I was memorizing too.

I was a memorizing machine by the time I had mastered the discussions, and I didn't want to stop. I understood that effective memorization included a systematic review process. I bought a small wooden file box and filled it with blank index cards—a size that would fit in my shirt pocket. I wrote down scripture verses on the cards—chapter and verse on one side, and the actual words on the other. At first I just wrote down the scriptures we used with our lessons, but then I started adding others; anything I thought was interesting or meaningful.

My personal study time was between six thirty and seven thirty every morning, and most of it was spent reading scriptures in German. My companion and I had our study-together time between seven thirty and eight thirty, which also was spent reading scriptures. My companion would read five verses, and then it was my turn. We would do this every morning, seven days a week, month after month after month; and while doing this, I was constantly finding scriptures I wanted to memorize. These I wrote down on the index cards.

Every day I would put half a dozen scripture cards in my pocket to memorize while we were traveling, waiting for lunch, eating a meal, or getting ready for bed. Every spare moment, I had a card in my face. About once a day I would take a few minutes to number the cards I had memorized that day and put them in the box. The system required that every time I numbered a card and put it in the box, I had to review the one behind it. Then I would skip a number to find the next one to review, skip two numbers for the next one to review, skip four, then eight, and so on. I stuck with it, month after month, until there were over five hundred scriptures in the box, and I knew them all. I could quote them verbatim and cite their locations. At first the memorization was hard work, but in time I learned to enjoy it. Everything is hard before it is easy. If a district or mission leader wanted to know how well I knew any lesson, I would tell them to recite part of a sentence anywhere in the lesson, and I would continue from there. They couldn't stump me. I always knew what came next.

Some of the missionaries thought I had a photographic memory, but I knew better. I had a reasonable system for learning scriptures, and I worked hard at it, like when I was stocking shelves and working bottles at Safeway. Anyone else could have done the same. I think it was just a matter of me working harder at it and staying focused.

My first companion was Elder Blaine Zollinger from Logan, Utah. We worked in Singen, a little town near Germany's southern border. I believed him when he told me that Conrad Adenhauer (Add-an-hour), the chancellor of Germany, had invented daylight savings.

Then I went to Karlsruhe as junior companion of the district leader, Elder Craig Wentz. His idea of a great breakfast was to prop himself up on one elbow while still in bed and eat liverwurst and oranges. He could crack two or three knuckles on each finger of each hand: crack, crack, pop, pop, crack, crack . . . A more detailed and somewhat fictionalized account of this portion of my mission is in my book *A Thousand Souls*.

I was getting real tired of the situation where everyone else seemed to *know* the Church was true while I only *believed* it to be so. I began to think if the Lord would not give me the testimony to *know*, then maybe I ought not to be doing this. I decided to put *Him* to the test. I began a three-day fast. We weren't supposed to fast longer than twenty-four hours, but I had been doing that once or twice a week since the beginning of my mission, and I decided it was not enough.

In the middle of the second or third night, after praying at the side of my bed for some time, I was filled with a hot tingly feeling from head to foot that unleashed a watershed of tears, almost like my bones were being consumed by fire. I decided my prayers had been answered, that I had received a confirmation, and that now I knew in my heart that the gospel was true and Jesus is the Christ.

Since that time I have considered that warm, burning feeling a confirmation that I was on the right course. In fact, later on when I began to write, I would never begin a book unless I had a similar feeling, a confirmation that I was doing the right thing. Not all the books were good sellers, but I wrote them because I had a strong, warm feeling that they were stories I should write.

Behold, I say unto you, that you must study it out in your mind; then you must ask me if it be right, and if it is right I will cause that your bosom shall burn within you; therefore, you shall feel that it is right. (D&C 9:8)

Not long after this experience, they made me a senior companion and transferred me to Reutlingen with Elder David Egli, a junior companion fresh from Salt Lake City. He had learned to ride a bike just before his mission and had some horrible wrecks that first month, but he was a good sport and didn't complain.

At first I didn't know how effective we would be in teaching and winning converts, but I knew we could work hard, so that's what we did. We were logging in about seventy hours a week of proselyting time and managing to give thirty or forty screening discussions. We led the mission in these categories most weeks. And guess what, after a couple of months, we began to have baptisms—not many, but one here and there. We felt especially blessed because some missionaries never had any baptisms. And just when it looked like we were going to start having many more baptisms, they transferred me to Stuttgart to become the district leader over ten missionaries.

I was about halfway into my mission. They were two and a half years in those days if you had to learn a language. When you are working so hard and under so much pressure to do the impossible—getting people older and more mature than you to change their religious beliefs and lifestyles—you tend to make some really good friends among your fellow missionaries. They truly become your brothers.

Such was the case with Elder Darrell Krueger. Both of us were senior companions in Stuttgart. Sometimes we would swap companions for the day and work together. One day when we were going somewhere on a streetcar, he started telling me about his patriarchal blessing and how much it guided his life.

As a teenager I had been active in the Church and had been given several opportunities to receive a patriarchal blessing, but for one reason or another had never done it. I suppose I never felt the time was right, but as I discussed the subject with Elder Krueger that afternoon, I suddenly felt an urgent need to get mine.

I called President Gardner and asked him for permission to call the Stuttgart stake patriarch, who lived in Heilbronn, to make an appointment. I was pleasantly surprised when the president gave me permission to take a day off and travel up there for my blessing. I called the patriarch and made the appointment.

It was a beautiful spring day when we rode the train to Heilbronn. Fields were being planted, new crops were starting to grow. The German countryside was alive with new life.

We walked from the train station to the patriarch's house. It was an older home, one that hadn't been bombed during World War II. The yard was neat and the sidewalk and steps had a freshly scrubbed look.

Brother Emil Geist was probably in his seventies; a short, thin man with snow-white hair. I don't think he spoke much English; at least he didn't with me.

Whereas most patriarchs will interview the proposed recipients of their blessings before giving the blessing, Brother Geist didn't spend any time getting acquainted. He didn't know I was studying physics with the intention of becoming an engineer. He didn't know I disliked English classes and was determined never to take another as long as I lived.

He ushered me into the room where he gave the blessings and invited me to be seated in a chair in the middle of the room while he made sure his tape recorder was ready.

I remember looking up at the ceiling and being surprised to find it bright red. Everything else in the old house was brown and beige—subdued colors—but the ceiling in the blessing room was bright red. I couldn't guess why that was so, if it had something to do with the blessing or not, and I didn't ask.

He placed his hands on my head and gave me a long blessing, which included the promises that I would find great success in life through my words—both inside and outside the Church; that through my words I would strengthen the poor and the weak and the lazy; that the Lord would put words in my mouth that would be of great meaning to my fellow men; and that through my words I would be blessed with the things of this world. He didn't say anything about me building dams and roads in exotic places.

In a few weeks I received a written copy of the blessing in German. I read it again and again and decided that when I returned home I would change my college major from physics to English and become a writer.

When Elder Spencer W. Kimball set me apart as a missionary, he promised me success and that I would be instrumental in bringing a thousand souls to the truth. Since I baptized only a dozen or so individuals on my mission, I wonder if his promise had a longer time frame, such as in my whole life, even in the eternities, that I might reach a thousand souls.

After Stuttgart, I was district leader in Esslingen. Lots of hills were in and around town. I asked the zone leaders if there was a chance we might get one of the mission motor scooters to make it easier and faster to get from place to place. They said it couldn't be done; all the scooters were spoken for, and there was no way we'd get one in the foreseeable future. We went to work using our bicycles. We gave a lot of lessons, and it wasn't long until we had some good people preparing for baptism.

One morning during our study-together time, while reading in the New Testament, we stopped reading to discuss a parable in Luke 11. Starting in verse 5, it told about a man who visited a friend at midnight to borrow three loaves of bread for unexpected guests. The friend said the door was locked, his children were in bed, and he didn't want to be troubled. Then Jesus said,

> I say unto you, Though he will not rise and give him, because
> he is his friend, yet because of his importunity he will rise and
> give him as many as he needeth. (Luke 11:8)

We figured Jesus was saying that the visitor refused to be turned away by his friend. He continued to ask for the bread until his friend finally got out of bed and gave it to him. Importunity means refusing to give up, to persist until you get what you want. Some of my children and grandchildren were born with this character trait.

Once we felt we understood the parable, it didn't take long to come up with a plan, one inspired by Jesus' parable on importunity and centered on our weekly reports to President Gardner.

At the bottom of the weekly report there was an open space where the missionary could write personal comments for the president to read. We knew the president read our reports, so we started making comments about the need for a motor scooter. We mentioned the hilly country around Esslingen, how we could visit more people and find more potential converts if we could cover more country, something only possible with motorized transportation. We explained how some of our best contacts were far from town, how a scooter would enable us to visit them more often, thus increasing the likelihood of them eventually joining the Church. We tried not to be pushy or demanding like spoiled children. We just politely and intelligently pointed out how a scooter could help us do the work better. We figured that we could keep this up for six months if need be. In fact, it was fun thinking up new reasons to send to the president each week.

It didn't take six months. Early one morning, about three weeks into the project, the zone leaders showed up at our door, delivering a brand new motor scooter. We'd take turns on who got to drive and who rode behind. It was wonderful. We really could cover a lot more country and visit more people. The importunity parable in Luke 11 became our favorite passage of scripture.

Over the years, however, I was reluctant in telling this parable to my children. One of them might mention at the dinner table that such and such friend just got a new hot tub and that we ought to get one too. Of course, the other children would all agree with the first. "Could we?" "Could we have one too?"

I'd say something about hot tubs needing lots of maintenance, being too expensive, and how they demanded lots of costly hot water that we couldn't afford. Then I'd try to change the subject. In a few days the idea would be forgotten and would not come up again for another year or so. On the other hand, if my children were familiar with the importunity lesson in Luke and together worked out a plan whereby they took turns reminding me each day how the family could benefit from a hot tub, eventually Sharon and I would have caved in and figured out how to buy one. I didn't want them to know this, so the parable in Luke was seldom talked about in our family. I mention the parable here in my personal history because my children are raised and gone. If my grandchildren and great-grandchildren learn this priceless lesson, it's not me, but their parents who will have to deal with it.

After about five months in Esslingen, I became first assistant to the president, in charge of member activities. I spent the remaining nine months of my mission traveling to all the cities in our mission, working with missionaries, and speaking in church meetings.

I'd been such a shy and quiet boy growing up and was always terrified when asked to speak in a church meeting. My palms sweated and my knees trembled. At first I would read the talks my father wrote, never looking up at the people in front of me. Then as I got older I would sometimes memorize the talks, forcing myself to look up at the audience once in a while. I was always well prepared because I was terrified at the thought of having to think and speak spontaneously on my feet, something I knew I could not do. I took a public speaking class in college, hoping that would help. I was always impressed with Church leaders who could get up in front of a congregation and speak for an hour or more without notes. I couldn't figure out how it was possible to do such a thing.

Now, because I was a hard worker, President Gardner picked me to help oversee the small branches in the mission, the ones outside the Stuttgart Stake organization. There were fifteen or twenty of them, with average sacrament meeting attendance ranging from ten to about fifty people.

It was difficult for the local Church leaders to find enough people to give speeches at the meetings each week. They needed two speakers at Sunday school, and three or four for sacrament meeting. Members got tired of hearing from the same people and local missionaries all the time, and the leaders and missionaries who could speak well didn't want to be doing it in almost every meeting.

I let them know they could call on me at any time. I was only twenty-one years old and not an accomplished speaker, but I had memorized over five hundred scriptures, had read hundreds of books, and had some interesting stories to tell. But most of all, I was happy to do it if they needed me. Leaders needing speakers would call and make arrangements for me to come. In time the leaders knew that if I attended a meeting where the other speakers gave unusually short talks with a lot of time left over, or if a certain speaker didn't show, they could call on me to fill whatever time was available.

I spent my personal study time each morning developing

speaking outlines and ideas and making a lot of notes. I didn't write out my speeches anymore but spoke from outlines. One week I spoke in a Sunday School and sacrament meeting in one branch, and later that same day in two other sacrament meetings. At the same time I found myself having to speak at one or two missionary gatherings each week. I didn't think my speeches were any better than those of the local leaders and missionaries, but in time I became more comfortable doing it. I was losing my fear of standing up in front of groups.

In time I found myself sometimes wandering from the prepared outlines, telling a story, quoting a scripture, or teaching a lesson for which there were no notes on the page in front of me. I realized I was actually thinking on my feet, something I thought I would never be able to do. Perhaps I was even opening myself up to respond to promptings from a higher sphere.

After returning home to Walnut Creek, I was asked to report in sacrament meeting on my mission. I had a lot of mission experiences I wanted to share with the people in my home ward. I had been talking about ten minutes when I noticed a man in the back row trying to get my attention. It was my father, and he was holding up his left hand so I could see him tapping the face of his wristwatch with the forefinger of his right hand, a clear signal that he wanted me to shut up and sit down. I was no longer the confident missionary, but the timid and humble son who quickly concluded his remarks and sat down. Later in life when I asked my father why he did that, he insisted he had done no such thing, but I can still remember him tapping on that watch as clearly as if it had happened yesterday.

Later in life, when my *Storm Testament* and *Beyond the Veil* books were good sellers, I was asked to give speeches again, sometimes more than a hundred a year. I usually didn't get paid to do it, but sometimes I was able to sell books. For subject matter I had the research I had done for my books.

Sometimes, before I got up to speak, I wished I hadn't accepted the assignment. Giving a good speech requires energy and effort, no matter how often you do it, and after I was finished, I was always glad I did it. Most of the time, I think the people who didn't listen to me very often found my words interesting, educational, and somewhat entertaining. During the late nineties, when I finished speaking to middle or junior high school assemblies, students sometimes asked if I had been in the movie *Mrs. Doubtfire*. I was amused that they thought I looked like actor Robin Williams, but only while I was talking and telling funny stories.

CHAPTER VII

If one took no chances, one would not fly at all. Safety lies in the judgment of the chances one takes. That judgment, in turn, must rest upon one's outlook on life. Any coward can sit in his home and criticize a pilot for flying into a mountain in fog. But I would rather, by far, die on a mountainside than in bed.

—CHARLES LINDBERGH
American aviator, author, inventor,
explorer, and social activist
(1902–1974)

Upon returning home, I transferred from the University of California to Brigham Young University. I moved into the Robert E. Lee Apartments with Kent Price, David Conley, and Ki Shields as roommates. I changed my major from physics to English. For the first time in my life, I began to get good grades on a consistent basis—probably a result of the study habits I developed as a missionary.

Sometimes on the weekends I drove up to Bountiful to visit Pop and Nana. One afternoon in early spring, as I was riding a horse through one of the lower fields, I heard some rustling in the dry grass. I stopped and looked closer. I could see water snakes—lots of them. I guessed I had come upon a spot where the snakes had hibernated, and the spring sun had just begun to bring them out.

Later, when I said good-bye to my grandparents, I threw a gunnysack and bucket in my trunk and drove down the lower road near the spot where I had seen the snakes. They were still there. I managed to slip forty-three of them into the gunnysack, which I placed in the bucket. They ranged in size from eight inches to about three feet. Some people call them blue racers. I didn't know what I was going to do with them, but I knew forty-three snakes in a girls' dorm or the Wilkinson Center might stir up some excitement.

I didn't have time to do anything, because by the time I arrived back in Provo I had to get ready for a date. I called a friend at Helaman Halls, who didn't have anything going on for the evening, and asked him if he thought he could find homes for forty-three snakes. He said he could, so I dropped them off. He spent Saturday evening wandering up and down the halls dropping snakes in toilets, showers, drawers, briefcases, and between bed sheets. We heard all about it at church the next morning. I believe he said they recovered only twenty-nine of the snakes, the rest remaining unaccounted for.

On another Saturday afternoon at Pop's, I built a mongoose cage out of 1 x 12 boards. It was about two feet long, with a screen over the front half and a wooden door over the back half. A wood partition with a little crawl hole separated the two halves. If you looked closely when you peered down through the screen, you could see a food dish and a patch of fur through the hole leading to the covered half of the cage. I told curious onlookers that the cage contained a mongoose named Ricky; that a mongoose was a furry mammal from India that killed cobra snakes. These little animals were very fast and liked to bite people, so when Ricky got out, we had to catch him by throwing a blanket over him. People would whistle and coo trying to get Ricky to come from the enclosed half to the screened half so they could get a better look at him.

Of course, there was no mongoose in the cage, just an old raccoon tail tied with a string to the back of the trapdoor, which was pressing against a bent-over spring. When the time was right, I would jerk out the nail which held the trapdoor shut, allowing it to fly forward, slinging the raccoon tail into the face or chest of the person who was trying to coax the mongoose out of his den. People would jump and scream, and I think some of them almost had heart attacks. Sometimes a girl would run screaming out of the apartment. We had a lot of fun with that mongoose for two or three years.

One weeknight, our ward went to a local park for a picnic and to participate in a demonstration by a young man from China or Hong Kong who was said to be skilled in martial arts. He was smaller than all the young men in our group, weighing perhaps 130 pounds.

He began by demonstrating some defensive and offensive fighting moves. He was lithe and quick in his movements. Then he gathered us in close, both men and women, and began to explain the mental or spiritual power involved in fighting. He called it *chi* or *key*. He said that with proper use of *chi* he could defeat men two or three times his size. He could see from the looks on some of our faces that some doubted what he was saying.

He stood erect, feet apart, arms bent at the elbows, fists clenched, elbows pressed tightly against his ribs. He invited us to crouch behind him, place palms under his elbows, and try to lift him off the ground. He said he would not use *chi* to hinder our efforts.

Most of the men in the group, including me, crouched behind him and lifted him up. It was not hard lifting such a small man.

When all who wanted to had demonstrated their ability to lift him up, he spread his feet a little wider, took a deep breath, and clenched his fists a little tighter. He said he was now exercising *chi* to attach himself to the earth. Then he invited all who had lifted him off the ground earlier to try to do it again. We all tried, and we all failed. Some tried several times. None of the big strong men who had lifted him a few minutes earlier could elevate the little man even a fraction of an inch off the ground, and from what I could observe, we had all tried very hard to do it. While the others were laughing and talking about what had happened, I was feeling both amazed and humbled, like I had witnessed the application of a profound spiritual truth, but I didn't understand it, and knew I hadn't learned enough from the young man to do it myself. Though I had been a missionary and studied the scriptures a lot, I realized there was a lot I didn't know about the potential of the human mind or spirit.

During that first year at BYU, Kent was taking flying lessons at the Provo airport. He had worked on a pipeline in Alaska the previous summer, where in addition to earning enough money for school, he had been able to afford flying lessons.

The Provo flying club had an airplane they wanted to sell. They were having little success finding a buyer, so Kent offered to fly it to Alaska and sell it for them up there since everyone believed it would be easier to sell an airplane in Alaska than in Utah. The flying club agreed to let Kent take their Piper Tri-Pacer, and I agreed to go with him as his copilot.

When our final exams were over, we threw our sleeping bags, some food, a box of books, and a change of clothes into the back of the plane and headed for Alaska. The airplane was not equipped with instruments for flying at night, or in clouds, so we stayed low, about three thousand feet above the ground, visually following known highways. Cruising speed was about a hundred miles per hour. We could fly about four hours on a tank of gas—actually two tanks, one in each wing. At night we'd land at little airports, roll the sleeping bags out under the wings, and go to sleep. Usually the airports had an old car we could borrow if we wanted to drive into town to get a hamburger.

We were about three hours out of Whitehorse, Yukon Territory, following the Al-Can Highway, an eleven-hundred-mile dirt road connecting Canada with Alaska, when a severe thunderstorm blocked our way. We were flying up a valley between two mountain ranges with the clouds above us getting lower and lower until they were touching the mountaintops. We were flying through a tunnel with a cloud ceiling and steep mountain sidewalls. Then ahead of us we could see the clouds dropping even lower, all the way to the ground. In a few minutes we wouldn't be able to see any of the landmarks, not even the ground.

We had only an hour's worth of fuel remaining, so we couldn't go back to Whitehorse. If we flew above the clouds we would lose sight of the highway and might not be able to find it again. To just keep going, and lose visibility, with the steep mountains on both sides, would likely be suicide. So we decided to land on the highway and wait for the storm to pass.

There were power lines on one side of the road, so it was imperative that we land quickly while we still had good visibility. If we turned around and landed with the wind instead of into it, landing would be much more difficult too. So down we went.

A Mounty with the Northwest Mounted Police saw us coming down and raced to the end of the strait stretch of highway that we intended to use as our runway, his lights flashing in an effort to get the attention of any approaching vehicles that might get in our way.

The landing went without a hitch, and the officer helped push the plane off the road. Then he drove us sixty miles to the nearest telephone so we could call ahead to explain why we would not be arriving at the time listed on the flight plan we had filed. When we got them on the phone, they said they were about ten minutes away from sending out an aircraft to look for us. By the time the Mounty drove us back to the airplane, the storm had lifted and we were able to take off and resume our journey.

When we arrived in Alaska, we discovered that planes like ours with the third wheel attached to the nose instead of the tail were not very popular. They were much harder to land on ocean beaches and rough dirt runways in the back country. Plus, because there were so many small planes in Alaska, the values were lower than in Utah. We couldn't sell the plane at the desired price, so we continued using it as we looked for work.

While in Anchorage we spent several nights in the local LDS Church meetinghouse. One evening one of the stake clerks showed us a map of Alaska with colored pins showing where the members in remote areas lived. He pointed to some pins in a town called Dillingham at the head of Bristol Bay. There was a member there named Lyle Smith who came to stake conference once in awhile but had never in his life been visited by home teachers. We said we would do it. There was a fish cannery at Nak Nek, also on Bristol Bay, where we wanted to inquire about work, so while we were in the area, we would hop over to Dillingham and home teach Lyle Smith.

The next morning we flew over the remote and majestic Brooks Range and landed at Nak Nek. The salmon had not yet started running, so the cannery wasn't hiring. We headed over to Dillingham. We radioed ahead and Lyle Smith met us at the airstrip, along with a herd of Eskimo children.

He was a thin, pink-cheeked, robust man in his mid-thirties, with jet-black hair and beard. He drove a brand new yellow Mercedes Benz. We had seen from the air there were no roads going in and out of Dillingham. People came and went by water or by air. There were about three miles of dirt roads in and around the town, so there was nowhere else the Mercedes could go.

He took us to the little white house where he lived with his German-born wife and children. His parents were buried in the backyard.

For supper they served us their favorite during the fishing season, fish head stew. They threw some salt, carrots, and onions into a pot of boiling salmon heads. The best part was the meat on both sides of the heads, the jaw muscles.

We stayed overnight, and since the next day was Sunday, we had church with them—folding chairs and a small podium in the living room. They had five or six hymn books, and several neighbors joined the group. Kent and I got to say prayers, bless and pass the sacrament, and give the talks.

Lyle had a fishing boat and earned his living during the summer salmon runs. He had joined the Church at BYU, if I remember correctly, and then returned to Alaska to fish.

His future wife was a German nurse at the medical center in Dillingham when he first met her. About the time he decided she was the one for him to marry, she left to return to Germany. He followed her to Hawaii, and then the rest of the way around the world, eventually catching up with her when she arrived home in Germany. He convinced her to marry him, join his church, and return to Alaska with him.

He took us down to the harbor and showed us his fishing boat. The thing I remember most was him telling us he didn't know how to swim. He made his living on a boat and didn't swim! I couldn't believe it. He said most of the other fishermen didn't swim either. How were they supposed to learn to swim in forty-degree water? Besides, they wore so much clothing, and in water so cold, he believed even good swimmers would have a hard time getting back to the boat if they fell overboard.

The next morning we headed back to Anchorage, but as we flew up over the Brooks range, we met eighty-mile-an-hour headwinds. The rugged mountains below us seemed to be standing still. We started to get real nervous about our rapidly diminishing fuel supply. Finally, we passed the highest part of the mountains and began our downward descent toward Anchorage. We had to cross Cook Inlet before reaching the airport.

When we reached the inlet, the gauges on both tanks registered empty.

Kent radioed ahead to let traffic controllers know of our predicament. Kent decided to fly on one tank until we began the landing pattern and then switch to the other. He wanted to minimize chances of the engine sputtering while landing. If the first tank ran out before we reached the airport, we'd to go to plan B, whatever that was.

While Kent was worrying about fuel supply, I reached behind the seat, unrolled our air mattresses, and filled them with air. We knew if we landed in the water, hypothermia induced by the icy waters could kill us in about four minutes. We hoped the air mattresses might slow down the hypothermia process long enough for us to be rescued.

When we reached the airport, Kent switched to the other tank and we enjoyed a smooth landing. The first thing we did was check the tanks. The one we had just switched to had about three gallons, and the other less than half a gallon.

Eventually, I ended up working for an oil tool company in Soldotna, south of Kenai. We supplied drill bits and hole openers to the many offshore oil-drilling platforms. I spent my time swinging a sledgehammer, painting drill parts, loading those parts onto trucks, and making deliveries to piers and helicopter pads.

Kent found a job on Kodiak Island installing cable television in homes. Sometimes on our days off, Kent would pick me up and we would go exploring in the airplane, landing on the beaches of remote islands or visiting people we had met. I bought some cherry bombs that I would light and throw out the open door as we flew over houses of people we knew.

Along the Kenai beach, people had fishing claims, about like mining claims, which were sections of beach where they had rights to commercial salmon fishing. Typically, the fisherman would install an anchor with a pulley several hundred yards out in the inlet. Another pulley would be anchored near the high tide mark on the beach. A continuous loop of cable passed through the two pulleys connecting them to each other. Attached to a portion of the cable was a gill net perhaps several hundred feet long, with floats tied to the top of the net to keep the top near the surface of the water, and lead weights secured to the bottom of the net. By attaching the cable to a tractor, the fisherman could pull his gill net into the water when he wanted to start fishing, and out of the water when he wanted to remove fish.

Three or four Mormon families had side-by-side fish claims on the same beach. The locals called it Mormon row. Sometimes after work I would go down and help them harvest the fish. During the silver salmon run, they were getting $1.27 a fish, and sometimes one net could catch over a thousand fish in a night. I built a little smokehouse, and using cottonwood, smoked some of the salmon.

Sometimes Beluga whales or seals would follow the schools of salmon. Whales and seals could ruin the gill nets, and since one could often see the approach of the whales and seals because they frequently came up for air, efforts were made to drive them away, usually shooting at them with a 30-30 rifle. I soon established myself as the best shot on the beach, and on several occasions found myself shooting holes in whale and seal fins to scare them off. I don't think I ever killed any of them. If I missed the fin I was aiming at, the report of my rifle would usually send them fleeing to deeper water.

One of the ward members who didn't have a fish site on the beach but lived back in the woods ran a gill net across a remote stretch of river behind his house. This was totally illegal, and he could have gone to jail, but he caught a lot of fish, and the missionaries helped him do it.

The fish cops tightly regulated the fishing times in an effort to ensure the safe return of the required number of fish to the spawning grounds. There was controversy among the Mormons over allowed fishing times that began on Sundays. Some believed it was all right to have your nets in the water on Sunday, even while you were in church. Others thought that in order to observe the Sabbath, the nets shouldn't go in the water until midnight when the Sabbath was over. The other side argued that since there were only a few weeks in the entire year when large numbers of fish could be caught, the Lord understood if you fished on Sunday.

The branch president was one who waited until midnight to start fishing. On the other hand, he would let his sixteen-year-old daughter watch television and go to the movies with one of the missionaries. I don't remember the missionary's name, but he sometimes wore Bermuda shorts and asked us to call him Governor instead of Elder. He wasn't exempt from holding hands with the branch president's daughter, nor did he see anything wrong in poaching fish with the ward member. When we called the mission president to report this elder's unorthodox behavior, the president didn't appear very concerned. He seemed to want to tell us that maybe we ought to mind our own business.

I brought with me to Alaska a box of books. One of the requirements for an English degree at BYU at that time was to take a comprehensive test on the content of over four hundred books considered to be the foundation works or classics of English and American literature. Some of these works were covered in our course work, but many were not. I think I read about a hundred of those books that summer. I remember *The Scarlet Letter*, *The Leather Stocking Series*, *Wuthering Heights*, *The Great Gatsby*, and many more.

When the summer was over, Kent flew back to Provo, but I bought an old Cadillac for $275 from Dave McFadden, another BYU student who had been a cook at the Nak Nek cannery. I found three other BYU students willing to share expenses. We drove from

Anchorage to Bountiful in 71¾ hours. We stopped for fuel and bathroom breaks only. All four of us took turns driving. A case of canned goods in the middle of the back seat kept us fed. Since I already had a car, I sold the old Cadillac for $350, earning a $75 profit.

CHAPTER VIII

I said that the great public was the only tribunal competent to sit in judgment upon a literary effort.

—MARK TWAIN, author
(1835–1910)

The first week of school I attended a dance at the Wilkinson Center and met a pretty freshman, a German major from Pleasant Hill, California. She was a convert to the Church and had driven to BYU in her sky blue Volkswagen. She was wearing a turquoise sweater to match her big sparkling eyes. She had short, blondish hair. I danced with her quite a few times, but she wouldn't let me take her home because, of course, she had her own car. Her name was Sharon Anderson.

A few months later, at Christmas vacation, I left my car at school and rode home with her. We held hands much of the way, causing my heart to beat more rapidly. When I met her family I learned that her mother's maiden name was Storm. I liked that name, not realizing that one day I would use it in a series of historical novels called *The Storm Testament* that would launch my writing career.

The following February, as we were sitting on a stone bench on the east side of the Joseph Smith building between classes, I put a ring on her finger and asked her if she would marry me.

Her response caught me by surprise.

"Wrong hand," she said. In my excitement I had placed the ring on the third finger of her right hand. Quickly, I changed it to the left hand, and she agreed to marry me. We set a date for the following September. I figured I couldn't go wrong with a girl who loved asparagus as much as I did. She had grown up in California too. That's when I learned that no one is perfect until you fall in love with them.

I was finishing up my degree in English and had been accepted into the MBA program. My first short story, *Stronger than Reason*, had just been published in the *Y Magazine*. I still had dreams of becoming a writer but didn't know how I could make a living at it, so I figured I needed the MBA.

I remember taking a creative writing class from a young professor named Douglas Thayer. He wrote short stories and had self-published some of them. I was pleased the first day of class when he opened a copy of the *Y Magazine* and read some excerpts from my story. But my joy quickly turned to horror as he began to rip apart my first published work. He made fun of it, saying that he thought it was sentimental gibberish. My ears throbbed as I slouched down in my chair.

After a while the teacher said it seemed strange that so few people were laughing at what he thought were very funny jokes he was making at the expense of the story's author.

"It's probably my bad fortune to have the author in this class," he guessed. Affirmative nods from some of the students told him that was indeed the case. I felt so humiliated, so sorry I had submitted the story to the magazine. Who was I to presume I could be a published author? I hoped the few remaining copies of the *Y Magazine* in the BYU Bookstore would soon be gone and nobody else would ever see my story. Another threshold guardian had ambushed me in an effort to prevent me from realizing my destiny.

But I was wrong in thinking that my story would disappear into the sunset when the last copies of the *Y Magazine* sold off the shelf. After a few years of silence, my sister called from Texas to report someone had read the story in her sacrament meeting. I soon received another call from Florida. Apparently my story was read in a fireside. A parent of a missionary called to report that the missionary was handing the story out to investigators, insisting it was true. I assured the parent it was fiction. Three or four authors compiling LDS-theme stories for books requested permission to publish it. Somehow the story found its way into a seminary manual. I never made any money from the story, and possibly the mean things Doug Thayer said about it were at least partially true. The story has something to say about love and loyalty that rings true and profound with many readers. The story found a way past the threshold guardian and found a life of its own, without any push or promotion.

I learned from that experience that you can't please everyone, so there's no need trying. I also learned that the true value of a story or book is not decided by the critics, but the everyday people who are willing to spend their hard-earned money to read what you wrote.

That summer I stayed with my parents in San Jose, finishing up a few correspondence courses needed for graduation, and Sharon stayed with her parents in Pleasant Hill, working in a candy store. We were about an hour apart, usually spending our weekends together. Our courtship felt comfortable and right for both of us.

Sharon later admitted that she almost broke off the engagement that summer. But we did love each other. Neither of us doubted that, and we felt good about marrying each other, so we did it.

We had a civil marriage on Friday, September 7, 1967, mainly for the benefit of Sharon's family, all of whom were nonmembers except her brother. The next morning we went to the Oakland temple to be sealed for time and eternity. I felt bad my parents couldn't come in the temple. Later, my mother became a temple worker.

We set the wedding date a week before the start of the MBA program, but the MBA starting date was moved up so group therapy could be done up near the Sundance Ski Resort before the beginning of classes. This shortened the honeymoon to only a few days.

On our wedding night my sister had made reservations at a place called The Chicken Coop in a resort town on the northern

California coast. Upon arrival we discovered it was a real chicken coop converted to a guesthouse, with too many windows and too few curtains. There was no view of the ocean, just storage sheds and metal buildings, though the ocean was only a block or two away. The floor was covered with dead flies, so we had to be very careful where we stepped.

The next day we drove through the redwood forests of Northern California while beginning to work our way back to Utah. We settled into a little white house at 350 North 680 East in Provo, and I began work for my MBA degree. Sharon continued her school that first year too.

Our courtship had been smooth and uneventful, but now we were married we began to experience the challenges of living together, and some of the little differences we hadn't noticed during courtship seemed large.

We were asked to co-teach a Gospel Doctrine class in our ward. I had done this before in my singles ward. I was comfortable and thought it was easy, but Sharon, a new convert to the Church, was totally intimidated by a class full of people who had mostly been raised in the Church, many of them returned missionaries. She was so careful. She worried about every word that came out of her mouth, and I was the opposite. It was hard doing it together, and I was frustrated that I seemed unable to make it easier for her.

That winter I broke one of the rules of the MBA program that prohibited students from taking classes outside the required curriculum. I signed up for a magazine writing class offered by the communications department. The thing that intrigued me and made the class irresistible was an article in the *Daily Universe* by the instructor Herb McLean who said the class was "sell or fail," meaning any student who didn't sell an article for cash money would receive a failing grade.

I had taken plenty of writing classes from professors who talked about how easy it was to sell articles and short stories, but it seemed none of them ever did it. And none of the students in their classes seemed to be able to do it either. Here was a teacher who obviously knew how to sell magazine articles and how to teach students to do it. I signed up for the class, and by the end of the semester I had sold two articles; one to *Western Livestock Journal* on chariot racing, and one to *Organic Gardening and Farming* on the thirteen varieties of peaches my grandfather raised. Having received money, I was now a professional writer. The total income from both articles and the accompanying photos was $130.

Later that same year Herb McLean announced a summer work experience for writing students. He called it Operation Midnight Sun. Students who signed up would accompany him on a six-week tour of Southeast Alaska, gathering material for magazine articles. I signed up and made arrangements for Sharon to come with me, even though she was pregnant by this time.

So north we went. We weren't very far out of Provo when we heard the news that Robert Kennedy had been shot. We followed the developments on this story all the way to the Canadian border.

Instead of going north on the route Kent and I had followed in the airplane two years earlier, we headed up through British Columbia to the southern tip of Southeast Alaska and then took the ferry north through Ketchikan, Wrangle, Juneau, and Skagway.

Some nights we slept on the ferry; others we camped on beaches and in forests. Herb had made arrangements for some of us to fly out to logging camps, wilderness resorts, and uninhabited islands. We took pictures and wrote down our thoughts and observations in notebooks.

One time, with another student named Cliff, we camped out in a remote area where there were lots of Alaskan brown bear sign. I took my 30.06 along for protection. We had little food with us, so we caught and cooked a porcupine for our supper and breakfast. I don't know why we didn't have any salt, but we had plenty of mustard to spice it up. We roasted it on a revolving spit over the fire and it tasted quite good. But roasting juicy, dripping meat over an open fire in bear country was a stupid and careless thing to do. We were very fortunate that the scent of our roasting porcupine didn't bring a bear into camp.

I wrote a number of articles for *The New Alaskan*, a tabloid published in Ketchikan. The publisher arranged some amazing flights with bush pilots to remote fishing and hunting lodges. Following the trips, I sold six articles to magazines and trade journals and decided this was not the kind of writing I wanted to do on a permanent basis.

The following December our first child was born. I don't think my grandfather approved of us naming him Richard, because whenever we went up to Bountiful to visit, Pop would call him Little Dickie. Since he was born just before Christmas, our first picture of him was in a Christmas stocking.

Richard was born on a Sunday, and I remember having a major paper due in one of my classes the next day. Of course, I didn't get it finished on time, so I asked the professor for an extension, explaining that my wife having a baby had interrupted my work schedule.

"Should have thought of that nine months ago," was his only response.

I began to see a new side to Sharon. She was the perfect, nurturing, loving mother, and she just seemed to get better as more children came along. She became angry with me a few times, but hardly ever with the children. They felt loved and safe. I never noticed her pressuring them to do hard things, but all of them were reading and writing long before they entered school. Richard didn't start school until he was almost seven, and he was the one who went to Harvard.

We raised eight children: Richard, Robert, Marvin, Russell, Virginia, Sarah, Kristin, and Benjamin. Sharon made sure they brushed their teeth, did household chores, and said their prayers. She took them to doctor and dentist appointments and attended all the teacher conferences and soccer games. She read to the little ones every day.

I taught the children the important stuff like riding, roping, branding, shooting, hunting, skiing, camping, and how to catch and eat rattlesnakes. Plus I helped with English and algebra assignments and wrote talks for church, something they usually started doing without my help in the middle teen years. One time, hoping to toughen up my older boys, I bought a load of coal for the family room fireplace and dumped it out back by the barn. Along with making them do pushups and sit-ups, when it snowed I'd make them run in their bare feet to the barn to fetch coal.

We ate dinner together, all six, eight, or ten of us seated around the kitchen table. It was a noisy place with all the talking, laughing, and teasing. Sometimes one of the children would have a red dinner plate instead of a white one like everyone else. After the blessing on the food, one of the children would ask why so-and-so had the red plate. Perhaps that child had earned a part in a school play, received a Boy Scout advancement, won an award at school, or had a birthday. The child with the red plate had everyone's attention as we talked about the reason for the red plate. One of the small children might get the red plate for going all day without sucking a thumb or wearing a diaper.

If one of the children had the red plate because of a birthday, after the cake had been eaten, everyone would form a straight line in the family room or outside. The one with the birthday would quickly crawl between the spread legs in an effort to receive as few spanks as possible.

If I noticed that a child seemed to be complaining a lot about something that was going on at school or in the home, I'd quote Dale Carnegie. "Any fool can criticize, condemn, and complain, and most fools do."

If that didn't do the job and the complaining seemed to be spreading to the other children, I'd print out a verse found in Doctrine and Covenants 78:19:

> And he who receiveth all things with thankfulness shall be made glorious; and the things of this earth shall be added unto him, even an hundred fold, yea, more.

After taping the verse to the refrigerator or on a wall I'd make everyone memorize it. I wouldn't take it down until everyone could say it from memory. I probably did this five or six times while the children were growing up. I'm sure they can all recite that verse even today.

CHAPTER IX

To retain the dignity of your being you must avoid
subservience to human nonsense.

—Ian McCoy

Prior to graduation, I began to interview with various corporations. Caterpillar Tractor out of Peoria, Illinois, offered me a
job as a sales rep and wanted to send me to their heavy equipment
school where I could learn to operate their big earth-moving
machines. That sounded like a lot of fun. Prentice Hall, a publisher
of textbooks, wanted me to be their Utah publishing rep, regularly
visiting the various universities seeking textbook material from
college professors. Their retirement plan consisted of a cash payment
of a million dollars when I turned sixty-five. On the day I turned
sixty-five, I wished I had accepted their offer.

I took a job with Ford Motor Company in Dearborn, Michigan,
in public relations, thinking I would get more writing practice there.
I hate to admit it now, but I think the fact that Ford offered me
more money had something to do with it too. My classmates were
competing to see who could land the best jobs with the most money,
and I wanted to garner some respect, I suppose.

We bought a brand new bright red Ford Maverick and headed

to Michigan. We rented an apartment in Taylor, a little town south of Dearborn, and I went to work on the ninth floor of corporate headquarters. I was a trainee, helping write news releases, speeches, and copy for slide presentations. Everything I wrote was edited by an old newspaperman named Bob Hefty. No matter what I handed him, it came back covered with red marks. At first I thought I was back in high school English and didn't know a thing about writing, but in time I began to believe that by finding mistakes or possible mistakes or different ways to say things, Hefty felt important and needed.

The truth was that none of us in public relations were really needed at all. We were a luxury available in prosperous times, flunkies to help executives with speeches and hold their hands at media events. We were soft money, expendable, all two hundred of us. The environment was artificial and the executives around me were a nervous lot. My boss had three or four ashtrays on his desk, and much of the time there was a smoking cigarette in every one of them. Men at his level knew that if car sales slumped we would be the first to go.

The company used more than money to keep people working. Status symbols were everywhere. How close to the main building you were allowed to park was a symbol of your importance. Whether or not your desk was metal or wood, a potted plant, or a window in your office set you apart from lesser employees.

Bob Ford, no relation to Henry Ford, had an office much nicer than his station warranted. The reason for it was his name. It seemed every day people came to world headquarters seeking donations and sponsorships. Some of these people had legitimate requests, but many of them were absolute kooks, like wanting money to drill a hole to the center of the earth to find the lost tribes mentioned in the Bible. The problem was how to separate the wheat from the chaff or how to get rid of them without making them so mad they would want to come back and blow us up. Of course, none of the executives wanted to talk to these folks, so they were sent to the ninth floor where the lucky ones were given a chance to chat with Mr. Ford whose name was on the building. His job was to listen for a while before sending them away.

A guy in personnel named Dick Cook was the reason so many BYU students were coming to Ford. On any given day, five or six of us would get together for lunch. There were Mormons in almost every department and on every floor it seemed, and sharing information opened our eyes. The real Mr. Ford—Henry Ford II, the CEO—had an LDS secretary.

I remember the guys in finance one day explaining how the company kept three sets of books: one for the IRS showing how poorly the company was doing, one for the stockholders showing how well the company was doing, and one for management to show what was really going on.

One day a wonderful writing opportunity fell in my lap, but I couldn't think fast enough to grasp it, and then it was gone.

The president of Ford Australia had recently returned to Dearborn to retire. I was sent to his office to interview him and write up a news release for the local newspapers.

The problem was that he wasn't in the mood to do a news release. He was on the way out and really didn't seem to care if people knew about all the cars he built and sold. He wanted to tell me about a great adventure he had in Australia before coming home, and I was all ears.

When it was time for him to come home, he knew he would never go back to Australia, so he wanted to do something special. He hired a guide, with mules, who was supposed to take him to the most remote area of the continent where he hoped to see some primitive aborigines, ones who had minimal or no contact with the outside world. The guide promised he could deliver.

The Ford executive described riding a mule four or five days beyond the end of the road and finally coming to a remote aborigine village. The guide told him that these savages would not know any English. As they approached, little boys saw them coming and ran to greet them. The boys started yelling, "You see Boss Man. You see Boss Man."

The guide was both surprised and embarrassed that the boys spoke such good English. Impossible, there were no civilized people in the area. But the boys kept talking about their Boss Man. As the Ford president and guide entered the village, they saw more aborigines—short, squat people with pudgy round faces. The boys led them to the Boss Man's dwelling, a grass hut.

When the Boss Man stepped out, the guide and the client were equally surprised and amazed. He was black like the aborigines, but that's where the likeness ended. He was over six feet tall, weighed about two hundred and fifty pounds, and was muscled up like a linebacker in the National Football League. When he spoke, he sounded just like a football player in the NFL.

Boys were sent to the mules to fetch a case of beer. The three men stretched out in the shade of a tree and began to talk.

The Boss Man grew up in Philadelphia, on the street, always fighting and in trouble with the law. At age eighteen or nineteen, to avoid jail time, he became a merchant seaman. A year or two later, as his ship was cruising through the Indian Ocean, he got in a fight and killed a man. There was no jail on the ship, but he knew when the ship returned to the homeport in Philadelphia he would stand trial for murder and probably go to prison.

One night he gathered up some provisions, quietly lowered a large wooden crate overboard, climbed aboard, and set himself adrift. When morning arrived, he was nowhere to be seen. The ship continued on its charted course to port.

A week or so later, the Boss Man's crate washed up on the east coast of Australia. He hiked inland and found aborigines. The little chief was no match for the street fighter from Philadelphia, and Boss Man became chief. He instructed his new family to call him Boss Man. He introduced the guide and Ford executive to his three wives and growing herd of children. After three days, almost out of supplies, his guests headed back to civilization.

As the Ford executive told me this story, all I could think was what a great magazine article this story would make. I thought that if I got the name of the guide from the Ford executive, I could head off to Australia, find the Boss Man, scribble down a hundred pages of notes, take a bunch of pictures, and start selling magazine articles. But how would I fund it? How could I leave my young family to head half way around the world on a hope and a prayer?

Knowing what I know now about book advances from major publishers, it would have been possible to make this a sound career move. I possibly could have landed a ten-thousand-dollar advance from a New York publisher, which would handle my expenses and keep my family comfortable while I went to Australia to get the story of the Philadelphia black man who became king of the aborigines. When I finished the book, we could bring the Boss Man home on an all-expense-paid vacation so he and maybe his wives could go on every talk show in America. Seven years had passed since his fight on the ship, so he would be protected by the statute of limitations. The book would be a bestseller, and my writing career would be on the fast track before I was even thirty years old. But I didn't know about book advances, so I kept my nose to the grindstone, missing an excellent book publishing opportunity.

But sometimes a good story will find a way to be told anyway. When I started writing my *Storm Testament* series, this Boss Man story inspired a character named Ike, an escaped slave who went west with main character Dan Storm, eventually finding a home as chief among the Goshute Indians in Utah's west desert, helping his new people defend themselves against the Ute Indians who were constantly stealing their children to sell into slavery.

After a few months, Ford sent me to Los Angeles to learn about public relations in southern California. There were three of us with two secretaries in the office on Wilshire Boulevard. Little writing was required there. We just passed out news releases from headquarters and took members of the media to lunch and professional football games. We had a garage full of new Ford products, which we loaned out to reporters and movie producers.

My boss was a short, nervous type who never sat down at his desk. He paced back and forth, leaning over the desk to open mail or write notes, but never, ever did I see him sit down.

Soon after I arrived he explained the importance of being loyal to the company. He was dead serious when he told me that his relatives knew they were not welcome at his home if they did not drive a Ford vehicle. I asked him about our secretary who drove a Chevy Impala. He explained that she had been hired because she was beautiful, but if she hoped to have a future with the company she would eventually have to buy and drive a Ford.

One day I thought he was going to fire me. A week earlier while he had been out to lunch I took a call from the wife of one of the corporate vice presidents in Detroit. The family was coming to LA and she wanted to know if we could help her with Disneyland tickets. I called the park and arranged to buy tickets for her to pick up at the gate and called her back with the details. No problem. I forgot all about it. A few weeks later when my boss received a thank you note from the woman, he became unglued, not because the lady did not receive her tickets, but because I did not include him in the process. He made it clear I was never to do anything for people at the vice president level without him knowing about it and telling me what to do. I shrugged my shoulders, believing my days at Ford were numbered.

They brought me back to Michigan and transferred me to Philco-Ford in Philadelphia. Philco made home electronics and appliances, nothing new or original or very exciting, no cutting edge stuff, just some of the same old appliances everyone else made. The company had been losing money for a number of years, and if a breakthrough didn't come very soon, Ford would shut it down. The first day they took me on a tour of the assembly plant. I could see only a handful of workers. The conveyer belts and assembly lines were empty. Very little product was being built and sold. The media was not interested in our products because there was nothing new or different.

Sharon and I rented an apartment in Audubon and became members of the Valley Forge Ward. There was a stream with lots of geese and thick woods bordering our backyard. It was a nice place to live. By this time Bobby had arrived, so we had two little boys.

I would drive into the city every day. Philco was located in a dangerous neighborhood. You drove with your doors locked, praying your vehicle did not break down. High cyclone fences topped with barbed wire surrounded the company parking lot, and you couldn't get in or out of the twenty-four-hour security gate without the proper ID. Everybody stayed inside, even for lunch. We had our own barbershop so no one would have to venture into the war zone for a trim.

I frequently had reason to drive into the main part of town, usually to pick up print jobs, develop film, or buy office supplies. I tried to plan these trips around the lunch hour when I was hungry. On some of the

street corners, guys in T-shirts with little white baker caps would stand
behind big, black, cast iron grills resting on cinder blocks, heated from
underneath with torches attached to propane bottles. The cooks threw
blocks of thinly sliced frozen beef on the left side of the grill. When
the meat started to thaw, they'd separate the slices with a big spatula as
they pushed them to the middle of the grill to finish cooking. After the
meat had been turned over and was hot, they threw on slices of Swiss
cheese. While all this was going on, big hoagie buns were toasting
on the right side of the grill. When the cheese was melted, the cook
scooped up a generous portion of meat and cheese and placed it on a
toasted bun. He squirted catsup on the top, wrapped the whole thing
in waxed paper, and sold it to you for a buck. For fifty cents more you
could grab a can of pop from a washtub full of ice.

When you had to stop at a stoplight, sometimes a guy would
run to your driver side window with a cardboard flat covered with
soft pretzels still warm from the oven of a nearby bakery, which he
would sell to you for a quarter. For no extra charge he would squirt
on a little mustard. These were every bit as good and perhaps better
than the soft pretzels we'd buy at the corner bakeries in Germany. As
far as I knew, Philadelphia was the only city in the world where you
could buy cheese steak sandwiches and soft pretzels on the street. I
loved to go there for lunch.

At church they made me the elders' quorum president, so we
decided to have a Halloween party. I bought an ugly rubber mask—a
Frankenstein-like face that fit entirely over my head. David Fickes, a
neighbor, bought one too. We put on our trench coats the day before
Halloween and went knocking on doors. We stopped after a while
realizing that sooner or later someone would have a heart attack or
shoot us since some of the people were so frightened. People expected
goblins at their door on Halloween, but not the day before.

So Dick and I came up with a better plan to scare people. I
told him about the party we were going to have for couples from
church. I made up a story about miners, many years ago, who had
died mysteriously in the woods next to our apartment, and how their
restless spirits had stayed behind to haunt people. I told the story to
our guests and suggested we take a short hike into the woods so I
could show them the miners' graves. I assured them that the stories

about the spirits lingering to haunt were fictional, I was sure of it, or at least I thought I was. So we took a hike into the woods, some of the women continuing to ask questions about my story. I assured them that the part about the ghosts was fictional, but the graves were real. Still, they continued asking questions. I had set them up perfectly for what was about to happen.

At a place where the woods were especially thick and dark, the path narrowed to get around the end of an old gate. I knew Dick was hiding in the bushes, wearing one of the grotesque masks under a hood. He had taken a flashlight with him, so everyone would be sure to see his face when he stepped forward.

As three or four of the women were squeezing around the end of the gate, Dick stepped forward, not more than three feet in front of them, with the light shining on his masked face. It was pandemonium. People were screaming and scrambling to get out of the way. A few seconds later, I told them it was only a hoax, and Dick removed the mask so they could see his smiling face, but it was too late. One woman, refusing to be soothed, ran screaming all the way back to the apartment, falling down several times. When her husband finally caught up with her, she insisted he take her home immediately. I think she had an accident in her pants. Sharon was mad at me and so were some of the other guests. A party was ruined. I hoped we would never have another Halloween party as long as I lived.

Work was so frustrating. Our products were not selling, and the company was losing more money. In public relations we tried to look busy, going here and there, making reports, reading newspapers, calling reporters, looking for news about Ford and Philco Ford, and finding very little. We had a lot of meetings, but as far as I could see, no meaningful developments occurred at the meetings. About the only productive thing I did was write speeches for executives who were too lazy or incompetent to do it themselves. The president of the company, Leo Bebee, was a personal friend of Henry Ford II and didn't seem to have a plan for turning things around. From my MBA studies, I knew what I would do if I were running the company—fire all the soft money employees like me who were not building or selling product.

In an effort to continue developing my writing skills, I started getting up at four or five in the morning and writing poetry and songs. Maybe I just needed an outlet for my frustrations at work. The problem with getting up so early is that I would get drowsy about mid morning. During one of our meetings I started dozing off. The next day they fired me. They gave me a job with no responsibility and no opportunity to make a difference and then fired me for not doing it well. It was an environment where everyone was hurrying to meetings where there were always lots of things to talk about, but nobody was doing anything that made any difference as the company continued to lose more and more money. They went out of business shortly after I left.

I had believed for a long time that good writers had to have an understanding of human psychology and behavior, and I felt bad that in my many years in college I had not taken psychology classes. So I drove over to Villanova, a Catholic university in Philadelphia, and enrolled in three psychology classes. I found an afternoon job handling advertising for a heavy equipment school. I would place posters and response cards in delicatessens and barbershops. If I hustled, I could earn close to fifty dollars an hour. I was earning almost as much as at Ford and furthering my education. Life had taken a turn for the better.

The next term I took an upper division psychology class from a Dr. Larry Furst. He was a laid-back professor, wearing open-necked polo shirts to class and encouraging us to play volleyball during class time. I thought I had made a mistake taking the class. Then he made an assignment for us to do a psychology project or experiment, one that would count for a large portion of our grade. He tossed out a lot of ideas to get us thinking.

I was one of the first to come up with a plan. I figured out a way to quantify and scientifically test what I had learned with the IQ game when I was eleven. As long as I believed the writing on the box, after hundreds of attempts, I could never play the game with less than four remaining pegs. After Dr. Roberts convinced me the writing on the box was made up by advertising guys who knew nothing about IQ and that I was perfectly capable of doing it with one peg remaining in the middle—even a blue one if I desired—it was just a matter of time until I could do it every time with only one peg left in the middle. The core idea is that if you really believe you can do a difficult thing, you are more likely to be able to do it. Likewise, if you don't believe you can do something, you probably won't be able to do it.

On the day set aside for my presentation, I showed up to class bringing a contraption I had built to measure arm strength used in arm wrestling contests. It consisted of a handle with a rope passing over a pulley to a platform where my assistants could add weights, making it increasingly difficult for the person being tested to hold up the platform. For weights, I used bricks.

I measured the arm strength of all the male students in the class by having them seat themselves in front of the contraption one at a time. They would grab the handle and hold it as long as possible while two of the prettiest girls in the class added weights to the platform below the pulley. (I used pretty girls to do the measuring, thinking the men were more likely to want to impress them by demonstrating superior arm strength.) When a particular student could no longer hold up the platform, I would write down the number of weights the girls had put on the platform. The platform was out of the line of vision of the subjects, so they did not know their score, and neither did anyone else in the class except me.

When the measuring was done, I had an arm strength number for each boy in the class—the higher the number, the stronger the subject. Next, I passed out a paper to each of the subjects, listing the names of all the men whose arm strength had been measured. They all knew each other, but none of them knew any of the strength measurements. I asked each boy to make a mark by each of the other student's names, guessing whether he thought that particular boy had a higher or lower arm strength measurement. When they were finished, I gathered up my data, not telling anyone what I was trying to accomplish, including the professor.

The next day I came to class announcing we were going to have arm wrestling contests.

In going over the data, I found about a dozen paring opportunities where contestant A had scored higher than contestant B in the strength measurement, but both A and B in their personal evaluations thought the B contestant was the stronger of the two. In other words, in each contest I had a situation where both contestants thought the weaker contestant was stronger. I wanted to know which was most important—expected strength or actual strength—in determining the winner of arm wrestling contests. I wrote down the results of all the contests.

The next day I explained to the class what I had been attempting to measure and why I had paired the young men in arm wrestling contests the way I did. I explained that I was comparing real strength versus perceived strength in determining the outcome of athletic contests. I reported to the class that eighty-two percent of the time the weaker man won the arm wrestling contest. Eighty-two percent of the time, when both contestants thought the weaker man was stronger, the weaker man won. Perception played a bigger role in determining the winner than did actual strength.

The professor seemed pleased and asked me to conduct the experiment in his other classes. Each time we came up with about the same result: over eighty percent of the time the weaker man won.

Dr. Furst helped me write up the results. We sent the paper to the *Journal of Psychology* and they published it. They didn't pay me any money, but I started getting letters from military and academic researchers and graduate students asking for more information. Not only had I been published in one of the most prestigious academic journals, but I was also getting straight As in all my classes. I started writing to various universities inquiring about PhD programs in psychology.

Forty years later, my daughter Sarah called one night to ask a question. She was working on a master's degree in psychology at Utah State University. In her new textbook there was a chapter discussing a study of arm wrestling contests comparing expected strength versus actual strength in determining winners. Coauthors of the study were Leland Nelson and Larry Furst. She knew I wrote historical novels and some nonfiction books about near-death experiences, but now she wanted to know if I had anything to do with the *Journal of Psychology* article discussed in her textbook. Of course, I said I did, and she seemed surprised. Once again I confirmed the need to write a personal history, because you want your posterity to know things like this.

I suppose there's another lesson here. Some of the good things we do develop legs and a path of their own, refusing to die. Like the story in the *Y Magazine* that my professor didn't like that ended up being published in a lot of places. Some of the things we do have a rippling effect, finding legs and going places we can't imagine, reaching people and doing good that we probably won't see until perhaps the next life. On the other hand, the bad things we do can come back to bite us in unexpected ways too.

I hesitate sharing another experience that happened during our short stay in Pennsylvania. In March of that year I went on a camping trip with the Scouts in the mountains west of Valley Forge.

I had to laugh at one of the boys as we hiked along a clear flowing stream to our camping spot. I called the boys' attention to some mallard ducks flying in to land on the stream. One of the boys yelled at me, insisting I was wrong. He said the birds we saw were not ducks because ducks were white, and ducks couldn't fly.

I tried to reason with him, explaining that these were wild ducks that are different than the white domestic ducks he had seen, but he refused to listen because ducks are white and ducks can't fly. I felt like I was back in Germany trying to tell people about Joseph Smith and the Book of Mormon. No matter what I said, this boy was not about to let me shatter his belief in white ducks. I suppose I was used to adults defending such beliefs, but it surprised me to find a twelve-year-old boy, who goes to school every day to learn new things, to be so entrenched in a partially correct but false belief.

As we were driving home, we found ourselves in a wooded valley that was full of smoke. It had been unseasonably warm for a few weeks allowing the leaves that had fallen from the trees the previous fall to finally dry out. Apparently the leaves in this valley had caught fire. Through the smoke we saw a fire truck that was blocking the road. We had to stop. Men were unloading five-gallon water cans equipped with shoulder straps and nozzles. Other men were putting the water containers on their backs, picking up shovels, and marching to the downhill side of the road on our right where they would step off the road and disappear into the woods below.

Since we weren't going anywhere, after telling the boys to stay in the vehicles, I got out of the car to check things out. The first thing I noticed was that the smoke-filled air was moving down the mountain, from left to right. The men with the water-filled backpacks were going the wrong way. The fire responsible for the smoke had to be up the hill to our left—or did the men who lived here know something I did not know about fire? I tried to explain my reasoning to some men who stayed behind with the fire truck, but they weren't about to be distracted by a grown man wearing a Boy Scout shirt. For the second time that weekend I was talking about ducks to deaf ears, so I walked over to the row of water cans, strapped one onto my back, and headed up the hill. The men by the truck didn't seem to notice.

The heavy water canister made the uphill climb difficult. The hiking was a little easier if I followed a small game trail that veered in an uphill direction to the left, toward a rocky ridge. When I reached the ridge, my little trail joined a larger trail, and since it was still going uphill, that's the way I went. I liked being close to the ridge because it looked like a good firebreak.

I began to see yellow flames and wondered if I should hurry back to the fire truck to tell the men I had found the fire, but not wanting another duck conversation, I continued along the edge of the ridge, finally reaching a brush-filled saddle, a perfect pathway for the fire to spread from the little valley on the right to a much larger and more thickly wooded valley on the left. The breeze was pushing a wall of flames, perhaps two feet tall, in my direction. It was time to make a stand. I removed the canister and used the attached hand pump to build up the pressure. Then I started spraying water on the flames.

At first I seemed to be having good success because there were no big trees burning, just grass and short brush. I had only five gallons of water, so I was careful to make sure to spray only the grass and brush at the bottom of the flames. I guessed the other men would figure out where the fire was sooner or later and come up to join me. All I had to do was keep the flames from getting through the saddle.

But nobody came. The breeze turned into a wind, and then I ran out of water. My first thought was to run to the cover of the rocks, and then it occurred to me that there was one more thing I could do.

I had given a lot of blessings on my mission, mostly attempts to heal the sick, and while not all the blessings succeeded in a noticeable way, some did. I believed priesthood power was real. I raised my right arm to the square, thinking I was going to command the wind to stop, but instead I commanded it to change directions.

If I'd thought very much about what I was doing I probably would not have done it, but I did, and the wind immediately changed directions, blowing the fire back on itself, away from the saddle. I was no longer in danger. Feeling weakness in my legs, I sat down on a stump, trying to ponder what had just happened.

Sure, the wind could have changed on its own at the exact moment I raised my arm to the square, but the chances of that happening were like winning the lottery—one in a million, or one in ten million.

Such were my thoughts when I heard the crunching of boots. Three men with full water tanks were huffing and puffing into the saddle, ready to spray water on the remaining flames in the event the wind changed again. One of them said something about me being lucky, that if the wind hadn't changed I'd have been a dead man.

I thought I'd earned some respect by reading the wind and finding the fire before they did, but they just thought I was stupid in heading off by myself without proper leadership and tools. They were probably right, and with me not wanting to continue another white duck conversation, I picked up the empty canister and headed down to the road. Because of the wind change, visibility had improved, and traffic was allowed to start moving again. I didn't say anything to my companions about what had happened up on the mountain.

At first I thought I had discovered something mysterious and wonderful, that if I had the faith to do it once I could do it again, but as I tried on other occasions to command the wind, it refused to obey. Sometimes I'd read John 14:12.

> Verily, verily, I say unto you, He that believeth on me, the works that I do shall he do also; and greater *works* than these shall he do; Because I go unto my Father.

In time I realized I probably didn't have as much faith as I thought I had. I figured God indulged me once because my life was in danger and He didn't want me to die.

Still, my faith in priesthood power and blessings continued. I gave a father's blessing to each of my children when they were babies, promising them health and strength and protection from evil and danger. At the beginning of most school years I'd line them up in the living room and one at a time bless them that they'd get along with teachers and friends, be good examples, and be able to understand and remember the things that were taught. As the children grew older, sometimes they would ask for blessings at difficult times in their lives, and sometimes miracles happened.

One time a mare I was keeping for Ross Boundy, a missionary companion and friend, ran into a fence and ran a wire into her left eye. When I'd move my hand suddenly and quickly toward the eye, she would neither blink nor try to move her head away. The eye had gone blind. The veterinarian who examined the mare said he had no training to repair this kind of injury. He gave me some antibiotic eye drops to squirt onto the eye once or twice a day. After several weeks of treatment I could see no improvement.

When Ross, a bishop, came down from Washington for a short visit, I suggested we lay hands on the mare and give her a blessing. We anointed her head with oil and pronounced the blessing. A few weeks later, I e-mailed Ross, telling him that every time I raised my hand toward the mare's eye, she blinked and moved her head away. Her vision had returned.

One time I attended a lecture by Jack Houk, an aeronautical engineer from southern California. Everyone attending the lecture was supposed to bring a bunch of forks and spoons. His intent was to teach us how to use our minds to bend silverware.

After telling everyone to toss their spoons and forks in a big pile in the front of the room, Jack proceeded to explain the principle of spoon bending. I was in the first row. He was standing directly in front of me, holding a fork in his right hand, the tines pointing toward the ceiling as he talked.

While Jack was talking, I noticed that the fork tines were beginning to bend forward, looking soft and pliable like warm clay. This was not what was supposed to happen at this point in his lecture, so without calling attention to it, he reached up with his other hand

and quickly straightened the tines. This happened several times.

This guy was not slick and polished like a David Copperfield. He wore a white shirt and tie with a black suit that looked like it had been slept in. He had a crew cut and thick glasses. He earlier told me how he had mounted spring steel in the heels of his black shoes so there would be a spring in his step. He looked and acted like someone who would hang out with Albert Einstein. When he wasn't bending dinnerware he was building rockets and missiles.

In contrast, the audience was full of women in brightly colored Gypsy dresses with strings of beads hanging around their necks, and many of the men had ponytails. The audience did not fit the speaker.

Jack explained that the atmosphere in the room was extremely important. He said if we were serious, reverent, and religious, the experiment would fail big time. He wanted a party atmosphere with lots of smiling, laughing, and talking. He said if we were feeling happy and having a good time, we would destroy a lot of good silverware.

Finally he asked everyone to select four or five pieces of dinnerware from the big pile. He then told us to hold a fork or spoon in front of our face and yell at it to bend. Then we were to relax and let go and look around at what everyone else was doing. He wanted a lot of happy noise in the room.

When I yelled at my spoon nothing happened, so I looked around. Some people were bending their dinnerware, especially a skinny little lady right next to me. My spoon didn't seem to want to do it so I kept looking around.

After a few minutes I noticed that my spoon felt warm, almost hot. As I pushed my fingers against it, determined not to force anything, it started to bend. I twisted it in circles and tied it in a knot. I was able to do the same with the next three spoons.

After the last one had been destroyed, I yawned and started looking for the refreshment table. Almost everyone was bending forks and spoons by now, and it just didn't seem like a big deal anymore. Anyone could do it. When I returned home and didn't have the happy party atmosphere, I couldn't do it.

Another time I attended a lecture in Salt Lake City on psychokinesis, the skill of influencing the physical world with your mind. The lecturer started handing out florescent lights to most of the people in the small audience. The overhead lights in the room were turned off as the lecturer talked lovingly to his light bulb, asking it to glow for him. He told us to try to do the same with our lights. Pretty soon the lecturer's light was glowing, not brightly, but in the dark room its glow was unmistakable. Pretty soon another light started to glow, then another, and then there were lights glowing all over the place. When mine started to glow, I wondered if they had given us trick lights with little batteries hidden inside.

To make sure this was not the case, I stopped in at the neighborhood Walmart store on the way home and bought a florescent light similar in appearance to the ones used at the lecture. Sharon was already in bed when I arrived home, so I quickly undressed and crawled under the covers, bringing the light with me. Sharon demanded what was happening when I held the bulb above our heads and began talking to it. I said I had learned to illuminate light bulbs at the lecture and wanted to see if I could do it at home.

She told me I should stop going to these lectures because they were making me crazy, and then the light began to glow. She was upset and wanted me to turn it off. I told her not to worry, that the Jaredites used glowing rocks without power cords to light their ships thousands of years ago. This wasn't much different—just glowing glass instead of glowing rocks. A few days later she moved the light from the bedroom to the office, hoping I'd forget about it.

As far as the spoon bending and light bulbs go, I believe the yearnings of the heart assure us that miracles are possible, but natural law does not show us how to accomplish them. It is for us to uncover the spiritual and natural laws that bring them to pass.

CHAPTER X

Hast thou given the horse strength? hast thou clothed his neck with thunder? Canst thou make him afraid as a grasshopper? the glory of his nostrils *is* terrible. He paweth in the valley, and rejoiceth in *his* strength: he goeth on to meet the armed men. He mocketh at fear, and is not affrighted; neither turneth he back from the sword. The quiver rattleth against him, the glittering spear and the shield. He swalloweth the ground with fierceness and rage. . . . He saith among the trumpets, Ha, ha; and he smelleth the battle afar off, the thunder of the captains, and the shouting.

—JOB 39:19–25

One night I received a very interesting call from Reno, Nevada. My childhood friend, Syd Smith, was purchasing an automobile dealership in Hamilton, Montana. While I was over in Germany doing missionary work, he was going to dental school. Now he was practicing medicine in Nevada, but he was getting ready to move to Montana where the fishing and hunting were better. He wasn't ready to move up there yet, but he had found a business for sale, a Dodge car and truck agency, and felt like he needed to move quickly before someone else picked it up. That's why he was calling me. He knew

I had experience in the car business, plus I had an MBA degree. He thought I would be the right guy to run his new car and truck business.

I told him I had never sold cars before and that I wrote speeches and read newspapers at Ford. He insisted we could learn the business together. A few weeks later he picked me up at the Missoula airport, and we drove down through the beautiful Bitterroot Valley to check things out.

Mellott Motors was a little business, not on a main street, and had sold only sixteen new trucks that year. Harry Mellott, the owner, was getting old and wanted to retire.

Shortly after Christmas, Sharon and I threw all our earthly possessions into a U-Haul truck, and with our two little boys, we headed west to our new home in Hamilton, Montana. I started work January 2, 1971. I was wearing a white shirt and tie and my best suit, ready for two events that would help set the course of my future in Montana.

First, a young man named Bob Maloney, who had been severely wounded in Vietnam and was now confined to a wheelchair, came in to look at new Dodge Chargers. We had one in stock, and it was loaded. He had a substantial disability benefit, so after an hour or two of talking and test-driving, we filled out the papers and he drove away in his new Dodge. I had sold my first car. I believed I would sell many more. I was glad we had moved to Montana.

The second event that shaped my future was a get-acquainted visit by the other car dealers in town—the Cadillac-Olds dealer, the Chrysler dealer, and the friendly Ford dealer. All of them were men twice my age. None of them wore suits. They weren't nervous and jumpy like some of the executives I had known at Ford. They were self-confident small business owners, used to doing as they pleased.

I was impressed until they began to explain what they perceived to be the reality of doing business in Montana's Bitterroot Valley. They said 80 percent of the cars and trucks were purchased by farmers and ranchers, men and women whose grandparents killed Indians to get their land. These folks had deep roots and traditions and did not like buying cars and trucks from city slickers like me.

My fellow dealers knew I had moved to Montana from

Philadelphia. Others before me had come from the big cities to sell vehicles, and all had failed. I was an outsider, a city slicker; the farmers and ranchers would not buy from me, and I would fail. They said it couldn't be done. They told me I seemed like a nice young man, but I ought to start looking for a different way to make a living because the car and truck business was not going to be kind to me.

I explained all this to Syd on the phone that evening, and he thought they were bluffing. We knew about that from our childhood poker games. I wasn't so sure. In the weeks to come, though I was selling a reasonable number of new and used vehicles to the townspeople, the absence of the farmers and ranchers was apparent. I didn't know what to do about it.

Sharon and I were renting a house a mile or so east of town, up against the mountains. We had a barn and nineteen acres of pasture and woods. Though I was nervous about the warning from the other dealers, I wasn't about to pass up the opportunity to start riding horses again, the activity I had loved so much as a child.

A local racehorse breeder named Darrel Cozad was in the Hamilton ward where we went to church. I told him I wanted to buy a horse that both my wife and I could ride. He said he had several like that for sale and I ought to come and take a look. I did, and the least expensive one was $650. In 1971 that was a lot of money to pay for a horse, at least it seemed that way to me considering the precarious nature of my new profession, so I decided to keep looking.

A few days later I found a four-year-old quarter horse mare advertised in the newspaper. The owner wanted only $225 for her. She looked every bit as good as the more expensive horses Darrel Cozad had tried to sell me. There were two reasons for the low asking price. She didn't have any papers, and she had been ridden only twice. I figured I was a good enough horseman to finish the training, so the purchase was made and I took her home.

After that, when I ran into Darrel at church, he would tease me about my mongrel horse, wanting to know if she had bucked me off yet. Sharon was a little nervous about me bringing home a horse that was not broken. The horse was nervous too, trotting back and forth in the little pasture outside our kitchen window. We named her Sundance.

The second or third morning after we brought her home, as we sat down for breakfast, two-year-old Bobby turned up missing. He was nowhere in the house. His huge Tonka dump truck was missing too. Then we saw him, outside in the pasture with the new horse. Bobby was bent over his dump truck, trying to push it under the horse's belly. One of the mare's feet was in the way, and our boy was ramming the truck against the foot. The horse appeared relaxed and calm and made no effort to kick Bobby. Quietly, we went outside and persuaded him to come in for breakfast.

At first I rode Sundance in a corral, and then I started taking her out on the logging roads through the forest above our house. In time I started galloping her, faster and faster. She liked to run, and seemed very fast. She never tripped or stumbled. I was very pleased with my purchase. In time I let Sharon ride her around the yard. At church, Darrel continued to tease me about my mongrel horse, while telling me how well his Appaloosa racehorses were doing on the tracks in Montana and Washington.

Then one Monday morning, Darrell Cozad showed up at my place of work. We had changed the name from Mellott Motors to Smith Motors. Darrell had a lot of miles on his Chevy pickup and wanted to trade it in on a new Dodge. He was a tough customer and worked hard to get the best possible price. I wanted so much to sell him a new truck, but I wasn't about to give it to him.

After more than an hour of dickering back and forth, a strange and wonderful idea entered my mind. We were about fifty dollars apart, the difference between what he was willing to pay and what I was willing to accept.

"Let's stop dickering over price," I said. "We're only fifty dollars apart. I'll race you for the difference, my mongrel pony against any one of your fancy racehorses. I'm tired of you giving me a bad time over my cheap horse. I believe I can beat you in a horse race. If you win you can have the new truck at the price you have agreed to pay. If I win, you will give me an extra fifty dollars. Do we have a deal?" I extended my hand.

He looked at me like I was nuts or that maybe I knew something he didn't. He was sure my little mare didn't have a chance against one of his racehorses, and I guessed he was probably right.

"Do we have a deal?" I asked again, still holding out my hand. Finally he reached out to shake my hand. We both smiled, the tension between us gone. He gave me the title to his old truck, and we filled out the papers with the understanding that he would give me another fifty dollars if I won the race.

"Let's get our horses," he said when the deal was done.

"Not today," I said. "How about Thursday night, eight o'clock at the fairgrounds?"

"Why wait?"

"I want to invite a few people to watch."

"Fine, see you Thursday at eight." He climbed into his new truck and drove away.

I went to my desk, opened to a clean page on my yellow note pad, and scribbled out the copy for a radio advertisement announcing a grudge race between a Montana rancher and a city slicker car dealer from Philadelphia, two men who could not agree on the price of a truck, so they were settling their difference the old-fashioned Montana way, a horse race at the Ravalli County fairgrounds, Thursday night, eight o'clock, public invited.

I called the fairgrounds to make sure we could have our race there and then took the ad over to radio station KLYQ, the only one in the Bitterroot Valley at the time. They started running the ad ten or twelve times a day. By Thursday everyone in the valley knew about the race.

I had no idea how many people might come to watch. I didn't know for sure how the farmers and ranchers would respond to a publicity stunt like this, but I had a good feeling about the whole thing. Besides, it was not a publicity stunt. It was an honest and courageous way to settle a legitimate difference. If I had not challenged Darrell to the race, he might not have signed the papers. Nothing was faked. It felt right, win or lose. After the race things would be different between me and those farmers and ranchers who wouldn't even talk to me about their car and truck purchases.

I was pretty sure I would lose, but I told myself it didn't matter. The important thing was letting everyone know that this city slicker was willing to have a horse race to settle a dispute over a new truck. I hoped they would no longer think of me as a city slicker but someone who belonged in rural Montana.

Since the ads described me as a city slicker, when I headed down to the fairgrounds Thursday evening I dressed the part—white shirt, suit and tie, and polished church shoes. Nobody in the Bitterroot dressed that way unless they were going to church or a funeral.

Darrel showed up, smug and confident, his horse saddled and ready to go. He was wearing a big white John Wayne cowboy hat.

I chose as the course for the race the straightaway in front of the grandstands. We would start at the north end and run to the middle of the grandstand, a distance of nearly four hundred yards. Since there was no starting gate, we would ride to the end of the straightaway, turn around, and start back toward the grandstand. I had arranged for a mounted cowboy with a loaded Colt .45 to ride behind us. When it looked to him like we were even, he would fire his gun to start the race. This kind of start, I later learned, was called *lap and tap.*

As I was explaining all this to Darrel, I noticed that the grandstand was filling up. Hundreds of people were coming to watch, including newspaper reporters and photographers. One was from *The Missoulian*, the largest newspaper in western Montana, fifty miles to the north.

I was beginning to think I had made a terrible mistake. What if my horse started bucking? She had never raced before. What if I fell off, looking like a true city slicker in front of all these people? My palms were sweating.

Slowly, Darrel and I rode to the end of the straightaway. The old cowboy rode with us, slipping a slug into the cylinder of his gun. We turned and started walking real slow toward the grandstand. The gun went off.

Grabbing the saddle horn with my free hand, I leaned forward and rammed both heels into the little mare's ribs. In a second we were running full speed. My suit coat was flapping in the breeze. My necktie was a red streamer over my right shoulder.

I couldn't see Darrel. I worried that he was holding back, waiting to pass me just ahead of the finish line. I hoped he was struggling to keep up. It seemed like Sundance was running really fast. I loved the sound of the hoofbeats.

The race was over almost before it began. I beat him by three or four lengths. I was so proud of that little horse. I was glad I hadn't fallen off. The reporters were asking questions and photographers were taking pictures as Darrel handed me a check for fifty dollars to complete our transaction. Our picture appeared on the front page of the Sunday *Missoulian*.

My good feelings had led me right. Farmers and ranchers wanted to meet the city slicker who defeated Darrel Cozad in a horse race. They brought in their old Chevys and Fords to see what kind of deal I would make them on a new Dodge. I sold eighty-three new Dodge trucks that year, compared to sixteen the year before. I believed if I had spent a million dollars in advertising I could not have accomplished as much.

CHAPTER XI

If one advances confidently in the direction of his dreams, and endeavors to live the life which he has imagined, he will meet with a success unexpected in common hours.

—HENRY DAVID THOREAU

The bishop asked me to teach early morning seminary, and since I was the elders quorum president, we tried another Halloween party that fall. I promised Sharon I'd behave myself—no scary stories and walks in the woods. I could chat with the guests, bob for apples, keep an eye on the boys, and nothing else. Sharon dressed up like a witch, dyeing her face and hair green with food coloring. She was the most beautiful witch I had ever seen.

I was in the kitchen behaving myself when I heard a strange noise out front. It was kind of a clanking, clickety sound. I remember standing by the kitchen sink wondering what could make a noise like that.

We had a pet goat named Gadianton. We had raised him from a kid. He was a frisky little fellow who would run into the house if we gave him half a chance. If we left a car or truck door open, he would jump right in, and one time he did that right after Sharon had placed a cake on the front seat. He had his nose and both front feet in the cake before she could get him out of the car. Normally he just munched on flowers and nibbled the bark off our fruit trees.

As the noise out front continued, I decided to check it out. Our guests had parked bumper to bumper along the street in front of the house, and little Gadianton had discovered what great fun it was jumping from hood to trunk as he journeyed back and forth along the tops of the cars. It was too dark to see if any damage had been done, but I quickly got a rope on his neck and tied him out back. Eventually the happy guests went home, and none ever reported any dents on their hoods and trunk lids. Finally, we had pulled off a Halloween party without serious mishap.

The second winter in Montana, I bought a two-wheeled cutter or chariot that was designed to be pulled by a team of horses. We sponsored chariot races at the fairgrounds. Syd and I caught a seven-year-old bay mare that had been running wild since birth on a place Syd bought, and we hitched her to the chariot with Sundance. Fortunately, the first time we let them run was at the fairgrounds, so when they ran away with me, all they could do was run around the track, I believe eight times before I finally got them stopped.

About a dozen other teams showed up on Saturday afternoons to participate in the races, and lots of people came to watch. I had Dodge signs all over the place. We sold Coke products and hot dogs.

To help our races appeal to more people, I started announcing special competitive events during the breaks between races. One week we had pie jousting. Business people from the community, armed with cream pies, would gallop horses toward each other and try to hit their opponent with the pie as they galloped past—a takeoff from medieval jousting, using pastry instead of wooden poles.

Then I mounted a plywood buffalo on the side of a truck that was driven around the track. As it came to the straightaway leading to the grandstand, a mounted rider with bow and arrows would gallop alongside. The objective was to shoot as many arrows as possible into the buffalo before reaching the finish line. Four was the best anyone ever did, which was achieved by a local pharmacist.

One week we offered fifty dollars and a hundred pounds of dog food to the fastest dog in the Bitterroot Valley. Two people—a holder and a master—accompanied each dog. The holders held their dogs among the fifty or so other dogs at the starting line at one end of the grandstand, while the masters walked to the finish line at the other end of the grandstand. The masters started calling their dogs. That's when the gun went off, the signal for the holders to let go.

Confusion reigned. Maybe the starting gun was too loud. Dogs ran in every direction. Some just stood still and cowered. A fight broke out. Some disappeared under the grandstand. One little lap dog about a foot tall trotted to his master and won the prize.

One week we announced we were going to do an experiment to determine if Levi Strauss, the largest jean manufacturer in the world, was guilty of false advertising. Back in those days, cowboys and farmers for the most part wore Levis instead of Wrangler jeans. Between the belt loops on the back of every pair of Levis was a leather patch showing two men with whips trying to get two horses or mules, one hitched to each side of a pair of Levi jeans, to pull the trousers in two, implying that Levis are so tough that not even horses can rip them apart. By sewing that patch on every new pair of jeans, the company was claiming such a thing couldn't be done.

Darrel Cozad agreed to bring a pair of small draft horses to the fairgrounds, and a local clothing store gave me a brand new pair of Levi jeans. On Saturday afternoon a record crowd showed up to watch. We took our time securing the horses to the trousers. Some spectators were absolutely sure no pair of jeans in the world could withstand the pull of two strong horses. Others were equally confident that a large, reputable company like Levi Strauss would not sew a lie on the back of every pair of its jeans, if indeed it could be done. Those on the side of the company thought the jeans would be like a thick rope and the horses would not be able to rip them apart. I could see a lot of people placing bets.

Finally, with a horse hitched to each pant leg, Darrel was ready to give it a try. I nodded for him to proceed. With a big grin on his face, he clucked to his horses. The Levi jeans ripped in two like they were made of tissue paper. It seemed the horses didn't even have to lean into their collars.

Some of the losers were bad sports, insisting that the jeans had not been properly attached to the horses. There had not been an even amount of pull from belt line to crotch as depicted in the drawing on the leather patch. I thought they had a valid point, so I announced we would do it again the next week.

Darrel was more than happy to bring his horses again, but the store owner would not give me another pair of Levis. He was probably afraid that if I kept doing this, people would stop buying his best-selling jean product. So I had to buy the second pair of jeans.

The next week we ran a wooden fence post through each pant leg and attached a horse's harness to both ends of a corresponding fence post. The critics agreed this was a fair way to do it since the pull would be uniform from belt line to crotch. As Darrel hitched up the horses, I could tell the amount of betting was greatly reduced. Few people wanted to bet against the horses two weeks in a row. Their work had been too easy the previous week.

For the second time the jeans easily ripped in two. The critics disappeared. We had proved beyond any reasonable doubt that Levi Strauss was guilty of false advertising. I sent them a letter suggesting they might want to change their logo before the whole world knew about their lie. The company never responded to my letter. I thought the folks at Wrangler might send me a box of their jeans, but that didn't happen either.

Not long after that, the entire cowboy community nationwide began switching from Levis to Wranglers. Wranglers were more cowboy-friendly in that they had a thinner inside seam that wasn't as likely to rub sores on your legs on long horseback rides. The hip pockets were deeper and sewn tighter across the top to keep a wallet in place while riding a horse, but any kind of aggressive riding in Levis, like roping or cutting, tended to work a wallet out of the pocket. I like to think that maybe my little experiment in false advertising had something to do with cowboys switching from the deceptively advertised Levis to a more honest kind of jeans like Wranglers.

Our cutter races were held in the winter and were so popular that when summer rolled around we sponsored Friday night match races with only two horses involved. It was a double elimination series, with the finals taking place at the county fair in August. Lots of people who thought their horses were fast had to eat humble pie. The fun part for me was watching the kids and women on their pet horses beating the millionaire horse breeders. Some people, hoping to compete, entered Arabian or Morgan horses, but quarter horses and thoroughbreds won all the races. The only weight requirement was that every horse had to carry a western stock saddle.

By this time Sharon and I had moved out of the rented house east of town. I traded two new vehicles for sixteen acres south of town. The property was located up on the bench and had a lot of ponderosa pine trees and a little stream running through it. It was a great place to ride horses and a favorite wintering area for deer and elk. I borrowed money from the bank to pay for the two vehicles and took out a construction loan to build our first home.

We were selling a lot of cars and trucks, but Syd and Mindy weren't happy with the bottom line or the profit picture. We didn't have anyone with experience to guide us. It was a case of the blind leading the blind, even though by this time I was pretty good at selling cars and trucks. The sales rep from Dodge came by about once a month to help with the paper work and give advice, but he wasn't much older than I was and had never actually operated a dealership.

Syd and Mindy figured we needed more product. They rented a lot on the highway and brought in a bunch of Circle J horse trailers and a line of campers and camp trailers. I could sell a horse trailer once in a while but was lost when it came to campers. I'd never owned one and didn't know the first thing about them. Someone would ask me about winterizing a certain unit, and I didn't even know what they were talking about, at least not at first. Overnight our overhead doubled—more rent, more insurance, more interest, and more maintenance costs. Then, for the first time, we started losing money. Syd decided to sell out, and I landed a job as used car manager at the Chevy dealership, my former competitor.

As soon as I started working there, I cornered the general sales manager, Jim Porch. I wanted to know how he had beat me so many times on truck deals when I was with Dodge, selling trucks to people who paid cash with no trade-ins. There were times when I had wanted a deal so bad that I had shaved the margin to two hundred dollars and the customer still ended up buying a Chevy from Jim instead. Now that I worked with Jim, I wanted to know how he beat me so many times.

He just laughed and turned around and pulled open a file drawer containing invoices on all the new pickups. He pulled out an invoice on a truck that the dealership had paid about four thousand dollars for. He rustled through the invoices again until he found one for a truck that the dealership had paid about eight hundred dollars more for. He folded under the bottom of the first invoice so one could not see the total cost of the vehicle and then laid that invoice on top of the more expensive one. Then very carefully he laid both invoices on the glass top of the copy machine. The copy that came out showed all the features with prices on the less expensive truck, the one the customer wanted to buy, but the bottom line showed the total amount to be eight hundred dollars higher than it was supposed to be.

"This copy is what I show the customer," Jim said. "I tell him he can have the truck for $50 over invoice. Because of the phony bottom line, the customer thinks we are making $50 when we are actually making $850."

"What would happen if someone added everything up and discovered the total was wrong?" I asked.

"They never do," he said confidently.

This guy is really a shyster, I thought, but there was more. One day we were out in the little shack in the middle of the used car lot, the place where we waited to pounce on used car customers.

Jim was explaining why it was so important to win a customer's trust before trying to sell them something. We noticed a young couple looking at a bright red Pontiac Firebird. Jim quietly opened the shack's back window so I could hear what he was saying to the couple, and then he headed out the door to show me how to win trust.

He walked up to the couple and looked around like he was making sure no one else could hear what he was saying.

"You don't want this car," he said. The young man looked back at him in surprise.

"The transmission is about to go, and that's why it's priced so low. It's a lemon. You'll have nothing but problems."

The young man and woman stared at him in amazement.

Jim continued, "They'd fire me if they knew I was telling you this. But come over here. Let me show you a really good car . . ."

After the happy couple drove away in their new purchase, Jim returned to the shack.

"I didn't know the Firebird had a bad transmission," I said.

"It doesn't," he said. "I just told them that to win their trust."

I decided I had learned enough from Jim. I did well enough without using his techniques. My best month there I sold nineteen vehicles.

Then one day I was presented with what many people would consider the business opportunity of a lifetime. The Dodge sales rep, the one that used to come by and help me with the paperwork, stopped in and took me to lunch. He explained that the owner of the Dodge-Chrysler agency in Dillon, Montana, a hundred or so miles east of Hamilton, was getting ready to retire, and there was no one to take over the business. The sales rep said Dodge-Chrysler would sponsor me if I wanted to be the dealer in Dillon. They would provide financing for my new vehicle inventory, and I was already approved. All I had to do was come up with a down payment for the real estate and a line of credit for used cars. Wow, I had enough equity in my house to do that. Dillon was larger than Hamilton, had a college, and was on Interstate 15 just above the Idaho border. I had an MBA, car selling experience, had worked for Ford at the corporate level, had the startup capital, and the backing of the mother company. It was a perfect opportunity. I'd probably never have a business opportunity like this again as long as I lived. It was being handed to me on a silver platter. All I had to do was reach out and take it.

I believed I would enjoy selling cars in Dillon and be successful. But deep in my heart I felt uneasy. If I accepted the offer and moved to Dillon, I would probably be locked into that wonderful business opportunity for a long time.

Deep down I wanted to be a writer. According to the blessing from the German patriarch, I would find success in life through my words, not by selling cars.

CHAPTER XII

My salvation is to write, write, and write some more. To hammer keys until I am finger worn to the second joint and then to hammer keys some more. To pile up copy, stack up stories, roll the wordage, and generally conduct my life along the one line of success I have ever had. I write.

—L. Ron Hubbard
Sailor, adventurer, photographer,
philosopher, educator, and author
(1911–1986)

I decided not to go to Dillon. I thought if I were going to give up that kind of opportunity so I could be a writer, then by darn, I'd better start writing. So I scraped a little money together, quit the car business, and started a monthly tabloid magazine called the *Bitterroot Journal*. I wrote the stories, took the pictures, sold the ads, and Sharon helped do the typesetting and layout on the kitchen table. We printed ten thousand copies of the first issue and gave them away at the county fair. From that beginning we garnered about a thousand paid subscriptions. We had feature articles on Bigfoot and UFO sightings, fishing and hunting, Montana's log home industry, skiing, and historical subjects. A serialized story, which was historical fiction, was at the end of each issue. Of course, I wrote that too.

I learned how to dig through newspaper archives and dusty journals in search of historical information. I learned all about Lewis and Clark's journey through the Bitterroot in 1805, and how Chief Joseph fled through the area in 1877 while being chased by the United States Army. I learned how to interview people who did not want to be interviewed. I figured out how to put words in people's mouths—with permission—so they would sound intelligent when quoted in articles. I was turning research into articles and stories. Finally, I was a writer. The Bitterroot Valley and its people were my classroom.

We were no longer in the Hamilton Ward after we moved to our new home south of Hamilton. We were in the Darby Branch and had to drive eighteen miles to church. They made me elders quorum president. There were plenty of inactive men for me to worry about. By this time Sharon and I had learned our lesson about Halloween parties, so no more of them.

Darby was a logging town, surrounded by millions of acres of national forest. Some of our inactive men worked in the logging industry. They were working men—traditional, conservative, and Republican. They had little respect for the hippie protestors they saw on the news each night. More than one hippie hitchhiking through Darby found himself in a bar, getting a free haircut with a chainsaw.

Our stake president didn't like the hippie look either. The long hair, beards, sandals, and headbands were symbols of immorality and rebellion. In the Missoula Stake, a man could not get a temple recommend if he wore a beard, a mustache, or had long sideburns.

I didn't know the same grooming code was enforced for church athletics when I rounded up a bunch of inactive loggers for our elders' basketball team. They were mostly clean shaven at the time I recruited them and started the practices, but what I didn't know was that men who work in the woods start growing facial hair along about October when the weather turns cold. A tradition in Darby was that when the fall hunting season started, they would stop shaving until they had killed their winter meat supply. This took a while for some, and in the meantime, their beards continued to grow longer and longer.

I explained to the new members of the basketball team that in order to play in a church league they had to go to church, and the attendance at our weekly elders quorum meeting suddenly doubled.

When we drove the seventy miles to Missoula for our first game, a well-meaning high councilman pushed my boys into the bathroom, handed them razors, and ordered them to start shaving. Maybe the Church could do this to high school kids trying to grow a little peach fuzz, but not a bunch of loggers. I feared for the safety of the high councilman as I herded my boys outside. They weren't about to shave, and the Church wasn't about to let them play basketball, so we went to McDonald's for some food and drove home. Most of them stopped coming to church.

There was another church rule that frustrated me. We were instructed through letters read in sacrament meetings not to associate with Mormon fundamentalists who lived at Pinesdale, a tiny community a few miles north of Hamilton. The people there believed in polygamy. The letters were very specific in that we were not to do business with them, shop at their stores, or hire their tradespeople. I suppose the Church was afraid they might recruit us, the mainstream members.

In time, some of these people sought me out when it came time for them to buy cars and trucks. They knew I was a Mormon, and I suppose they thought I would be an honest person to deal with. I didn't like the idea of turning them away, sending them to people like Jim Porch for their auto needs, so I tried to help them as much as possible.

With most of them the relationship was strictly business, but one well-meaning brother would bring me articles to read. He was trying to recruit me. The Church had been right about that. Seeing nothing wrong in being nice to him in the hope that he might buy a car from me someday, I didn't turn him away. Besides, I found the articles he brought me very interesting as they discussed the Mormon roots of modern polygamy.

Then one day I asked the man how many wives he had. His answer was a total surprise, something I never could have guessed ahead of time. He said he didn't have any wives, not even one. When he told his first wife that he believed in "the principle" and was going to start looking for a second wife, the first wife divorced him, leaving him with none.

I had met my first bachelor polygamist. I met more after moving to Utah. "Bachelor polygamist" is probably one of the most ironic terms ever coined. But after thinking about it, one can see why there would be such men in the fundamentalist communities where there are very few single women, if any, available for such a man to marry. The more dominant polygamists—those with engaging personalities, money, and ecclesiastical power—snatch up the available females, even the teens, leaving slim pickings at best for the shy, funny-looking guys with bad breath, no money, and average personalities. They are the ones who become the bachelor polygamists, or more harshly put, the eunuchs of modern polygamous society.

When I started the *Bitterroot Journal*, I published a feature article on polygamy in Montana. I think the stake president was a little worried about me after that, but I enjoyed his first counselor who claimed to be the only Mormon in the world who had permission from Church headquarters to go fishing on Sundays. He explained that when the Pinesdale fundamentalists were having a big conference, the Church sent him down there on Sunday mornings to fish in the stream alongside the road leading to Pinesdale so he could write down the license plate numbers of the vehicles from Utah bringing people to the conferences. At that time the fundamentalists encouraged new recruits to stay in the main church as long as possible so they could continue going to the temples. I suppose the Church wanted the license plate numbers so they could ferret out the wolves among the flock.

I didn't make near as much money doing the *Bitterroot Journal* as I did selling cars, but I was gaining valuable experience for my budding writing career, and I learned other things too, like when an archery store traded me a recurve bow and a bunch of arrows for an advertisement. I had never hunted with bow and arrow before. The guy in the store told me to hunt like an Indian—two looks, one step, two looks, one step, instead of the white man way, one look for five or ten steps taken.

I saddled my two horses and tied on a sleeping bag and some food. My neighbor, Bill England, was from back east, a preacher of sorts, and had never been on a camping trip in the mountains, so I invited him to come along. If he had known this was the first time I had been hunting like this, he might have decided against tagging along. We headed west up Roaring Lion Canyon into the Bitterroot Mountain Range behind my house. At the head of the canyon was the boundary for the Bitterroot-Selway Wilderness, the largest wilderness area in the continental United States. If you started on one side and headed straight for the opposite side, you'd ride a hundred miles.

The stream was crystal clear and only a few feet wide in most places. The fall colors were upon us—red maple, yellow aspen, and golden tamarack. The grasses had already turned yellow, like straw. The sun was shining in a cloudless, deep-blue Montana sky.

We made camp about ten miles into the canyon. Bill was one of those people who has to be talking all the time, especially when he gets a little nervous, so I left him in camp to tend the horses and keep an eye open for bears. We had seen some bear sign on the trail.

I followed the advice of my mentor—a lot more looking than walking, knowing I had to get real close to even have a chance for a shot. I spent an hour going a few hundred yards. I knew I had come to a good place because elk sign was everywhere. To my amazement, because I was going so slow and so quiet, I began to see animals. I saw two or three mule deer, a small band of cow elk, and even a white mountain goat with a kid at her side. I began to believe I might actually see a bull elk.

Eventually I came to a fork in the trail. With only an hour or so of daylight left, I would not have time to hunt in both directions. The small canyon to the left looked really good with a little stream and patches of aspen and pine lining small meadows. The main canyon to my right looked good too—more of the same kind of habitat.

I didn't know which way to go, so I said a short but sincere prayer and asked for guidance. Sharon and I couldn't afford a lot of meat on my meager salary, so a couple of hundred pounds of elk meat would be wonderful to have.

As soon as I opened my eyes, the prayer was answered. The shrill bugle of a bull elk echoed between the canyon walls. He was up the main canyon, to my right, so that's the direction I went—not in a hurry, but two good looks before each step.

The elk didn't bugle a second time, so I just continued along the trail where there was little or no plant growth to make noise. By the time the sun went behind the mountain, the trail was winding its way into some very dark and deep woods. The tall trees blocked out the light, adding to the rapidly darkening situation. I knew it was time to start heading back, but I kept telling myself to go just a little bit farther, and then a little bit farther again.

I heard a thrashing sound, like someone beating a bush with an axe handle. I couldn't see the source of the sound but didn't think it was very far away. I knew bull elk this time of year rubbed antlers on trees to get rid of the velvet. I also knew that bears would claw at trees with their long, sharp claws.

I walked a little closer. The thrashing sound continued. If it was an elk, I might be close enough to shoot. If it was a bear, I was too close and needed to retreat. I just didn't know what to do. Then I saw movement above where I had been looking earlier. The top of a small pine tree was waving back and forth. Now I knew where the noise was coming from—about thirty yards in front of me.

I didn't dare get any closer, so I moved slowly to the left, into a somewhat open area, hoping that by changing my angle I might see the source of the thrashing sound. There were a lot of dry leaves on the ground, so I walked along a fallen log in order to be more quiet.

Then I saw it, at least a small piece of it. It wasn't a bear, but a young bull elk—a spike. He was aggressively and carelessly rubbing off his velvet.

I could see his head and antlers but not his body, so I stayed on the fallen log and slowly inched my way back to the trail. Whenever the elk stopped thrashing to look around, I remained perfectly still. When he went back to work, that's when I moved.

The log ended about eight feet short of the trail, beside a huge fir tree, its trunk about six feet in diameter. Walking on the leaves, I had to move slower, constantly keeping my eye on the elk or his tree. It would soon be dark.

Without warning, he abandoned his little tree and began sauntering down the trail, in my direction, occasionally grabbing a mouthful of grass. He was twenty yards away and closing. The thick fir tree was hiding me and blocking my view of him. I had an arrow on the string but couldn't see clear to shoot, and I didn't dare move with him so close. He was ten yards away, and I couldn't see any part of him, but I knew he was there.

Reason told me that if he continued along the trail, he would emerge from behind the fir tree, about ten feet away. I decided to wait until he did that. I slowly turned my body just enough and pointed my arrow toward the spot where I guessed he would appear. I didn't dare pull the string back, because I didn't know how long it would take before he walked into the open. The bow had a sixty-five-pound draw, so I knew I couldn't hold the string back very long. I waited.

I couldn't figure out why he was taking so long. My feet were going to sleep, and I didn't dare move. It was almost dark. It was so quiet that I thought I could hear my heart beating.

Then he stepped out from behind the tree. He didn't see me, in the open only six or seven feet away. I knew as soon as I moved he would be gone. I didn't have time to pull the arrow back and take aim. I was so close I didn't need to aim. I thought, *Just jerk the string back, not even all the way, and let go, all in one motion, using maybe a fourth of a second, before the elk can react.* So that's what I did.

The arrow plunged between two ribs, not far behind his right shoulder, and he was gone, back up the trail, toward the battered tree. I didn't move, thinking maybe he hadn't seen me. All was quiet, so I knew he hadn't gone far. My mentor at the archery store told me that if I put an arrow in an elk I should sit down and wait half an hour before going after it. He said if you chase an elk with an arrow in it, its adrenalin starts flowing and it might run for miles. If you didn't chase it, it might lay down, stiffen up, and soon not be able to get up and run at all. That's when you finish it off.

I moved just a little so I could see beyond the tree. He was standing in the trail about ten yards away, looking to the right and then to the left. He still didn't know I was there. Then he reached back and tried to pull the arrow out with his teeth. I waited. It was mostly dark now.

Finally, he laid down, first on his belly, and then his side. I could hear his forced breathing. By now I was feeling very sorry for him.

He was dying. I was taking his life, and it wasn't quick and fast. It was a slow, probably painful, death.

It was time to hurry things up. I decided to put another arrow in him. Then he would die quickly. I stepped up on the log. He saw me, but he couldn't get up. I let another arrow fly, then another. I waited some more. He rolled on his side again, his head flat against the ground. He didn't move again. I could no longer hear him breathing. I thought he was dead. Because of the dark, there was no time to lose in dressing him out. I set down the bow, and removed the quiver of arrows.

Pulling the knife from my belt, I walked toward him, stepping behind his head, bending over, grabbing one of his antlers with my left hand, reaching forward with the knife to slit his throat.

Without warning, his left hind foot shot forward, striking me in the wrist, knocking the knife out of my hand. I walked over and picked up the knife and waited some more. It seemed there was no more life in him, but I didn't want to be kicked again, so I waited a little longer. Finally, I was able to cut his throat and dress him out. I was careful and determined to do a good job. I had taken the life of this forest animal so his meat could provide nourishment for my family, and I didn't intend to waste any of it.

When he was cleaned out and I had wiped away most of the blood from the cavity, I dragged him onto some brush and broken limbs in order to get him off the ground, knowing the meat would cool down better if it wasn't touching the ground, which was warmer than the night air.

Now it was time to worry about getting back to camp. I didn't have a flashlight. The bottom of the canyon, with towering mountains on both sides, was a darker than normal place. I picked up my bow and arrows and hurried down the trail.

Eventually it was so dark I couldn't see the trail at all. I walked more slowly, feeling my way with my feet. I could have felt my way better without shoes, but my feet were too tender for that. With increasing frequency, I wandered away from the trail, occasionally tripping over rocks and logs. Several times I had to get down on my hands and knees, feeling my way back to the trail.

It was almost midnight when I finally saw the reflections of a campfire on some tall trees and granite cliffs. Not long after that I strolled into camp, showing Bill my bloody hands and forearms, acting nonchalant, like this was just another normal day in the life of a backwoods scout like me. I don't remember telling him this was the first elk I had ever killed and that I was so excited about it that I probably wouldn't sleep.

He was so glad to see me that I thought he was going to cry. When I hadn't returned at dark, he was sure I had been mauled to death by a bear. He had built up a big fire in the hope that it would prevent the bear from killing him too. He had been praying that I wouldn't be dead. Hallelujah, his prayers had been answered.

Borrowing his flashlight, I went down to the stream to wash my hands and arms. When I returned, he asked if we could return home at first light. I said we could not. We had to return to the elk and load the meat onto the horses, and then we could go home. He didn't seem at all happy about that. We cooked some things to eat and tried to get some sleep.

At first light I got on my horse and headed up the trail, a reluctant Bill following close behind. Every little while he would ask how much farther. I said I didn't know since the country looked different in full daylight. He looked from side to side, like he was worried something might be getting ready to ambush us.

When we stopped for a break, Bill asked how much meat I intended to take home.

"All of it," I said.

"But how many pounds?"

"I don't know, maybe two hundred."

"Does a beef weigh that much?"

"Maybe a hind-quarter of beef."

"I'll buy you a hind-quarter of beef if we can turn around and go home right now," he said.

That's when I realized that Bill was really afraid. We hadn't seen any more bear sign, so perhaps he was afraid of being lost.

"No," I said, "We must get the elk before turning back."

After riding a little longer, he raised the offer.

"If I buy you half a beef, can we turn back?"

I stopped. A half a beef was a lot of meat.

"No," I said. "I took the life of a beautiful animal. You are asking me to let its meat go to waste. I will not do that."

I told him he could stay behind if he wished and wait for me to come back with the elk, but he didn't want to be left alone again, so he continued following me, even when the woods became thick and dark. We were getting close.

Then we found it. No predators had disturbed the carcass. The meat had cooled nicely. Without removing the skin, we cut away the quarters so we could tie the two front ones over one saddle and the two back ones over the other saddle. We cut off the rest of the meat, placing it in canvas bags. In an hour we had the horses loaded and were leading them down the trail toward home. The journey consumed the remainder of the day.

Bill was all smiles once we hit the road and began seeing signs of civilization. But the day was not over. We spent the evening hours skinning the quarters, cutting the meat into steaks and stew meat, and wrapping it into clear plastic packages. We did all this on and around our kitchen table. We filled our freezer and when Bill finally left, he had a heavy bag for his freezer.

The next evening we had our first elk steaks. The meat didn't have a gamey flavor like some of the deer meat I had tasted. The main difference between our elk and Grade A beef was that the elk meat was more tender. One didn't need a knife to cut the steaks; the edge of a fork was sufficient. The meat lasted most of the winter and we didn't waste a single morsel.

By this time we had three boys. Marvin was born one April night in the old Hamilton hospital. I still remember sitting in the waiting room reading an article about a famous race horse, Secretariat, in *Sports Illustrated.*

Because Marvin liked to put wood chips in his mouth, Sharon sometimes called him Woody. As he became old enough to talk, he began making up his own words, like when his older brothers got their blue scout shirts, he called them "scub scouts." And when we'd take him to McDonald's he'd order "Chicken McMaggots." When his older brothers received the Aaronic priesthood, he called them "dinkons."

As I began trying new ways to cook our elk meat, I met resistance from Bobby, who was five. I thought I made a pretty good stew, but he didn't like it. I thought the steaks and roasts were perfect, but Bobby resisted eating them also. It seemed like he ate most of the things his mother cooked, but anything I made, especially if it had elk in it, we'd have to make him chew and swallow every single bite, and it was ten times as hard if onions were included. He hated onions. I had grown up eating raw and cooked onions every way possible.

One night I made a sweet and sour elk goulash to go over rice. I figured the kids would like it because it had sweet pineapple in it. Bobby locked his little hands onto the sides of his chair and announced he wasn't going to eat elk goulash. *Here we go again*, I thought.

It occurred to me that a straight-A psychology student, who had published in the *Journal of Psychology*, ought to be able to get a five-year-old to eat his supper. Instead of just forcing Bobby to eat the goulash as I was inclined to do, I figured out a way to make it a matter of choice for him.

He beamed when I told him I was not going to make him eat his dinner. I told him he had a choice. He could eat a bowl of goulash over rice like the rest of us, or he could have three lashes across his behind with a green willow stick. The choice was his.

Showing no emotion, he thought about what I had said. Then he raised his hand, like in school.

"Question?" I asked.

"If I choose the whipping, do I still have to eat the stew?"

"No," I said. He disappeared outside and returned a few minutes later with a nice green willow stick, plenty heavy to do the job. There was a defiant look on his face, like he was the one in control now, not me. This isn't what I thought would happen. I had the distinct feeling that the parent, not the child, was being manipulated, but it was too late to turn back. When he bent over, I applied the willow with enough force to punish a fifteen year old. Instead of crying out, he looked up at me and smiled.

I hit him again, harder. Still, he did not cry. I knew now the five-year-old was getting the best of the psychologist, and he knew it too. After I hit him the third time, he pushed back the bowl of goulash and headed over to the sink to fix himself a bowl of cold cereal. I decided right then and there I would never make this kid eat anything he didn't like ever again. Food was not going to be a source of conflict in our relationship. In the years to come, we bought a lot of vitamin-enriched cold cereal, Wonder Bread, and tubs of peanut butter. Bobby never learned to eat onions either, but fortunately he married a girl who disliked them as much as he did.

One Sunday Larry Dean Olsen came to Darby to speak in our sacrament meeting. Larry had started the modern survival movement while a student at BYU. Growing up in Idaho, south of Twin Falls, he had learned to live off the land like an Indian. While working his way through college at BYU, he persuaded the school to let him teach a class in outdoor survival. Soon students were following him into the desert with nothing more than a pocketknife and blanket. He taught them how to stay alive on ants and field mice and thistle stalks, how to build fires without matches, and how to get a good night's sleep in sub-freezing temperatures with nothing more than a blanket.

After a few terms of teaching the class, the school approached Larry with an interesting proposal. Due to poor classroom performance, about eight hundred students were flunking out each year. Some of these students wanted a second chance, but the school had no way of knowing if they were really ready to work harder and if they would indeed take advantage of a second chance. The school sent a letter to these second chance candidates, telling them if they would go on a thirty-day survival trip with Larry Olsen, they could get back in school. It seemed a wonderful surprise to parents and school officials when these students wandered in from the desert, signed up for classes, and began getting mostly As and Bs on their report cards. After that, parents began sending wayward teenagers out with Larry, hoping for similar changes.

BYU Press published Larry's book, *Outdoor Survival Skills*, which became a bestseller. His program received a ton of publicity and grew and grew, until one of the students died. That's when Larry moved to Montana.

As I listened to his talk, explaining how eating ants and

grasshopper cakes and learning to build fires without matches turned juvenile delinquents into honor students, I was so enthralled with what he said that I cornered him afterward and convinced him to take me on one of his upcoming survival trips in northern Nevada. I agreed to do a story about it in the *Bitterroot Journal*.

There were about ten of us in the group when we stopped at a little café on Highway 93 south of Twin Falls. Larry told us to enjoy our last civilized meal before heading into the wilderness. It being morning, I ordered three eggs, bacon, ham, hash browns, toast, and juice. An hour later they had to stop the van so I could throw it all up. I had the runs too—food poisoning, I suppose. By the time we reached the trailhead at Murphy's Hot Springs and started hiking down the Jarbidge River, my insides were empty, which is not a good way to begin a survival trip.

Larry pointed out plants along the way, like dogbane. "First you're high and then you die," he said of the poisonous plant that could be twisted into very strong string. We followed the river awhile and then wound our way onto a sagebrush bench where one of the girls almost stepped on a large rattlesnake. We killed it and ate it for supper, but divided ten ways, there wasn't much to enjoy.

To keep warm that night we stuffed mounds of grass into little crawl-in caves and then crawled in ourselves. Fortunately, no snakes were in the caves. The next morning we learned how to make deadfall rodent traps using dogbane string, sticks, and flat rocks. We caught a few mice, but it was soon evident we would not catch enough meat to sustain us. Some of the students began cooking weeds in old cans left behind by sheepherders. None of this tasted very good to me, though I was very hungry.

They had let us bring along a few fishhooks and some line, so I headed down to the river and tied my line and hook on a willow. I found a half-rotten cottonwood log and began tearing it apart with my hands until I found a big fat grub. I began to fish, not knowing what kind of fish might inhabit a remote desert river, but was pleased when I pulled out a cutthroat trout. I was so hungry by this time that I didn't bother to cook before eating. My muscles were weak, but my senses seemed very sharp.

As I swallowed the raw flesh, I could feel strength surging into my starved muscles. A fifty-dollar prime rib dinner would not have been more satisfying. I built a little fire and caught three more fish. These I cooked, on pointed sticks, like one would roast a hot dog. After six fish were in my belly, I felt like a new man. I caught nineteen more and headed back to camp, throwing fish at the feet of the starving students. I was the hero, the provider, as everyone went to work cleaning and cooking the fish.

When we were finished, all huddled around the same fire for warmth and light, Larry said he wanted to teach us a lesson. He said we ate fish like we were in a fancy restaurant, not like we were surviving in a hostile wilderness desert. Nobody knew what he meant by this.

Instead of telling us what he meant, he reached over to a pile of fish remains, and popped a fish head and skeleton, including fins and tail, into his mouth, and started chewing.

"What about the bones?" someone asked.

"Rich in protein," Larry said, continuing to chew. He said nobody ever choked on a fish bone that had been chewed to mush. And so he continued to chew, saying that if we didn't get more fish tomorrow, we'd be sorry for wasting so much today. Some of the students began chewing on bones too.

We lived on fish for the rest of the trip. We learned to chip arrowheads from obsidian rocks that we'd found in a field near the little café that had poisoned me. We used deer antler points to flake and shape the arrowheads. We built fires without matches. We learned to use wild onions as insect repellent. It was a great trip, and I enjoyed writing the story. Larry and I became good friends. I sold my house in Hamilton and bought 120 acres just up the road from Larry in Stevensville, Montana's oldest settlement.

We lived only one year on the Stevensville property, but we have some interesting memories. For example, the first year we hired a farmer to plow up forty or so acres of flat farm ground that we planted in oats. It was fertile ground, and the oats grew thick and tall. When the crop was between three and four feet high and about ready to develop the grain heads, we lost Marvin. He was about three years old at the time but not nearly as tall as the oat stalks. We could hear him crying somewhere far out in the field, but we couldn't find him, and he couldn't seem to find his way back to us. We knew he was all right, but still it was so frustrating to know he was lost and scared, and we couldn't help. Eventually, after tromping down some of the crop, we found him and carried him out of the field.

We lived in a twenty-foot camp trailer that summer while I was working on the house. Russell had just been born, so we had four boys. Conditions were cramped, so I set up a fourteen-foot Blue Star tepee down by the stream. Richard and Bobby moved in. They had little cots to sleep on and boxes for toys and clothing. There was a fire pit in the center. The boys ran around barefoot and shirtless most of the time—regular little savages.

One time when I came home, they had a porcupine cornered between the trunks of two trees and were trying to kill it with their BB guns. The BBs penetrated the skin, but not the flesh. The poor animal had about three hundred BBs under its skin and was still alive.

I helped them finish it off and then explained that the rule of the mountains was that you had to eat what you killed. We weren't going to waste a life. We dragged the carcass home, skinned it very carefully, and then wired it on a spit over an open fire. Bobby wasn't very happy about eating rodent, but I explained he had made his choice when he fired the first BB. I thought the boys had learned their lesson and were going to eat it all until I discovered that whenever I turned my back they were feeding pieces of meat to the dog.

One time when I was driving home from town I saw a family of skunks crossing the road in front of me. I braked to a stop, thinking I could take one of the baby skunks home to the boys. I figured we could make a pet out of if. I didn't think a little skunk had scent glands yet.

I had a basketful of laundry on the back seat, so I grabbed a clean blanket and ran after the skunks. They were scurrying up a steep bank on the side of the road, headed for some thick brush. I threw the blanket and dove on it. As I wadded up the blanket, I could tell by the feel that I had at least one of the little skunks in it. I threw the wadded-up blanket back in the laundry basket and resumed my journey home.

It wasn't long before I had to roll down the windows. I realized

I had been wrong about the skunks, that even little skunks had fully developed scent glands. The little guy was busy squirting his scent into our laundry basket.

When I arrived at the trailer, I called the boys and Sharon over to the vehicle, announcing I had a new pet for them. I tossed the rolled up blanket on the ground, and we watched as the little skunk wiggled free. We left him alone as he marched off into the woods, his tail high. We hung the scented blanket on the clothesline for the duration of the summer. The smell just wouldn't go away. The rest of the laundry in the basket had to be washed two or three more times with plenty of soap and bleach before it was usable.

One time when Sharon was out hanging up some laundry she had rinsed in the sink, she heard a snort on the hillside above her. She looked up to see a black bear, sitting on his haunches, watching her work. He didn't seem to be in a threatening mood so she finished hanging up the clothes.

There was a stream, Burnt Fork, which ran through a corner of the property. It was full of fish, and sometimes I would take the boys down there to catch our supper. It was a neat place to live, but I soon realized I would not be able to keep up the land payments from my *Bitterroot Journal* income. Plus the neighbor's cows ruined our oat crop before I could sell it. We realized we were going to have to make some changes and perhaps move again. I put portions of the property up for sale. The five acres with the stream went almost immediately, and soon we had another buyer for thirty-five acres.

About this time Sharon and I read an article in the Church magazine, the *Ensign*, which changed the course of our lives. It was a reprint of a talk Spencer W. Kimball had given at BYU about ten years earlier. He said the real story of Mormonism had not been told; that writers and artists would yet step forward to do this important work. I figured I was one of those writers, and Sharon agreed. I had a blessing promising me success through my words, and now this. The *Bitterroot Journal* had been a wonderful and exciting learning experience, but now it was time to move on.

CHAPTER XIII

I wrote because I was too lazy to work, too honest to steal, and too old fashioned to start an e-business.

—LEE NELSON

We said good-bye to our Montana friends, packed up our things, and moved to Provo, Utah. Another twenty acres of our Montana land sold, giving us enough money for a down payment on a nice home in the Edgemont area of Provo where many of the BYU professors lived. We had a good feeling about being there. Still, we had taken a huge leap of faith.

I remember how awkward it was explaining to neighbors and people at church why we had moved to Utah. No, I did not have a job to support my wife and four children. No, I was not going to school, nor did I have a teaching job. I was going to write books. People would look at me like I was nuts. Oh well.

We put the tepee up in the backyard, and soon the neighborhood boys were sleeping out with our boys. Within a month I was the elders quorum president, for the fourth time, but we didn't hold any Halloween parties.

Herb McLean, the magazine writing teacher who took us to Alaska, introduced me to Louis Crandall who had an advertising agency in Provo. Louis hired me to write radio and television ads and copy for display and direct mail advertising. Again, I fell into a wonderful learning environment. I would rewrite some of the ads fifteen or twenty times, until every word was just right.

About this time a new Superman movie starring Christopher Reeves was released, and everyone had Superman on the mind. I wrote a radio ad for a local bank that went something like this: *More powerful than a locomotive, with sixty million dollars in assets, faster than a speeding bullet in computing daily interest on savings, and able to build tall buildings with a single loan.*

The bank gave away Superman cloaks and comic books to the children of those who opened new accounts. I thought I was a great ad man. About this time I started writing some copy for an ad agency Herb McLean had started, now called Soter Associates, named after Greg Soter, the new owner.

Still inspired by President Kimball's talk, I bought a paperback set of *The Documentary History of the Church* by Joseph Smith and began doing research for a series of historical novels I intended to write. I did my research early mornings and evenings.

I wasn't very far into the documentary history when I realized it contained a lot of first-person writings by Joseph Smith. The first portion was the same as the *Joseph Smith Story*, the little booklet given out by the missionaries. But there was a lot more. The *Joseph Smith Story* could be expanded into a full-sized book. I sent a proposal to Deseret Book Company, offering to do the compiling for the book. Everyone would want to have it. We could call it *Joseph Smith's Diary* or *Journal of Joseph.*

They didn't think much of my proposal. Why would anyone want to buy my book when the material was already published in the documentary history?

One day I explained the idea to Greg Soter. I read him some advertising copy I had written that I thought would sell the book: *eloping with Emma, chopping wood with the brethren, wrestling Baptist ministers . . . Joseph's own story in his own words, available for the first time in a single volume.*

Greg thought it was a great idea, but like me, he had no experience in producing and selling books. He said a local typesetting company owed him some work, and if I would get the copy assembled, he would get it typeset.

Using Louis Crandall's antique paper cutter, I sliced the spines off my *Documentary History of the Church* volumes. Then I went through the loose pages, marking the first-person passages by Joseph Smith. I left out some of the long, boring, or redundant ones. Working evenings, it took about two weeks to get it all compiled. I gave the stack of marked pages to Greg who took it over to the typesetter.

In an issue of the *Ensign,* I noticed a drawing of Joseph Smith sitting at a desk, writing with a feather pen. Greg paid the Church fifty dollars to let us use the drawing on the cover of our book.

Finally the typesetting was done. We had the cover art. I wrote a two-hundred word introduction, telling what the book was about and how I put it together. Greg found a printer, and the price seemed reasonable. Of course, there were substantial variations in cost per copy depending on how many we wanted to print. We still didn't know how we were going to distribute the book to bookstores. Greg was an idealist who believed in the power of advertising. "If we can create a demand, the distribution will take care of itself." He repeated this statement every time I began to express concerns.

Since we would be extending ourselves financially to pay for the first printing, we decided to take our wives out to dinner and present the possibilities to them. We wanted to involve them in the decision on how many to print. We really had no idea what the potential market might be for such a book.

We were eating Chinese food in Spanish Fork, explaining the economies of scale to our wives: the fewer books we printed, the higher the unit cost and the less potential for profit. On the other hand, if we printed too many, our money would be sitting in a storage for the rest of our lives if the book didn't sell. Before going to dinner, Greg was arguing for a ten-thousand-unit first printing, while I thought five thousand would be a more prudent number considering our inexperience in book publishing.

After we explained everything to our wives, Sharon suggested that we ought to consider printing a thousand books. Be safe. I was so disappointed in her response and her lack of faith in a project Greg and I had been working on for almost a year. So we asked Greg's wife, Kit, what she thought, hoping her comments might bring Sharon to a more realistic number. Greg and I were flabbergasted when Kit suggested that we ought to print a hundred copies and see if those sold before we risked so much money.

Greg and I went to the bathroom where we decided we had made a terrible mistake by not involving our wives earlier when we were analyzing market conditions and economies of scale. A year of analysis had brought us to this point in time, and now we were ambushing our wives, expecting them to suddenly take a leap of faith with no advance preparation and with their mouths full of Chinese food. We decided to go ahead without them. When we returned to the dinner table we changed the topic of discussion.

When the book went to press for a five-thousand-copy first run, we still didn't know what the retail price on the book would be. We knew what it would cost to print it, and we knew that the bookstores selling it would want 40 percent.

We visited Rob Whitehead, who was running the Seventy's Mission Bookstore in Provo, and asked him what we could charge for such a book. He explained that President Kimball's biography was selling for $7.95, and most general authority books were $6.95. BYU professors could sometimes get $5.95. For an unknown author like Lee Nelson, the book would have to be priced below $5. If we wanted to sell this book for more than that—well, it couldn't be done.

We went back to the office and crunched some numbers. Unless we sold a million books, we were doomed to failure if we followed Rob's advice, and we knew that was not going to happen. So we priced the book at $8.95, a dollar above President Kimball. Our thinking was that this was not a Lee Nelson book; it was a new Joseph Smith book. If President Kimball could ask $7.95 for his story, Joseph Smith ought to be able to get $8.95 for his.

The Monday the book came off the press, we filled our trunks with books. The plan was simple. With the yellow pages of the phone book as our guide, I would visit all the bookstores on the north half of the Wasatch Front, and Greg would visit the southern stores. The ads were scheduled to begin on KSL radio on Wednesday. We had hired a man named Glen Shaw to record the ad for us. He had an old-time radio voice and was Elohim's voice in the temple ceremony.

Our visits to the bookstores were not very productive. They didn't know us and had never heard of our new little company, Council Press. In fact, we didn't sell a single book, though we were able to put out about three hundred on consignment, meaning if the books didn't sell, the stores would not pay us, and we would have to pick them up if we wanted to have them back. I made the largest consignment order—twenty books—at the downtown Salt Lake Deseret Book location. Mrs. Stevenson was the buyer there.

Two days later, Wednesday morning, I was in Salt Lake City and stopped by to see if Mrs. Stevenson wanted more books. I went to the place in the store where she had stacked the books. I counted them. Nineteen of the original twenty were still on the shelf. I didn't bother to go see her. I knew there was no way I could sell her more books when she still had nineteen on the shelf.

The ads on the radio started that morning. When I stopped in at Greg's office at one o'clock, there was a message for me to call Mrs. Stevenson at Deseret Book. *Oh no*, I thought, *she wants to return the books. The ad isn't working.* I was afraid to call her, but eventually worked up the courage to do it.

She was her usual nice, friendly self as she told me she wanted another three hundred books. The nineteen she had when they opened that morning were gone, and dozens of people were asking for the book. By the end of the day, almost all the stores that had taken books on consignment were calling to buy more. Consignment was no longer an issue.

That night I received a call from Richard Maher, an LDS book distributor who wanted a thousand copies. In nine days, all five thousand books were gone, and we had orders for thousands more, including a single ten-thousand-unit order from Bookcraft, a publisher who wanted to distribute it to all the LDS bookstores outside Utah. We ended up selling fifty thousand copies of *Journal of Joseph* in one year.

But it wasn't entirely a bed of roses. Some members of the BYU religion faculty and other historians were upset with me. They wanted to know who this guy from Montana was, who still had cow manure on his boots and dared publish the best-selling Joseph Smith book since the Book of Mormon. One of them, Michael Quinn, invited me to a meeting at BYU where he pointed out some of the problems with first person entries in the documentary history. Many were not recorded by Joseph Smith but by Willard Richards and Emma Smith. *So what*, I thought. He pointed out errors in some of the entries. *So whose journal doesn't have a few errors in it?* I thought. He wanted me to change the title from *Journal of Joseph* to *A Compilation of First Person Writings from the Documentary History of the Church, some by Joseph Smith and some by Willard Richards and Emma Smith.* One of the professors went so far as to put up a sign in a Provo bookstore claiming that the book was not Joseph's diary and that a lot of people helped write it.

I felt bad that so many people were upset over what I thought was a fine piece of work. Greg would just pat me on the back and tell me not to worry about the wolves who were nipping at my heels. Sometimes he would hand me a check for ten or fifteen thousand dollars to help me feel better.

When Greg and I went out to lunch, the most frequent question we asked ourselves was *Why is this so easy?* Greg insisted that there were things about the book publishing business we did not know. He felt we should be very careful. Instead of buying a big printing press and hiring a bunch of secretaries, as some people in our position might be tempted to do, maybe we ought to hang onto our money, buy a seventy-nine-dollar file cabinet, and very cautiously see if we could do it again. I agreed.

Shortly after the first of the new year, while the orders for *Journal of Joseph* were pouring in, Greg called the Brigham Young University football office and set up an appointment for us to meet with head coach Lavell Edwards. I had suggested to Greg that we do a book on how Lavell turned around the football program and how he had done it with a passing attack. BYU sports were the main events in Utah County. The new stadium filled up for home games, as did the Marriott Center for home basketball games.

Lavell seemed surprised when we told him we wanted to publish his story in a book. He had several concerns. First, he confessed that even though he had earned a PhD in education, he struggled as a writer. I told him I would write the book. All he had to do was approve the final draft. Second, he told us how busy he was, recruiting and preparing for spring training camp. He didn't think he had the time to work on a book. We suggested a plan that wouldn't compete with his busy schedule.

He agreed to do the book, and I started meeting him at his office at 7:00 a.m. each weekday when he was not out of town. I brought a list of questions and a tape recorder to each session. I asked the questions and recorded his answers. When the phone started ringing at 8:30 or thereabouts, I picked up my things and left. After about eighteen hours of taped interview, I couldn't think of any more questions.

I hired a typist to transcribe the content of the tapes onto paper, and then I went to work much like I had with the *Journal of Joseph* project. With a pair of scissors and a felt marker, I began marking and cutting apart Lavell's comments, organizing the pieces into about ten piles representing future chapters in the book. Then, attacking the piles one at a time, I wrote the first draft of the book.

The draft filled a little more than sixty pages, hardly enough for a book, but rather than seek more information, we decided to include forty pages of photos, set the story in large type, and print it on thick paper. By September, ten thousand copies of *Lavell Edwards: Building a Winning Football Tradition at BYU* rolled off the presses.

After our success with *Journal of Joseph*, the bookstores began to stock up on *Lavell Edwards*, believing they could sell a lot of books during the upcoming football season. The smallest single order I knew about came from the BYU campus bookstore. They took three copies and placed them on the bottom shelf in the biography section, spines facing out so nobody could see the books. It was as if the buyer didn't like Lavell or football or me, or just wanted to make sure we didn't enjoy two successful books in a row. But the rest of the stores in Utah loved Lavell and his football program, and soon books began flying off the shelves.

While working on Lavell's book, I went to the BYU library and compiled the first-person writings of Brigham Young that had been published in the *Millennial Star* in England during the late 1800s. Of course, this book we titled *The Journal of Brigham*. Ten thousand copies of this interesting work rolled off the presses about the same time we were starting to sell the Edwards book.

The ad for *Journal of Brigham* sounded just like the Joseph ad we ran the year before. Glen Shaw was our voice again. But an interesting thing happened. After the ads had been running about a week the stores were not ordering more books. Initially we had sold about seven hundred copies, but they were not moving off the shelves, even with the ads running. We called the radio stations and cancelled the ads. Those readers who had gobbled up fifty thousand copies of *Journal of Joseph* had no desire to read *Journal of Brigham*. I was surprised.

I remember one night in November that year, sitting up in bed, a yellow note pad and the *Journal of Brigham* in my lap. We had decided to write a new ad, one that might help us move all those books. I was thumbing through Brigham Young's journal, fishing for something—a new idea perhaps, or a new slant—something interesting that could be the foundation of a new radio ad.

While I was studying the personal journal entrees of Brigham Young, BYU football was much on my mind too. The BYU football team was in the middle of another winning season, and with Christmas still ahead, most of Lavell's books were already sold. The big item in the news that November day was the announcement that BYU would be playing Southern Methodist University (SMU) in the Holiday Bowl in San Diego. The two teams had never played each other before.

Suddenly I found what I was looking for and quickly scribbled out the beginning of our new ad:

The 1980 Holiday Bowl won't be the first clash between the Mormons and the Methodists. In 1840 in Manchester, England, Methodist ministers tried to get Mormon missionaries arrested. Brigham Young figured out a way to turn the tables and twenty Methodist preachers went to jail . . .

Greg didn't waste any time producing this new ad and placing it on KSL radio. The difference in audience reaction was amazing. The books flew off the shelves. Greg and I thought we were so smart . . . until we got a call from the sales manager at KSL Radio telling us he was taking the ad off the air. Apparently one of the general authorities, whose name could not be mentioned, had ordered him to do it because the Church was getting complaints from members of the Methodist community. They claimed the ad was offensive, and if it was allowed to continue, it would further widen the gap between the LDS and Methodist peoples living in the Salt Lake Valley. As soon as the ads stopped running, the books stopped selling.

We were discouraged, but unknown to us, BYU president Jeffrey Holland had heard the ad and purchased a copy of the book to take with him to San Diego. In a luncheon with the press a few days before the game, Holland told reporters the upcoming game was not the first contest between Brigham Young and the Methodists. Then he read the passage from my book that had been featured in the ad, where the Methodist preachers went to jail. Everyone had a good laugh, including the SMU officials, who were not offended in the least. The sports writers wrote about Holland's remarks, so I took clippings from the *Los Angeles Times* and *San Diego Union* up to KSL. They called us the next day to say we were clear to put the ad back on the air. By Christmas all the books were gone.

Of course, Greg and I watched the Holiday Bowl that year with more than the usual spectator interest. We knew that if BYU played well, Lavell's book would sell well too. But the team didn't play well. BYU got behind. The team seemed plagued with mistakes and just couldn't catch up.

During a third-quarter time-out, Greg called to remind me that I could relax. The books had been sold, not consigned, and the stores could not bring them back, no matter how badly BYU performed on the football field. His comments didn't make me feel any better.

With four minutes remaining, BYU was down by twenty points. Fans were leaving the stands. It appeared all was lost.

Lavell later told me that during this part of the game, with BYU facing a fourth down and eight yards to go, the punter was sent in. Quarterback Jim McMahon called a time out and trotted over to the coaches to tell them what he thought of their decision to punt, and how stupid that was considering the score and the time remaining.

Lavell said he told Jim that if he didn't like the play selection, then he could do it himself. And that's exactly what Jim did. The team went for the first down, and then went down and scored. After that, they recovered an onside kick and scored again.

With only a few seconds remaining, BYU was at midfield, down five or six points. McMahon threw a *Hail Mary* pass to the end zone as the time ran out. Clay Brown caught the pass and BYU won the game. Many of the SMU fans that left early didn't know BYU won until they read about it in the newspaper the next day.

By Christmas all the Lavell Edwards books were gone. I loved those Texas Methodists who made it possible. The Brigham Young books were sold out too. Our only concern was that one of the distributors owed us over eighty thousand dollars.

CHAPTER XIV

The idea that God is actively nurturing us so that we might grow up to be like Him brings us face to face with our own laziness . . . the force of entropy within us, pushing us down and holding us all back from our spiritual evolution. So original sin does exist; it is our laziness.

—M. SCOTT PECK, author

While I was learning so many interesting lessons about the book business, another significant event occurred to make sure my writing and publishing career didn't head down the wrong path.

When Sharon and I were first married and living in Provo, there was a young man living across the street who was preparing to go on a mission. His name was Don Oldham. I was his elders quorum president, and one night late he called to ask if I wanted to go on a midnight horseback ride. I never said no to anything like that, so we drove to his family farm in Santaquin, slipped bridles on two horses, and headed down through the pastures, bareback, at full gallop. It was nearly midnight, and in the cloudy darkness I could not see the ditches, fences, culverts, or anything else that got in the way. All I could do was hang on and trust that the horse was familiar with the terrain. If Don's objective was to scare me, he succeeded.

A few months later, Don headed off to southern Germany to do his missionary work. It was nearly ten years later, after I returned to Provo and my first books were beginning to sell, that Don called again. Instead of inviting me on a midnight horseback ride, he invited me to join him on a different kind of adventure.

Don and his brothers had started a shoppers' guide publication that was delivered free to about sixty-five thousand Utah Valley homes each Wednesday and Saturday. Income came from advertising revenues. Don said he was looking for a story he could serialize from week to week that would build readership and create interest in his publication. He explained how an army of school children delivered the papers each week, but once in a while a delivery boy or girl would abandon papers in a ditch or vacant lot instead of placing them on doorsteps. Don thought that if the paper published a continuing serial, readers would call the office if their paper did not arrive, which would allow Don to correct the problem of the disappearing papers. He remembered that I was a creative writer in college and asked if I had a story they could use for the serial. I said I would bring in something in a few days.

I sat down at the typewriter and wrote the prologue and first chapter to *The Storm Testament,* my first novel. It was the story of an orphan boy, a Huck Finn character, caught up in the Mormon persecutions near Far West, Missouri, in 1838. After getting in trouble with a Missouri mob, he went up the Missouri River with an escaped slave named Ike and ran away to the Rocky Mountains. Ike was patterned after the Boss Man I learned about from the retiring president of Ford Australia. I had learned a lot of LDS Church history in compiling the Joseph Smith and Brigham Young journals, and I had been reading about American Indians since I was a kid. I used a first-person narrative, which seemed to make the writing easier.

The prologue described Sam Storm going back to Philadelphia to find the lost journals of his great-great-grandfather, Dan Storm. Alex Haley, who authored the best-selling novel *Roots,* inspired me. He wrote about his African-American ancestors as best he could figure it out from a sketchy genealogy. His book was 99 percent fiction. Haley gave a speech at BYU, and as I listened to his story, I kept thinking, *This isn't fair. The Mormons are the most family history oriented people on the face of the earth, yet when they write or talk about it, everyone goes to sleep. Yet this Haley guy ferrets out two or three names on his family tree, writes a story about it, and is suddenly the most famous family history expert on the planet—and fabulously rich from his royalties to boot.* I decided right then and there that when I wrote my first historical novel it would have a family history theme, lending glamour and glory Alex Haley style to the formerly boring field of family history research.

I didn't want to take anything away from what Haley had done. I just thought that if he could write a book using his black family tree, I could write a book using my Mormon family tree. In fact, it would be much easier for me, because unlike Haley's ancestors, some of mine had been very diligent in keeping personal journals and histories.

I wrote a prologue describing the discovery of Dan Storm's lost journals in the attic of a Philadelphia delicatessen.

When the book finally came out, the words *novel* and *historical fiction* appeared on the dust jacket, but over the years I received over a thousand letters and phone calls from people who believed that the prologue was true.

People even came by my house asking if they could look at one of Dan Storm's journals. A woman told me how she spent an unsuccessful afternoon at the American Fork City Cemetery looking for Dan Storm's headstone. A tour guide at the Mormon Battalion monument in San Diego told me how a visitor chewed him out for not having the name of my fictional hero, Dan Storm, engraved on the monument. A plaque at the old state capitol building in Fillmore, describing early Utah before the arrival of the Mormons, mentioned Dan Storm as one of Utah's first white explorers. When a Payson woman, Madoline Dixon, published what she called a factual history of the Ute Indians, she claimed the first Mormon to live among them was Dan Storm in 1838. I heard stories of people burning their collections of *Storm Testament* volumes when someone finally convinced them that the books were fiction.

After Don had a few days to look over my prologue and sample chapters and discuss the matter with his brothers, he asked me to meet with him to discuss my fee for letting them serialize the story.

I went to the meeting thinking that since I was going to write the story anyway, anything they wanted to pay me would be acceptable. They were doing me a big favor, giving me motivation and deadlines to write my story and an audience to give me feedback. I decided to ask for $250 a month for serial rights while they were running the story. When we finally sat down face to face, Don expressed so much enthusiasm over the samples I had given him that I asked for $500 a month, and he readily agreed. A week later the first installment of *The Storm Testament* appeared in *The Shoppers Guide*. Don and his brothers called it their shopper soap opera.

The audience response was immediate and much larger than anyone expected. The first time a carrier ditched his papers instead of delivering them, over twenty calls were received, most from women reporting they didn't get their new installment of *The Storm Testament*. The problem with ditching papers was solved forever.

I was so nervous about so many people reading my first novel that I used a pen name, Sam Storm. Readers started calling, wanting to know the real name of the author. Some were sure it was Blaine Yorgason, a popular LDS author at the time.

When the book was finally released, the *Salt Lake Tribune* published a negative review. Howie Schindler wrote, "Nelson must think there were freeways in the 1830s, the way his characters romp around the west." At first I felt bad and wondered if I had not been careful enough with my research, but as time passed, I realized Schindler didn't know the first thing about travel on the frontier. If anything, I was conservative in describing my character's travels. Walkara could ride from Sanpete to San Bernardino in ten days, and he did it many times.

I got my revenge on the *Tribune* when *Storm Testament V*, which was about the anti-polygamy persecutions of the 1880s, was published. I spent six thousand dollars on a radio ad that began, "The *Salt Lake Tribune* called the first presidency of the Mormon Church a band of desperate thieves . . ." I thought the *Trib* would retaliate with a scathing review. Instead they waited until my Huck Finn book was released, claiming I should have called it *Huck and Tom among the Mormons*, like I was trying to twist a Mark Twain story to convert the world to Mormonism. The LDS Seagull Book and Tape chain, nineteen stores, banned the book for "graphic language." I was taking fire from both ends of the spectrum. Still, the book sold five thousand copies the first month, and another five thousand later that year.

Don and his brothers were so pleased with the response to my *Storm Testament* story that they asked me if I wanted to write some sports stories too, mostly concerning BYU football and basketball. Since I had written the book on Lavell Edwards, they thought I would be a good sportswriter. They gave me a desk and a computer. I moved my office into their metal building on 400 South, about 350 West in Provo. I remember many times hurrying to crank out a few more column inches of *Storm Testament* so they would have enough copy to fill the allotted space in the paper.

It wasn't long until they made me editor. I started buying columns, feature articles, humor, and political cartoons from freelance writers and artists. The Oldhams changed the name from *Shoppers Guide* to *Utah County Journal.* But no matter how many kinds of articles we added, *Storm Testament* was the anchor editorial item. Many thousands of people were reading every single installment.

Don's brother Levor invited me to go with him to Philadelphia to a convention of free-circulation newspaper publishers and tell them about *The Storm Testament,* our shopper soap opera. The response was surprisingly friendly, and within a few months, over a hundred publications in the United States and Canada were serializing *The Storm Testament.* The Oldhams figured I was the most serialized author since Charles Dickens.

The serializations resulted in book orders from all over the country, but the biggest out-of-state orders were coming from a hardware store in Elkhark, Indiana. I called the store, saying I didn't think there were very many Mormons in Indiana, so I was wondering who was buying so many books. The clerk said the Amish, who had read the serial in the newspaper, were driving to town in their horse and buggies to buy *Storm Testament* books.

My favorite fan letter came from a high school boy in Preston, Idaho. He said that one night at the dinner table he started telling his mother about *Storm Testament II,* which he had just finished reading. In order to explain the story better, he went to get the book. He opened it in front of his mother in order to show her the pictures. To his amazement, there were no pictures—not one. He had read an entire book thinking it was full of pictures only to find out there were none.

Some people say a picture is worth a thousand words, but after reading this letter, I say a thousand words can be worth more than a thousand pictures.

CHAPTER XV

Writing . . . is the great invention of the world.

—ABRAHAM LINCOLN

While writing *The Storm Testament* series, I was doing a lot of reading on Indians and Indian lore to find material to use in my continuing story. One day, in getting ready to write about my hero Dan Storm going on his first buffalo hunt with his Indian friends, I simply could not find the information I needed in the library. Nobody who had ever killed a buffalo from the back of a galloping horse with a bow and arrow had ever written about it. I found a Mormon pioneer journal entry where Porter Rockwell and some of his friends dared each other to ride horses in front of stampeding buffalo bulls to see if the balls from the rider's guns could penetrate the thick skulls. But no one had done it the Indian way and written about it. How hard was it to train the horse? Indians claimed their forefathers had sophisticated training methods that were now lost. How hard was it to kill the buffalo? How dangerous was it?

My research told me that before the horse came along, the Plains Indians and surrounding tribes lived a pretty much hand-to-mouth survival existence. But the tribes who learned to chase herds of buffalo on horseback, with a single warrior sometimes killing as many as half a dozen animals in a single hunt, now had plenty of food if they made pemmican and jerky to carry them through the lean months. With abundant food, these tribes had more time for war, religion, travel, trade, and harassing their neighbors by stealing horses and women.

I decided that since I couldn't find anything in the library, this was a research project I could conduct myself. The first thing I did was place an ad in the classified section of the newspaper announcing I was looking for a buffalo horse to do research on the hunting methods of the Plains Indians. I received a number of interesting calls.

One lady tried to sell me an Arabian mare because that breed has the most endurance, she claimed. A man said I should buy his thoroughbred, the only breed of horse in the world bred entirely for athletic ability and speed. A couple of quarter horse people called and said their horses had cow sense, which could be translated into buffalo sense. These horses were bred to follow their prey. Of course, someone wanted to sell me a mustang, the original breed used by Indians to chase buffalo.

In the end I didn't buy a new horse but decided to use a four-year-old quarter horse I had raised from a colt. He was athletic and seemed to have plenty of speed. At first I hired a professional horse trainer, Virgil Neeves, to start my buffalo horse, but when I saw Virgil trotting around in a pen with a bunch of cows, shooting an arrow here and there, I decided the horse needed a more aggressive brand of training, and so did I.

In an effort to develop my skill with the bow and arrow while riding a horse, I started galloping through Mapleton hay fields, shooting arrows into bales of hay on the ground. When I told Browning Arms in Morgan, Utah, about my research, they provided me with two Bantum compound bows, short and powerful. I had learned that when Indians started chasing buffalo on horseback, they started using shorter bows, because maneuverability was more important than the accuracy made possible with long bows.

Then I started taking my horse Sonny to roping arenas where team roping was going on. I talked the cowboys into letting me practice on their roping steers. I was using a plastic bow I bought for my son Russell at Kmart when he was six. I wrapped duct tape on the tips of the arrows to make them less dangerous. I would shoot one of the cowboys in the leg to show him my arrows would not hurt the roping cattle. Or course, I promised to buy any I might hit in the eye, but I never hurt any cattle.

When they let the roping steer out of the chute, I galloped out of the heeler's box on the right side of the chute. I rode Sonny into position, dropped the reins, and started shooting arrows. If the horse got too close or out of position, I would grab the reins and get him back to the right spot, his nose five or six feet to the right of the cow's right hip. From there my arrow could enter the chest cavity from behind the rib cage. In that position I was far enough from the steer's head that I usually did not head him off to the left. And from that position behind the running target, it would be harder for an angry buffalo to turn and jab me or my horse with his horns.

After a dozen or so runs, Sonny knew his job. Contrary to what some Indians had told me, no sophisticated horse training was necessary. Someone would let the steer out of the chute, Sonny would run to the desired position near the right hip and stay there while I shot arrow after arrow at the running steer, aiming at the soft spot behind the last rib. After a hundred or so practice runs, I could hit the target almost every time.

If I wanted him to get a little closer to the steer or move a little further away, instead of picking up the reins, all I had to do was apply leg pressure. He had learned to move away from pressure.

In my reading I learned that Indians who chased buffalo with bows and arrows quickly abandoned bareback riding and started using crude saddles with stirrups. I assumed this change was made so the riders would not fall off so easily, but as I continued to practice, I discovered that when I rode bareback style like an Indian, my behind was flat on the horse's back, going up and down, forward and back with the movement of the horse. My arrows were not very accurate. But when I rode like a cowboy, weight in the stirrups, my behind off the saddle, and my knees absorbing the up and down movement of the horse, my arrows were much more accurate. As I watched calf and team roping competitions more carefully, it became apparent that all the good and accurate ropers also rode with their stirrups. So that's how I practiced.

While Sonny and I were perfecting our skills, I started calling Indian reservations and ranches with herds of buffalo requesting permission to kill one of their buffalo the old-fashioned way. The reservation Indians were not cooperative at all. It was as if they resented a white man wanting to do something that only Indians had a right to do.

A Blackfoot Indian in Montana told me it couldn't be done by a white man like me, that what I was trying to do was too dangerous and I shouldn't do it because I would get killed. When I asked how members of his tribe hunted the buffalo on their reservation, he said they drove around in pickup trucks, shooting the animals with high-powered rifles.

The private buffalo ranchers weren't any more cooperative. Though they let hunters pay them high fees to shoot their bison with rifles, they weren't about to let me stampede the animals by chasing them on a horse. One Wyoming rancher told me that when he let a television crew from Hollywood stampede his herd, the frightened animals went through his fences and then the neighbors' fences. He said it took all summer to get them back home again. He wasn't about to let that happen a second time.

I ended up buying a buffalo, a two-year-old bull that weighed about nine hundred pounds, from Dr. Otto Jones in South Jordan. He was buying up bison to develop a ranch in Wyoming. I found a valley east of Stockton, Utah, south of Tooele, where the owner had maintained a herd of about three hundred buffalo at one time, though the valley was no longer fenced to contain bison. When I told him what I intended to do, he described how his buffalo had killed several of his prize quarter horses. With the sharp, upturned horns, the bison instinctively knew how to get under a horse's belly and rip it open, allowing the entrails to fall down. He said there was a good chance this two-year-old would do that to my horse. He said if I had any brains, I would let the buffalo out of the trailer, shoot it with a 30.06, shove an arrow in the bullet hole, and then start taking pictures. No one would ever know that I had cheated.

One of my concerns was that my horse, who had been trained

on live cattle, would think the buffalo was a different kind of beast and refuse to chase it. Sometimes when an otherwise good cow horse comes upon a goat or a llama for the first time, he is afraid of it. Plus I was worried that much of the valley where I intended to conduct the chase was strewn with rocks and boulders. I asked Virgil what I should do if the buffalo ran through one of the rocky areas and if Sonny would be able to run through the rough terrain. He said Sonny was horse enough if I was man enough.

I arrived at Otto's place in South Jordan early on a Saturday morning. After handing him a check for $550, we ran the buffalo into my two-horse trailer. He tried to run right on through, and then he spun around to test the rear doors we had just closed. He was a wild animal, not a domestic cow. I didn't have any breakfast that morning while driving out to Stockton.

I had plenty of help to conduct my experiment. Virgil came along to see how the horse would do. Bob Davis, a rodeo cowboy, was there with his rope. I had given him permission to rope the buffalo if I missed with the arrows. My neighbor Jeff Kennedy brought his 30.06 rifle with the intent to kill the buffalo and save my life in the event it charged me. My boys' scoutmaster Bruce Palmer had come along to help. My friend Ray Virchow had come too. Bruce Elm, a computer programmer from work, came to take pictures. I had also hired Rell Francis, a professional photographer from Springville. We set up two tepees so everyone would have a place to sleep if they decided to stay over. Jeff, Bruce, and I planned to stay the entire weekend, making pemmican and jerky, tanning the hide, and cooking up Indian recipes. My four oldest boys were there, along with a dozen or so children belonging to others who came to help.

When I pulled the trailer into an open area at the bottom of the little valley, everyone was there. My horse was saddled and ready for the action to begin. A quiver full of arrows was strapped over my shoulder. The photographers had moved to the upper end of the valley where we thought the buffalo would want to go. They were hiding in gullies and behind bushes so they would not alarm the buffalo, possibly causing it to turn in the wrong direction.

By this time I had heard so many stories about the dangers of free-roaming buffalo that when I looked around and saw so many children, I became concerned. We couldn't risk a child being gored. I ordered the children to crowd into Bob Davis's four-horse trailer where they could peer between the steel side panels. I gave them strict orders not to leave the trailer until the buffalo was dead.

With the children safely confined, I rode Sonny to the side of my trailer and nodded for the rear gate to be opened. The buffalo didn't hit the ground running. He wasn't sure of his new surroundings, so he cautiously stepped out of the trailer, looked around, and then started trotting to the open area away from the vehicles and tepees. I loped alongside, hazing him in the direction I wanted him to go. I drew an arrow from the quiver.

That's when I noticed a lot of noise behind me, the sound one hears when driving by an elementary school at recess. I looked back. The children had opened the rear door of the trailer and were running after me. About that time, the buffalo turned into my horse, like he was going to give me a jab with his right horn. I had dropped the reins, but before I could grab them, Sonny laid back his ears, a warning to the bison to stay away. Sonny then turned away himself so he could maintain a healthy distance between himself and the bison. The horse wasn't excited at all. This seemed routine business for him, just like when we chased the roping steers. I was glad for that.

By now the buffalo had stopped and was looking back at the gang of children who were running toward us. Virgil and Bob were galloping forward on their horses in an effort to get between the children and the bison.

The buffalo had seen enough. He turned away from the approaching hoard and started galloping toward the open part of the valley. I galloped alongside and let the first arrow fly. I didn't miss. The only part of the arrow I could still see were the feathers. It had penetrated that far, but the buffalo continued to gallop along as if nothing had happened, though I began to see red foamy blood bubbling from his mouth and nose. This told me the lungs had been punctured and that the wound was fatal.

I shot a second arrow, but I was closer to the buffalo's head by now. The arrow hit a rib and didn't go in very far. I later discovered the rib was broken from the impact of the arrow, but the arrow did not penetrate deep enough to do any real damage. Had that been the first arrow, I might have had one angry beast on my hands. But the first arrow was fatal. The buffalo's lungs were now filled with blood. He gradually slowed to a stop, turned around, and fell to the ground.

Everyone gathered around to watch the butchering. Rell Francis, the photographer, pulled me aside to let me know that he had become so frightened when he saw the buffalo galloping toward him that he had not taken any pictures. I was devastated until Bruce Elm assured me that he had taken a ton of photos. So had Ray Virchow.

Before beginning the butchering, I had to experiment with an old mountain man custom, founded in a belief that if certain parts of the dead animal were eaten raw, the virility of the animal would transfer to the man who had made the kill. I cut out a raw testicle, gnawed off a huge chunk of it, and began to chew. Kind of slippery tasting; I do not recommend it.

When I am describing this event in speeches, if the audience is comprised of adults, I say that the virility experiment was a failure. My wife said she didn't notice any difference at all.

Since we were out in the flat and, like the Plains Indians, had no way to hang up the animal for normal white man butchering, we went about it the Indian way. We skinned back the hide on the top surface, removed all the meat, and then rolled the animal over so we could remove the hide from the other side and get at those cuts of meat. When all the meat was safely and cleanly tucked in sacks, we finally cut open the inner cavity, removing entrails, heart, lungs, liver and so on. By saving the messy part to last, we were able to keep the meat relatively clean.

Bruce, Jeff and I, and our children stayed there for several days scraping flesh off the hide and rubbing raw brains into it, making pemmican and jerky, and trying recipes I had discovered in the books I was reading on the Plains Indians.

I had to try a favorite Blackfoot recipe called *Crow Guts*. You take a section of small intestine more than a foot long and turn it inside out so the fat is on the inside. You then stuff it full of pieces of meat and tie a knot at both ends so it looks like a big, bumpy hot dog. You cook it a long time on a bed of hot coals to allow the meat to simmer in the melted intestine fat.

I tried to make crow guts three times, but the meat always had kind of a manure flavor. Not very good—I didn't like it. Months later, when I described this process to a Blackfoot Indian, he guessed I forgot to wash the intestine before stuffing in the meat. It never occurred to me to wash the intestine. Maybe that was the problem.

When I got home, I wrote an article about my research with the bison and included plenty of photos. The *Journal* published it, as well as most of the newspapers that were serializing *The Storm Testament*.

This piece of publicity really set me apart from the armchair writers who never seem to get out and *do* the things they write about. While the research with the buffalo helped me be more realistic and graphic in my descriptions, I can't deny that there was a huge benefit in the amount of publicity it generated about my books and me as an author.

CHAPTER XVI

In the beginning was the Word, and the Word was with God, and the Word was God. The same was in the beginning with God. All things were made by him; and without him was not any thing made that was made.

—JOHN 1:1–3

One of the articles I wrote for the *Journal* was about *The Godmakers*, an anti-Mormon film that had just been released and was being shown almost nightly in the Orem High School auditorium. The Ex-Mormons for Jesus were bringing in announcements for the times of the showings and begging me to print them, which I did.

I thought it interesting that they would call their film *God Makers*. Obviously, they were trying to call attention to a basic Mormon doctrine introduced by Joseph Smith and later summarized by Lorenzo Snow, which says, "As man is, God once was, and as God is, man may become," which teaches people that they can grow up to become like God. In my growing up and missionary years, Mormons were usually reluctant to discuss this doctrine with nonmembers. The Christian world considered it outrageous, blasphemous, and heresy.

So the Ex-Mormons for Jesus called their movie *The God Makers,* believing that no decent Christian person would ever want to join a church that believed such a doctrine. They probably didn't know that a recently published book at Simon & Schuster, by a psychiatrist and religious philosopher named Scott Peck, claimed that all the trials and struggles we face in life just don't make any sense if we don't believe we are on a path to become like God. The book was called *The Road Less Traveled* and found a spot on all the bestseller lists for a record ten years. One of my favorite quotes in the book is,

> The idea that God is actively nurturing us so that we might grow up to be like Him brings us face to face with our own laziness . . . the force of entropy within us, pushing us down and holding us all back from our spiritual evolution. So original sin does exist; it is our laziness.

The Seven Spiritual Laws of Success, by Deepak Chopra, an Indian medical doctor, became the bestselling religious book of the 1990s. Chopra arrived at the same conclusion, that all of us are on a path to become like God. Now as I write this personal history, millions of people outside the LDS Church believe this formerly unpopular Mormon doctrine.

I attended one of the showings of the movie *The God Makers*. There were cartoon depictions of God and Jesus standing around with mobs of plural wives. It told how Mormon men had the goal of achieving that same status. The only problem was where all the plural wives would come from.

What really surprised me was how the movie argued that the Mormon Church was anti-family and that our Church leaders were actively engaged in breaking up families, especially in situations where one of the spouses might be inactive or a nonmember.

In one scene, there was a nice-looking man in a green shirt, telling viewers, very tearfully, how the local Mormon bishop told his wife and children to leave him, because he was not active in the Church. The bishop had caused a breakup of his family.

After the film ended, when people in the audience were allowed to ask questions, a young man stood up. When given the microphone, he said the man in the green shirt was his father. Yes, the bishop had told his mother to take the children and go, but the film didn't tell the rest of the story. It seems his mother had been hospitalized several times as the result of beatings by her husband. I think the young man also said something about the abuse of a little sister.

I took plenty of notes but didn't go to work right away on the article. The following Sunday evening Sharon and I attended a direct wire broadcast in the stake center, a fireside for adults in the Church. Gordon B. Hinckley was the speaker. He talked about marriage and family relations. His words were warm and sincere, and I could feel a kind and gentle spirit while he talked. The next morning I wrote the article.

Among other things, I chastised Orem High School officials for allowing a public auditorium to be used for religious persecution. When I called the school principal and asked him why he was allowing his auditorium to be used to air an anti-Mormon film and program, he said he was afraid the ACLU would sue him if he did not allow the movie to be shown. It was a free speech issue. A lot of people wanted him to say no to the *Godmakers* people, but he just couldn't do it if he wanted to avoid an expensive lawsuit.

In my article I informed the American Nazi party that if they wanted to hold a program defending Adolf Hitler's policies against Jewish peoples, the Orem High School auditorium was available for fifteen dollars. And if the Klu Klux Klan wanted to do a presentation on why descendents of former slaves should not be allowed to vote or share drinking fountains, restaurant tables, or bus seats with white people, the group could rent Orem High School for their program.

It was a strong article, in the end urging members of the peaceful and sometimes complacent Mormon community that if they were not afraid of the ACLU and didn't think *The Godmakers* should be showing at Orem High School, they should pick up their phones and call the Orem High principal, whose home and office phone numbers were conveniently listed at the end of the piece.

The day after the article appeared, the receptionist buzzed me to let me know there was a man on line two who wanted to talk to me, but the caller would not give his name. I picked up the phone.

"Hello, this is Lee Nelson."

"Did you write that story?" asked a serious, deep male voice.

"Which story?" I asked, explaining that I wrote lots of stories, including *The Storm Testament*.

"The one about the *God Makers*."

"Yes, I wrote that." The line was silent for a few seconds as I waited for the caller to respond.

"You're dead. We've taken an oath, and you're dead," were his exact words.

Click. He hung up the phone.

My first thought was that I must flee to Oregon, and I don't know what prompted that. Next, all I could think to do was call Swen Nielsen, the Provo chief of police. He took my call, and I told him about the threat. He said I should take the call seriously. Threats from religious nuts were not to be laughed off.

"What do I do, then?" I asked.

"The best advice I can give you," he said calmly, "is to hold your hands over your ears every time you start your car."

It took me a few seconds to realize he was joking. To me this was no joking matter. Later, as I thought about it, his comment was very funny.

On a more serious note, he advised me to look behind the tires before I got in my car, because a popular car bomb was the kind that went off when the victim backed over it. He said I might want to place a piece of gravel on the seam between the hood and fender whenever I left my car unattended. If the gravel was gone when I returned, I would know someone had been tampering under the hood. He said I should travel to and from work at different times each day, and take different routes. I should not be predictable. He said to watch for suspicious cars that traveled beside me at the same speed on the freeway.

That night I told Sharon and the older boys about the threat and what Chief Nielsen had told me so they would understand my new behavior. We all laughed over the chief's joke.

Bobby and Richard, then in their early teens, had a little bedroom with bunk beds off the family room that we passed through when coming in the back door.

That night when I went out to the boys' room to say good night, Bobby's upper bunk was ready for war. Beside him were his .22 rifle and my .22 pistol. At the head of the bed was a Rambo survival knife, two banana clips containing fifty rounds each, and five or six boxes of cartridges.

My initial reaction was to feel bad that I had frightened one of my sons. But instead of me comforting him, it was the other way around.

"Don't worry, Dad," he said, his innocent blue eyes bright and serious. "They won't get you through this end of the house." I knew he meant every word. If a bad guy forced his way through our family room, World War III would begin.

A day or two later, I asked Chief Nielsen if I could get a permit to carry a concealed weapon. I owned a snub-nosed .38 with a shoulder holster. He said under the current concealed weapons laws I could not get a permit, so I strapped the .38 with its holster on my hip, John Wayne style. I wore it for about three months and would sometimes get funny looks in restaurants and grocery stores.

Only once did I think I might have to use the gun. A man named Richard H. called, telling me he wanted a meeting with me so he could present some ideas that would be the basis of a very important article I might want to write. I told him that if he would come to my office at 1:00 the next afternoon, I would meet with him then. After he got off the phone, I started thinking about some of the things he had said that were not mainstream LDS. Perhaps he was an apostate or fundamentalist. Some of these people were not to be taken lightly. Rulon Allred, one of the most prominent fundamentalist leaders, had been murdered, execution style in his medical office by followers of Ervil LaBaron, the leader of another such group. The Lafferty brothers in Utah County had murdered their sister-in-law in a blood atonement ceremony for not wanting her husband to take a plural wife.

I began to regret I had invited Richard H. to my office, but I did not have a phone number to call to cancel the appointment. I called Jerry Scott, second in command at the Utah County sheriff's office, and asked him if he knew anything about Richard H.

Jerry knew a lot. He said that the man was another bachelor polygamist. His wife left him when he announced that he planned to take plural wives. The deputy believed Richard H. was stashing away guns, ammunition, and other survival items, anticipating the collapse of civilization as we know it. Jerry said he wasn't aware of Richard H. doing anything against the law—at least, not yet—but the sheriff's office was keeping an eye on him. Jerry thought I had made a mistake inviting the man to my office.

"So what do I do now?" I asked. "I can't get in touch with him to cancel the appointment."

"I'll come over and try to keep you out of trouble," Jerry said.

The next day when Richard H. showed up, Jerry was standing at the classified ads counter, just outside my office, pretending to be filling out one of the blank forms. Jerry was wearing a sport coat, his .45 loaded and ready in a shoulder holster.

When I invited Richard into my office, he was carrying a big brown briefcase that appeared quite heavy. I invited him to take a seat across the desk from me. The door was open, allowing Jerry to keep an eye on my visitor.

When I sat down behind the desk, I slowly removed the .38 from the holster on my belt, rested it on my thigh, and pointed it under the desk at my visitor.

My eager beaver visitor started telling me something about Joseph Smith that he thought regular members of the Church didn't know. Then he suddenly leaned forward and reached into the heavy briefcase. I cocked back the hammer on my .38, and glancing out the open door, could see Jerry's hand inside the front of his coat, ready to whip out the .45.

Richard pulled an old book out of the briefcase, opening it so he could read something to me. I eased the hammer forward to the safety position, at the same time noticing that Jerry had removed his hand from the front of his coat.

Richard read and talked for a minute and then reached into the briefcase a second time. Again, I cocked back the hammer while Jerry's hand went for the .45. My guest whipped out another book, and for the second time we quietly closed our hammers to the safety positions.

Richard's hand reached into his briefcase once or twice more, and each time we were ready for what might happen. But all we saw were books. Eventually I thanked him for coming to see me, telling him I had to get back to work. I sometimes wonder what might have happened had he pulled anything other than a book out of the briefcase.

Not long after that, while hurrying through Salt Lake City on Interstate 15, some crazy guy in a silver convertible sports car about ran me off the road as he shot across the lanes of traffic to reach an exit lane. I found myself reaching for the .38, not intending to hurt the man, but wanting to put a few holes in the side of his fancy little car. That would teach him not to run people off the road. Upon arriving home, I put the .38 away and never wore it again. And as far as I know, *The God Makers* was never shown again at Orem High School.

CHAPTER XVII

Lose this day loitering—'twill be the same story
Tomorrow—and the next more dilatory;
Each indecision brings its own delays,
And days are lost lamenting o'er lost days.
Are you in earnest? Seize this very minute—
Boldness has genius, power and magic in it.
Only engage, and then the mind grows heated—
Begin it, and then the work will be completed!

—JOHANN WOLFGANG VON GOETHE
Author of 133 books

Up until this time in my life, television viewing had always been in black and white, but color televisions were becoming more popular and more affordable, so one day I rustled up some money and bought our first color television, an RCA model with a nineteen-inch screen. We set it up in the family room in the back of the house next to Richard and Bobby's bedroom.

At first, of course, the children were watching it continually. Then one evening the boys surrounded me in the living room and announced that the new television didn't work anymore. Then Bobby told me why. Richard had shot a hole in the screen with his pellet rifle. Sure enough, there was a bullet hole, a little off center. I looked at Richard for an explanation.

He said they were watching a documentary on polar bears. He had been following the bears on the screen through the peep sights on his rifle. Then he had pulled the trigger, not thinking the gun was loaded.

"I hit the bear," he said as he apologized for his mistake.

I didn't punish him. I figured the natural consequence, that of not having a color television for a year or so until I could afford to buy another, would be sufficient punishment.

Richard's biggest mistake wasn't destroying our television set but picking up a gun and playing with it without first checking to make sure it wasn't loaded. There were real guns in the house, and they were not play things. Sometimes I would leave bullets in the magazine of my deer rifle, just so I could show the children from time to time that it really was loaded. That was something my grandfather did. He always said, "No one will ever get killed with an empty gun around here." Everyone knew his guns were loaded. I don't do that anymore, though, with all the grandchildren around. The incident with the television set was a good lesson for Richard and the rest of the children about the need to be careful around firearms.

We moved to Mapleton, Utah, in 1979, and while we were still living in the old house on Maple Street, Sharon decided to have another Halloween party—not for us this time, but for the older boys and their neighborhood friends. The guests were in the kitchen, bobbing for apples, carving pumpkins, and having a pie-eating contest. I think there had been some unsavory items on the news about people putting razor blades in apples handed out to trick-or-treaters, so Sharon's idea was to provide safe and fun activities at home where we could keep an eye on the children.

I couldn't leave well enough alone and soon came up with an idea that could really put some life into the party. When we purchased the house, Kenny Harmer, the previous owner, left behind a bunch of chickens. In fact, they were a special breed of chickens—fighting cocks. I knew from the farmers and cowboys around that some cock fighting was still going on in the valley. Apparently, Kenny Harmer knew something about that too.

Richard and I snuck outside, went into the chicken coop, and stuffed all the fighting chickens into a gunnysack. Richard climbed on top of the haystack in the old barn at the back of the yard, and I handed him the bag of chickens. He hid behind some hay bales, being careful to keep the chickens quiet while I went back in the house to get our Halloween guests. I told them to put on their coats and follow me out to the barn, because I had a special Halloween story to tell them.

When everyone was gathered around at the base of the haystack, I proceeded to tell them why it took so long for the early pioneers to establish a permanent settlement in Mapleton. It seemed there was a large colony of vampire bats residing on the Mapleton bench, and when people tried to build homes, the bats would attack them when they went outside at night. At first the settlers were frightened, but in time they learned that the bats, though very large, weren't deadly. When a person found himself under attack, all he had to do was lay flat on the ground and put his hands over his eyes and face. The bats would bite away a chunk or two of flesh and then fly away, never seriously hurting anyone.

I could see the boys' eyes were wide as I continued to tell the story. In time the pioneers killed off most of the bats, but a few still moved into some of the old barns when winter approached. There hadn't been any reports of bats in this barn for at least ten years, but if the bats were going to hang out in the rafters of a barn, they would come in the fall, when it started to get really cold in the mountains. I told the boys that every Halloween I would bring my flashlight out to the barn and check for bats. I told them that since moving to Mapleton I had never found a single bat in my barn, so there was really nothing to worry about, but I still liked to check every Halloween, just to be on the safe side.

Now that I had finished the story, I started to point the beam of my flashlight up into the rafters to check for bats. This was Richard's signal to release the chickens, which he did, and eight or nine big gray fighting chickens came flapping down from the top of the haystack on top of my Halloween guests. Some of the boys fell on the ground and held their hands over their faces. Others raced screaming to the safety of the house. One boy ran all the way home. When one of the boys started to cry, we decided to end the prank and tell them there were no bats, just some stupid chickens that Richard had dumped on them.

At work, I continued to slay dragons. When it came time for the big football in-state rivalry between BYU and the University of Utah, I decided to write about a problem that seemed to be getting out of hand in recent years—an inclination on the part of U of U fans and students to use sporting contests as an excuse to offend members of the LDS Church by flaunting obscene language and drinking all kinds of alcoholic beverages while mingling among the BYU Mormons attending the game.

I called the sports information officer at the U and requested press passes for my photographer and me. He seemed reluctant to grant my wish, but he gave me the passes anyway.

As my photographer Don Turley and I drove up there, I explained that I had no interest in the football game itself. I told him I was going to write an article about the fans, and I wanted pictures of Ute fans engaged in illegal and possibly obscene activities, such as consuming alcohol on school property, holding up offensive banners, and flipping off BYU fans. I learned from Lavell Edwards that it was a tradition for Ute fans at the top of the student section to spit, pee, and pour beer into garbage and trash cans and then attempt to pour the contents onto BYU players when they came out of the locker room through a door directly below the edge of the student section on their way to the playing field. I told Don to be sure to get a picture of that. While I was up in the press box taking notes, Don was down on the sideline taking lots of pictures.

Utah officials seemed concerned that while other photographers crowded around the line of scrimmage, the *Journal* photographer was wandering everywhere else, pointing his camera and telephoto lens into the stands. But they left him alone. By the time the game was over, we had lots of great photos and gathered a few more on the way to the parking lot.

In the article I said that when the BYU team ran onto the field I saw more birds than during the pheasant hunt. I cited the state law forbidding the consumption of alcoholic beverages at state-owned school facilities and showed photos of Ute fans chugging down cans of beer, mixing martinis, and opening metal pocket flasks—all on public property in violation of state law. We published a photo of two or three obscene banners. "Fan Filth" was the headline on the article, with a subhead that said something about people using a football contest as an excuse for religious bigotry and persecution. I mentioned in the article how some fans were chanting a slogan using foul language to describe LDS Church president Spencer W. Kimball.

At the end of the article, I laid out some financial information about the University of Utah. I broke down their budget to show how much was being spent to educate each student, how much of that was paid by the student, and how much was paid by the state. Then I showed how the state money came mainly from real estate taxes, with over 80 percent of it coming from members of the LDS faith. In other words, 50 percent of the money spent on educating each student at the University of Utah came from members of the LDS faith, the very people whose religious beliefs and values were ridiculed by the fans at the football game. Then I quoted Mark Twain, who said the main difference between a dog and a man is that a dog doesn't bite the hand that feeds it. I invited readers who didn't appreciate this immature and ungrateful behavior on the part of U of U fans and students to write to the president of the university. I provided his address.

A few days after the article was published, I received a call from a reporter at the student newspaper at the U. He said the president had already received over 230 letters from upset Mormon taxpayers. As I have observed this continuing rivalry, it seems my article hit the streets at the peak of the anti-Mormon behavior. It seems subdued today. Maybe the *Journal* had a role in helping that happen by calling attention to a problem that needed to be addressed.

I think the Oldhams, who didn't want to be part of what people termed "negative news media," were a little nervous about articles like this. I thought we were doing the right thing by carefully picking the bad guys who needed to be exposed. During the six years I was the editor, we never had a single lawsuit filed against us, though there were a number of threats.

One time I started digging into the background of Master Academy, an alternative school in Orem and Salt Lake City. Dix McMullin, the owner, was the majority leader in the state senate, and he had persuaded the state education system to pay him to provide a graduation alternative for high school dropouts. When he signed up a student, the state would pay him approximately twelve dollars a day, the same amount that was paid to each district for each child in school. About one afternoon each week, the students would come to Master Academy, which was a mobile home converted to an office. They would spend an hour or two going through workbooks and eventually earn high school degrees. No teachers, no music or sports programs, no lunch, or any of the other things provided by the public schools that had to operate on the twelve dollars a day they received for each student. Master Academy was making a ton of money and paying its owner a hefty six-figure income. The neat thing about it was that the state made it exclusive; no one could bid against McMullin.

The headline on my article was *Master Academy: The Real Home of Utah's Highest Paid Educator.* In the opening paragraph, I listed the salaries of some of the university presidents, showing how Dix McMullin was making more—much more.

The Oldhams were nervous about me taking on the top state senator. They set up a meeting with him and his lawyer, in which I read him the entire story before it went to press, giving him a chance to correct any errors I might have made. He didn't find any outright errors, though he disagreed with my conclusions. He begged us not to run the story, but we did, and in a couple of weeks, Master Academy shut its doors. I received a number of calls from *Salt Lake Tribune* and *Deseret News* reporters, all wanting to know how I managed to get information for the story. I felt bad about what we did to the guy, but at the time I thought we were doing the right thing. He was using his political influence to take a lot of money out of state school funds, most of it unearned. He deserved to be called on the carpet.

Many of the stories were easier and more clear cut, like the time a fellow came into the office and asked me to do a story about a new franchise business he had signed up for, wherein a lot of people in Provo were going to become rich. He showed me a list of businesses that sponsored his multi-level consumer research company in which participants could supposedly make forty thousand dollars or more a month by merely saving grocery receipts and filling out monthly reports on products they had purchased. The idea was that producers of consumer products, like Proctor and Gamble, were sick and tired of spending billions of dollars on consumer research conducted by major New York research firms and would like to pay all that money to the consumers themselves. The only hitch was that you had to buy a sixty-dollar instruction kit to get started. Anyone could afford that if it would bring a return of forty thousand dollars a month.

I gathered up the guy's materials and brochures and told him I would have to make a few phone calls to verify what he told me, and then I would write the story. He urged me to hurry because he was holding a public meeting at the Holiday Inn the following Thursday evening, and if the article came out before that, more people would be able to take advantage of this wonderful opportunity.

I went right to work, calling everyone whose name was listed in his materials, and it was soon obvious that no big corporations were gearing up to pay Provo residents to do product research. The guy was part of a scam to sell instruction kits which cost about fifty cents to produce.

The headline on the article said, *How to earn $40,000 a month saving your grocery receipts.* In the article I described how I had checked out the names in the brochures and nothing panned out. No large corporations were paying people to save grocery receipts. I mentioned the meeting at the Holiday Inn and invited readers to stop by and see firsthand how Utah Valley's latest scam was attempting to lure in the suckers. I felt bad doing this to the poor guy, who may have believed what he was selling was legitimate. But it wasn't, and the *Journal* had the power and duty to end it all right then.

On the afternoon before the meeting, the receptionist informed me that what's-his-name was in the lobby and wanted to see me. I figured he had come to punch me out for ruining his little scam. On the contrary, he tried to hug me for putting his article on the front page. It took me a minute to figure out that he had read the headline but not the article. He asked if he could have some extra copies of the paper to take to the meeting. I gave him an entire bundle and didn't have the heart to urge him to read the article.

The poor fellow was handing out my article to people as they came in the door. He could hardly believe his good fortune when cameramen and reporters from two Salt Lake television stations showed up. They knew about the story and had come to ask the same hard questions I had asked in the story. The meeting was a disaster, and nobody ever earned forty thousand dollars a month saving grocery receipts. Of course, nobody threw away sixty dollars on an information kit either.

The interesting thing was that over the next week or so we received a number of calls from people wanting to know how to get hold of the guy who could show them how to make forty thousand dollars a month saving their grocery receipts.

CHAPTER XVIII

He who knows himself knows God.

—St. Augustine or
Ali ibn Abi Talib (r.a.)
in *Hadrat Ali r.a.*

When Richard turned twelve and became a deacon, I decided it might be time for him to go on a vision quest, like some of the Indians and prophets in the scriptures had done. He had read the book of Mormon from cover to cover and was doing all the right things a boy his age should do.

So one evening we began a fast—no food or water—and headed to the top of Maple Mountain, a challenging hike even on a full stomach. We didn't ride horses or take packs with sleeping bags and a tent, just a light daypack with some drinks and treats to give us energy once we had ended the fast.

We arrived at the top of the mountain in the middle of the night, about the time a storm with the accompanying thunder and lightning rolled in. I built a little fire for warmth and light, while Richard went off by himself to conduct his prayer vigil. I was pleased at how long he endured, considering our weakened condition from a six-thousand-foot climb with no nourishment or liquid. When he returned he didn't report any heavenly manifestations, but we both felt good about what he had accomplished. I felt like Nathan, the ancient Hebrew priest, guiding the young Samuel along a spiritual path. We ended the fast with a prayer together, and since we had no shelter from the storm, we headed back down the mountain, arriving home around daybreak.

I didn't do this with any of the other children, perhaps because it was such a hard thing to do. Doing it eight times, again and again and again, would be hard. There wasn't any lack of toughness, willingness, or enthusiasm on the part of the children, even the girls.

I remember going with the boys on a Boy Scout backpack adventure to the Chain Lakes, east of Kings Peak in the Uinta Mountains, right after Bobby turned twelve. I loved to go to the Uintas, the huge mountain range in the northwest corner of Utah that goes from east to west. I had studied George Thompson's book, *Lost Treasures on the Old Spanish Trail,* and knew about many old Spanish mines and the Lost Rhoades Mine. When I went to the Uinta Mountains I often took a gold pan. I loved to prospect along the clear mountain streams and around springs like the Spanish had done. Sometimes I'd find little flecks of gold, and often I'd bring home rocks that seemed heavier than normal, thinking there might be gold or silver inside. I'd pile the rocks outside my tack room door and from time to time crush them on the anvil with a big hammer.

The trip to Chain Lakes was Bobby's first. He was a tough and determined little boy. He could run through the snow in his bare feet to get coal, and he didn't complain much when we did pushups and sit-ups. So even though he was one of the littlest Scouts, I thought he could make it. The weight of the boys' packs ranged from eighteen to about thirty pounds. The adults carried packs of about forty pounds each. I remember as we were preparing to leave from the church that scoutmaster Bruce Palmer pulled what felt like an eight-pound iron skillet out of one boy's pack. Some mothers just didn't understand. Even cans of soda and prepared foods were too much weight for the littlest boys to carry. The standard fare was Top Ramen and jerky.

If we didn't keep an eye on the little boys' packs when we stopped to rest, some of the older boys would put rocks in them to make them heavier. Such harassment would sometimes result in cries of anger when the rocks were finally discovered.

We were climbing a switchback trail in the afternoon under a hot sun. Every time we stopped for a break I would close my eyes and see my horses standing under shade trees behind my house, nothing to do but be lazy. I fed and took care of them all year so they could do that, while I worked my guts out. Never again. Next time the horses would be doing the lions' share of the work. That's the least they could do for the care I provided them.

By the time we reached the top of the switchbacks, Bobby and some of the other little ones were beginning to cry. Every few steps they wanted to know how much further we had to go. They wanted to stop. They wanted to go back. They didn't want to be Boy Scouts anymore. Everyone had blisters on their feet and on their shoulders where the straps from the packs rubbed against skin.

By the time we reached the first Chain Lake, it was almost dark and beginning to rain. We huddled under sheets of plastic, trying to build fires with wet wood to cook Top Ramen noodles. It rained for about twenty-four hours, while the boys questioned their decisions to become Boy Scouts.

Finally, the sun came out. The boys began fishing and exploring. I have a picture of Bobby submerged up to his chin in a black mud hole at the upper end of the lake. He couldn't get out without help from the other boys. What a glorious time it was. Steve Wiscombe and I hiked up to a higher lake called Okie Dokie and caught a hundred fish. There was no crying or complaining from the boys on the way back. We were going downhill with mostly empty packs. Hiking was easy now, even for the little ones.

One time, when the boys were older, we took them to the Jarbidge River in northern Nevada, the same place where I went with Larry Olsen on the survival trip. We parked at Murphy Hot Springs and followed the river downstream into the deep canyons leading to the Bruneau River, which eventually dumps into the Snake River.

I warned the boys to keep an eye out for rattlesnakes, reminding them this was not one of the well-traveled Boy Scout trails like the ones in Utah, but a real wilderness adventure. And it was. There wasn't much of a trail, and with high spring runoff water, we could not cross the river when the going looked easier on the other side. The hiking was rough, and with having to step over and around so many rocks, our feet soon became sore and tired.

Steve Larsen was the first to find a snake—a big, fat, coiled-up diamondback—on a fallen log at the water's edge. The boys were all fired up to catch the snake and bring it along for our supper, so I let them kill it.

When we finally stopped to make camp, my feet and legs were shot. We set up the tents and started cooking our Top Ramen supper. Some of the boys started asking me when I was going to cook the snake. I really didn't feel like it, but the boys persisted. Finally I told them I couldn't cook it until they cleaned it. So with a lot of noise and teasing, they cut open the snake's belly and removed the entrails. Of course, they enjoyed identifying the heart, liver, lungs, and so on as they threw such items at each other. I thought this activity might ruin their appetite for snake, but it did not. Soon they were pestering me again to start cooking.

"I can't cook a snake that has not been skinned," I protested. The boys went to work removing the skin. When they finished, I couldn't think of any more excuses, but still not feeling up to a lot of effort, I advised them to roll it up in the pan in which my boys and I had just finished cooking some noodles. I told them to cover it with water and put it on the coals to cook.

As the water began to boil, the color of the snake turned from pink to a light bluish gray. It didn't look good to me at all, but the boys were enthusiastic. I told them we were cooking it the way the mountain men used to cook snakes.

After it had boiled about twenty minutes I announced it was time to try a favorite mountain man delicacy. The snake still didn't look very appetizing, but the boys were game for whatever I suggested. I acted amazed that they had never heard of "snake soup." I told them the mountain men would usually throw away the snake and just drink the broth since they liked it so much. Now that I had explained it, the boys began pouring the snake water into cups and drinking it. None of them seemed to notice that I didn't have any.

A few days later, we were camped by a smaller stream where the boys could catch a few fish, and my son Richard and a friend ran into camp wanting to borrow my .22 pistol. They had found a big rattlesnake and wanted to bring it in for supper. I gave them the gun and followed them to see what they intended to do.

The snake had crawled under a flat rock, but they could still see part of its body, so they fired a bullet at what they could see. Assuming the snake was dead, they put down the gun down, grabbed both sides of the flat rock with their bare hands, and proceeded to pick it up.

What they didn't know was that there were two snakes under the rock. At first it appeared that they had killed one and not the other. Fortunately, their bullet had passed through both snakes, and both were dead.

We took the two snakes back to camp, and this time I was determined to cook them right. After the cleaning and skinning, we cut them into sections about three or four inches long. We had just cooked up a pound of bacon in a frying pan, so we had a lot of grease for deep frying. I rolled the sections of snake in a mixture of pancake flour, salt and pepper, and deep fried them in the bacon grease.

After three days of Top Ramen, the boys thought we had stopped in at a Kentucky Fried Chicken restaurant. They ate every single piece of snake, which resembled deep fried pieces of turkey neck. In fact, they fought over the last few pieces. I didn't get any, but I was happy the boys were so enthusiastic.

One May, Ben Gardner and I were exploring Fifty Mile Mountain on the Kaiparowits Plateau near Escalante, Utah. I was riding a big, hot-blooded ex-racehorse I had traded from Dave Nemelka. The horse was so big and strong that I named him Malone after the Utah Jazz basketball player. The horse didn't have a lot of brains, but he had a lot of heart.

The entire north side of Fifty Mile Mountain was a cliff, about fifty miles long, with two or three places where steep, rocky trails wound up through the cliffs to the mostly flat top of the mountain. We were hoping to find some big bucks living there among wild cattle and Indian ruins.

Ben and I were returning to the truck and trailer after three or four days of exploring and fighting spring snowstorms when I heard the unmistakable rattle of a snake. We were on a rocky, dangerous portion of trail that wound among some huge boulders. It was a place where a horse or man could easily break a leg if things got out of control. If a horse started bucking here, you could die.

Upon hearing the rattling noise, I stopped the horse and started looking around. Ben, who was leading the way, stopped too. In a quiet voice I told him I could hear a snake real close. The horses didn't seem to notice.

I looked and looked and looked as the rattling sound resumed, stopped, and resumed again. Then I saw it. A huge rattler was coiled up in the middle of the trail, right under my horse's belly. Somehow, the horse had stepped over it with its front feet. I had heard stories of good saddle horses dying from snake bite. I also knew my horse was capable of lunging ten or twelve feet in any direction if something startled him. Surrounded by boulders of various sizes, there was no place to go safely if one got off the narrow trail.

I was wearing my .22 pistol. Slowly, I removed it from the holster and cocked back the hammer. Carefully, I leaned to the right, taking careful aim at the snake. I had fired guns on this horse before so I wasn't too worried about him being startled by gunshot noise.

I took aim and pulled the trigger. *Bam.* The snake was dead. The horse never even flinched. The snake had ten rattles on its tail, which Ben took home to his children.

On that same trip, I found a perfect red flint spearhead covered with a thin layer of dust under a ledge. I brought home a set of the largest mule deer antler drops I have ever found.

A few years later, Ben Gardner and I bought a ranch on the Nevada-Utah border at a place called Pleasant Valley. The previous owner told us there was a rattlesnake den up near the base of the Kearn Mountains, across the road from the ranch house. He said we could find lots of rattlesnakes there on the first two or three warm days of spring when they came out of hibernation.

One sunny spring day Virginia and I went up there. She was nine or ten at the time and wanted to bring her .22 rifle. The den area consisted of a rock formation of decomposed granite about as big as a house, with lots of cracks, crevices, and little caves.

Immediately we started seeing rattlesnakes. Some were as big as your arm, some were as little as pencils, and others were every size in between—ten, twenty, thirty of them. The ones close to us would coil up and shake their rattles. It was a little scary, because when you walked close to the big rock formation, once in a while you would hear one rattling at eye level. You'd look into a crack in the rock, and there he was. Others would be out on the flat rocks where we were walking, quietly sunning themselves. No matter how hard we looked we couldn't see them all. I made Virginia walk behind me. I was wearing cowboy boots with extra high tops, but she was wearing sneakers, which made her more vulnerable to the ones on the ground.

I let Virginia kill one so she could take the rattles home to show to her friends at school. I was fascinated with the snakes but felt no enmity toward them. They had a right to live too—to hunt mice, sun themselves on warm rocks, and reproduce. If they were not going to harm me or Virginia, I had no desire to harm them. We explored the snake rock for about half an hour and then carefully worked our way back to the truck.

Later that evening I made the mistake of telling Bill Henroid, our neighbor, about our experience with the snakes. I told him where the den was so he could see them too.

A few days later when I took some of the other children up there, dead and decaying snakes were all over the place. The stench of rotting flesh was awful. Bill had gone up there with his shotgun and shot every big snake he could find. I remember counting twenty-two lifeless bodies.

Later when I asked Bill about it, he asked me if I had ever seen a mother cow that had been bitten on the nose by a rattlesnake, her nose swollen up like a basketball so she couldn't eat. I said I had not. He asked if I had ever watched one of my good saddle horses die from snake bite. I said I had not. Discussion ended. I have never been back to the snake den and have sometimes wondered if the rattlesnakes still spend winters there.

Sharon was always concerned about the children missing their church meetings when I took them to the ranch, because such trips usually lasted three or four days and included weekends. The ranch was in a remote location—fifty miles from the nearest paved road and a hundred miles from the nearest grocery store. When we returned home from these trips, we tried to make Mom feel better by telling her we had attended snake conference.

After the Chain Lake adventure, we started taking the Scouts to the Garfield Basin at the head of Utah's Yellowstone River. There were lots of lakes in the area where the boys caught all the fish a boy would ever want to catch.

We canoed from the city of Green River to Mineral Bottoms near the confluence with the Colorado River and rafted the fifty-two rapids in Desolation Canyon four or five different times. We even took the boys to the World Scout Jamboree in Calgary. Bruce Palmer was a tireless and patient scoutmaster, and under him and his replacement, John Crandall, my oldest four boys earned their Eagle Scout awards.

On many trips, over many years, I never saw Bruce lose his temper around the boys, though his patience would wear thin at times, like when we were on the way to the Jamboree in Canada. Bruce had most of the boys with him in a motor home, while I followed in my Suburban. When we stopped for food at a store in Montana, I remember Bruce warning the boys that if they played a certain audio tape one more time he would destroy it. As we were driving out of the parking lot, I remember seeing Bruce's window roll down and his arm extend as he threw the cassette tape as far as he could throw it, the brown tape streaming behind like the tail on a kite.

As we were driving through the Bitterroot Valley on the way home, we turned off the main highway to Lake Como, one of Montana's most scenic lakes, nestled up against a generous assortment of jagged, snow-covered peaks. We hiked to the inlet, where Tin Cup Creek gushed over a tangle of black ledges and huge boulders and into the lake at a place with a long row of cliffs where the boys could jump and dive into the clear, cold water.

While the boys were swimming, I built a big fire, hoping to establish a bed of coals. It wasn't a round bed, but a long bed, a little over a foot wide and nearly four feet long. I had picked up six whole chickens at a grocery store in Hamilton and hoped to cook a tasty lunch for the boys.

While the fire was burning down, I pounded into the ground two hefty forked sticks—one at each end of the fire. I cut most of the little branches and bark off a small pine tree and shoved it through the bodies of the six chickens. I pushed the chickens up against each other and tied up their wings and drumsticks with pieces of bailing wire to keep them from flopping around. Then I placed each end of the chicken-covered tree onto the forked posts I had planted earlier.

My biggest challenge as the chickens began to cook was to

prevent the boys, as they returned from their swim, from putting too much wood on the fire. It is the inclination and nature of every hungry boy I have ever known, when roasting a piece of meat over an open fire, to try to finish cooking it in five minutes instead of the thirty or forty minutes required to do a good job. If allowed to use his own judgment, a boy will burn up his meat before he can eat it. The boys helped by turning the spit and sprinkling on generous amounts of salt and pepper, but I tended the fire.

In time the chickens began turning a golden brown. Then hot juices and fat began dripping onto the coals. The scent of roasting chicken gathered everyone close around the fire, watching with keen anticipation as mouths began to water.

Finally, after what seemed like forever to the boys, I removed the spit from the fire and carefully slipped the chickens onto a large piece of white butcher paper. A roll of paper towels was passed around, and each boy tore off several squares to hold his dinner.

I served the two legs from the first chicken, and then the breasts. The fifth boy received the carcass with the wings without complaint. Then I started on the second chicken, the process continuing until all the chickens were gone. Nothing was wasted, not even a morsel of crispy, salty skin. It was a satisfying meal, following a vigorous swim in cold mountain water and a spectacular mountain hike—a wonderful way to end our journey to the North Country before returning to our homes in Utah.

CHAPTER XIX

If you don't do it, pretty soon you can't.

—JEFF KENNEDY

As a child, I developed a passion for books and reading. As an adult, I developed a passion for maps—the ones that show springs, rivers, pack trails, elevations, Indian ruins, locked gates, forests, and open desert country. I spent hours studying the Mount Moriah Wilderness on the Nevada border, where you find bristle cone forests older than the California redwoods and herds of mule deer and bighorn sheep. I spent countless hours studying locations in Utah's Book Cliffs, like Nutter's Hole, Moonwater Ridge, and the Tavaputs Plateau; and canyons with names like Flat Nose George, Rattlesnake, Rat Hole, and One Eye. I've studied the rapids in Desolation Canyon where the Ute Indians whipped Preston Nutter with the phalluses of trespassing bulls.

From maps I figured out the route to the largest Fremont ruin ever found at the head of South Franks Canyon. From maps I scouted a mustang trap on Flat Iron Mesa, still in good repair, because it's hidden in a juniper-pinyon forest, and because I'm about the only person in the world who can ride right to it. Maps show where the mustangs on the Copper Globe and Lynx Flat find their water. Maps give clues to the old Spanish mines at Moon Lake and Brown Duck Basin. I've learned that it's almost impossible from map study to find the Horse Thief Trail, which passes through the Waterpocket Fold to Swasey's Leap, but my son Russell and I found it.

If you're careful, a map can show you the way through Devil's Canyon to the Butch Cassidy hideout in the Badland Cliffs. Maps show the best way to find an old Indian trail leading to the ancient ruins in Fish and Owl Canyons. The right map can lead you to the mustang graveyard on the Slaughter Slopes. It takes an excellent map reader to stay on the Angel Trail across the Dirty Devil River to Robbers Roost. Without a map you could probably ride through the Little Grand Canyon a dozen times without finding Virgin Spring Canyon with its clear, turquoise swimming hole.

From careful map study I found places to prospect for gold, Indian ruins, Spanish mines, and big bucks. Map study inspired a hundred wilderness pack trips. In time, after I filled multiple file cabinet drawers with paper maps, my map study led to downloading the Google aerial photo of the world, where with the click of a mouse you can cruise like an airplane over your favorite places. For me, reading maps is like reading books. Map study fires up the imagination and stirs up passion, which make me want to visit the places I study on the maps, especially if the visit requires saddling up horses and mules to leave the roads, buildings, and concrete behind and heading into remote back country that looks the same today as it looked two hundred years ago when the first French trappers and Spanish explorers discovered it.

One day Jeff Kennedy, a neighbor, asked if I wanted to help him explore a remote area of the Book Cliffs he had been studying on maps as a possible hunting area for big bucks. Jeff taught at the junior high school, where the students called him Mountain Man Kennedy. His family ate a lot of wild game, including bobcats and beavers. We drove to Green River one Saturday, and then all the way to the head of a long desert canyon. We got stuck several times as we four-wheeled up the dry wash. There were no signs of human use, except for one empty pop bottle. We didn't actually see any deer, but as we glassed some of the more remote habitat at higher elevations, we were cautiously optimistic that this might be a good place to hunt where we wouldn't be rubbing shoulders with other hunters.

That fall I drew my first Book Cliffs elk tag, so back we went. Seth Boyer, another modern mountain man, went with us. We took our horses. Our plan was to drive to the end of the dirt road that followed the Green River upstream from the town of Green River, and to ride from there up a wilderness canyon by the name of Rattlesnake. It was 1984, the year of the big rains, even at Green River. The road was too muddy to get to the end of it. It was dark when we finally had to turn around. I remember checking a spot on a cliff above the river where a bunch of wet, sticky mud had slid down onto the road. There were huge bear tracks in the mud. We drove back to one of the dry canyons that came down from the high country, camped there, and the next morning began a twenty-eight-mile ride to some basins bordering the Ute Indian reservation. We waved at some grouse hunters as we began our journey.

Travel was easy, because a drilling company had punched a road up the canyon many years earlier. While spots were washed out, which prevented vehicular travel, it was easy going on horseback.

A gas well was at the end of the road. We could hear hissing sounds in the valves and gauges mounted on top of the casing and could smell leaking gas. From here the trail became rough and steep, so we decided to camp at the drill hole. Along the way we had seen some motorbike tracks, where some other hunters had been exploring the canyon before us. As we were making camp, I found where the bikers had stashed some quart-size plastic containers containing gasoline in the hollow of a tree. I threw two of the containers into one of the panniers, not sure why we would need gasoline, but it seemed a good thing to do.

With some daylight still remaining, we hiked up high on the rim to get a glance at a huge sagebrush flat at about a nine-thousand-foot elevation where we thought some deer and elk might be hanging out. We saw some nice bucks, but when we looked down into the deep canyon where our camp was located, we could see that my two horses had worked free of their hobbles and were starting to graze back down the canyon.

When we arrived back at camp, it was dark and the horses were gone. I grabbed a flashlight and headed down the canyon on foot. After awhile the batteries in the light were gone, but there was about a third of a moon in a clear sky, so I could see my way to continue.

217

I couldn't see well enough to find horses in the event that they wandered off into one of the many sagebrush flats to graze, so I just hurried along the canyon bottom, occasionally stopping to check for fresh tracks headed in the same direction.

It was well after midnight when there were no longer any fresh tracks headed down the canyon. I hadn't seen any tracks for some time, so I assumed I had finally gotten ahead of the horses, which I guessed were stopping to graze on their meandering journey back to the trucks and trailers.

I built a big campfire at a narrowing of the canyon where I didn't figure they could get by me without me seeing them. Then I stretched out on the sandy bank and waited.

In about half an hour, two curious horses approached the fire, expressions on their faces as if they were saying, "My goodness, what do we have here? Why it's Lee. How in the world did he get down here? I wonder if he has some oats."

I grabbed both lead ropes, hopped on Dan, and holding onto Thunder's rope, headed back to camp, arriving about five thirty, about the time Jeff and Seth were beginning to stir. By six thirty we had loaded up our camp and were leading the horses up the steep and dangerous trail to the edge of the big flat where we began our hunt at daylight. I was the only one with a tag. Jeff and Seth were going to help me get an elk.

We saw lots of tracks, but no elk that morning; but as we explored a large patch of timber along the rim, we found the biggest buck any of us had ever seen in the wild—ten or eleven points on each side. The deer hunt was about a month away, and we almost forgot about my elk tag as we discussed plans to come back and get the big buck.

Since we didn't find any elk, we moved up closer to the reservation, hoping to find a way over to the head of Rattlesnake Canyon, where we had intended to go in the first place before the muddy road stopped our progress.

To get to where we wanted to go, we had to cross a portion of the Ute Indian Reservation. We knew if the Indians caught us trespassing during hunting season they would probably confiscate our horses and guns and possibly take us to jail, so we didn't travel any of the dirt roads, and whenever we had to cross a road, we carefully wiped out our tracks with tree branches. We knew the Indians patrolled their reservation in airplanes at times, so whenever we heard the hum of an airplane engine we crowded the horses under pine trees. I felt like one of the characters in my books, constantly looking over my shoulder for hostile Indians.

We finally reached the spot we wanted, at the edge of the reservation boundary, high on a rocky rim where we could look down into the remote headwaters where Rattlesnake and Flat Nose George canyons began. There was elk sign everywhere, so we were confident our hunt would be a success. We had no plan as to how we would get back to the trucks and trailers, which were now about thirty miles away through some of the most rugged country on the face of the earth—at least, that is the way it looked to me. We knew there were elk on the Indian ground, but my tag was only legal on federal and state ground, so that's where we intended to hunt.

The main problem now was the huge storm rolling in. A strong wind was bringing thick black clouds, and it was beginning to rain. Little snowflakes were mixing in with the raindrops. To make matters worse, we hadn't planned to go so far or to stay so long, and our food was running out. We were mixing sage grouse with Top Ramen to make it last longer.

Wearing our rain gear, Jeff and I worked our way around the head of Flat Nose George. Late in the day we found two nice bulls on a steep hillside. I dropped one of them at four hundred yards. It took a long time to get to the dead animal, dress it out, and drag it down to a spot where we thought we might be able to get the horses. Dark descended before we could get back to camp. With the storm clouds blocking out the stars and moon, we could not see our hands in front of our faces, and with our flashlight batteries exhausted, we had no choice but to spend the night in the rain, huddled around a smoky little campfire.

When we reached camp about noon the next day, Seth announced he was sick and intended to hike back to the trucks by himself. He asked if we would take his horse and sleeping bag with us. He intended to take a direct route, which he assumed would be an impossible route for a horse. I didn't know what to think. It seemed a bad idea to split up like that, but Seth was determined to leave. We ate the last of the food, spent one last night together, and then Seth dropped over the rim into Rattlesnake Canyon and was gone. The rain was only getting worse, with no sign of letting up.

Jeff and I packed up the camp and led the horses off the rim, slipping and sliding into the deep hole that was the head of Flat Nose George. We did not worry about not having any food, because there would be plenty of meat for us once we reached the downed elk.

After cutting all the meat off the bones, we loaded it into the panniers and headed down the canyon. We couldn't make out any kind of trail, because little rivers of water were running everywhere. The brush was thick and tangled, and it took the rest of the day to cover only a few miles.

I remember finding myself in the middle of a brier patch—wild blackberries. The thorny vines were up to my horse's chest, and he couldn't back up because of the many vines matted around his back legs. I knew if I dismounted, I would be up to my chest in briers. So I grabbed the saddle horn with both hands, and kicked him hard. All he could do was lunge, like a bucking horse in slow motion. Eventually, he bucked his way out of the briers. There were bleeding scratches on his chest and legs, but there was plenty of rain to wash the blood away.

The cold and wet began to take its toll. Whenever I raised my right leg to get in or out of the saddle, the muscles in the back of the leg would cramp. Our teeth were chattering. The thick brush we had fought through all afternoon had shredded my sleeping bag, which was tied on top of the packhorse. A canteen was missing, and so was our frying pan and bow saw.

When dark finally came, the mixed rain and snow was still coming down. We thought we were past the thickest brush and that the travel would be fairly easy down the remainder of the canyon, though we figured we were still a good forty miles from my truck and trailer.

As we unpacked the horses and began to make camp, I realized my sleeping bag was not only torn, but also soaked to the core. Jeff's was in a little better condition. My muscles were cramping, my teeth were chattering, and it was still raining. We needed a fire in the worst way, and all the wood around us had been rained on steadily for several days.

We were at the edge of a big thicket of oak brush, which burns hot once it is started, but it has rough bark, which makes it better than other woods for soaking up rainwater.

As we were gathering sticks for our fire, I remembered the plastic containers of gasoline I had picked up at the drill hole. They were still in the bottom of one of the panniers. We stacked up a pile of oak logs and soaked them with a quart of gas, emptying one of the containers. When I lit it, the poof of flame burned my eyebrows off, and I could smell singed hair. The fire was bright and big. It lasted about five seconds and went out. The wood was simply too wet.

Using the same wood we tried again, this time with about a cup of gas to get it started. This time it burned about ten seconds before going out. We figured the wood must be getting warmer and dryer. Another cup of gas got us about twenty seconds, then about a minute. Only one cup of gas remained, and we still didn't have a fire. It was dark now, and more snow was mixed with the falling rain.

I don't know who suggested it, but we knelt down, facing each other, and offered a very sincere prayer, explaining our problem and our desperate need for a fire. Then we poured on the last of the gas and set it on fire. This time the fire kept going, and we piled on more wood, which would steam for a while and then start to burn. We were humble and grateful that our prayer had been answered. After awhile I wadded up the soggy remains of my sleeping bag and threw it on the fire, remembering that Seth had given us his sleeping bag to carry out. His was deeper in the pack and not damaged and soaked like mine. After roasting some meat over the fire, we spent a peaceful night, taking turns keeping the fire going. During the night we started seeing stars. The storm clouds were finally breaking up.

The next day as we headed down Flat Nose George Canyon, I realized that the horses were as tired as we were. My saddle horse, Dan, kept trying to go to the right, when I could see no reason to do it, like a car with a flat tire on the right side. A little while later, when I was leading the way across a stretch of flat sand, he suddenly sank in, almost to his belly. Due to the severity of the storm, a lot of water had gone down the canyon the day before and left behind some soft spots. Now I knew why Dan wanted to veer right away from the sandy bottom. He knew something I didn't, that the sandy flat part of the wash wasn't as solid as it seemed. I should have sensed that, when he was trying to veer to the right. We were more careful after that.

One time he started limping severely. When I checked his foot, there was a sharp rock wedged between the frog and the shoe. I was able to pry it out with my hunting knife, and then he was fine.

Thunder, my old bay horse, was carrying our camp outfit and some of the meat. The rest of the meat was on Seth's horse, the one he left behind for us to tend. We didn't know his name. Seth bought him just before the hunt and probably hadn't given him a name. He seemed a little hot-blooded and was afraid of things that didn't bother the other horses. I figured his inexperience was the problem and was glad he seemed to be getting a little better each day, until we got on the narrow trail winding along the edge of some cliffs in lower Flat Nose.

The trail was about a foot wide and was on the very edge of a rock formation that formed a cliff with a sixty- or seventy-foot drop, straight down to a rocky shelf. The other side of the trail merged into a steep side hill covered with loose rock and gravel.

As we were moving very carefully along this dangerous trail, knowing that stopping was probably the worst thing we could do to make our predicament more dangerous, Seth's no-name horse decided to look over the edge, maybe to see where he would land in the event he slipped off. The sight so frightened him that he made a ninety-degree turn to the right and tried to scramble up the bank away from the cliff edge. The hill was too steep and the footing too loose for him to succeed. He began to slide back down toward the narrow trail. It appeared that if his downward slide continued, he would go off the edge. There was nothing Jeff and I could do but stand and watch, and hope he didn't take our horses and us with him.

No Name apparently decided he did not want to meet his doom in reverse, so he spun around to face his doom head-on. The turning seemed to speed up his progress toward the edge. Just as his front feet hit the trail, only inches from the open space beyond the edge of the cliff, he did a ninety-degree turn to the right. He did it so fast that half his rear end went over the open space. I remember seeing his outside hind leg kicking at the empty air in a futile effort to get a foothold. The fact that he didn't go over the edge seemed to defy the laws of physics. But he stayed on the trail and was a very obedient and careful horse after that. We were grateful his fall hadn't converted my elk meat into burger. Then, like the Indians of old, we gave him a new name, one we felt suited his behavior and temperament. We named him Kamikaze after the Japanese suicide pilots in World War II.

When we arrived at the Green River, we figured we were still about fifteen miles from the truck. It was night and time to camp, but Jeff was worried about his unexcused absence from teaching school. Of course, we both wanted to get home as soon as possible, but he was the one who volunteered to ride ahead through the night and bring the truck and trailer as far up the road as possible to save us time the next day. So off he went, leaving me and my horses by the river, roasting strips of elk meat over a little fire. I found out later that his little mare, Tampico, was so upset at having to set off on her own without the company of the other horses that she shied at every rock and bush along the road, which forced Jeff to walk instead of ride.

Seth was waiting at the trucks and trailers. I met them on the road the next morning, and our great adventure came to an end. When we arrived home, several days later than anticipated, Jeff's wife said she had called Search and Rescue, but when they found out who was missing and where we had gone, they told her if we were not home by the end of the week to call again.

When the deer hunting season arrived a few weeks later, Jeff went back and bagged the monster buck. At that time, Sunset Sports was still holding a big buck contest, giving away a new Ford Bronco each season to the person who brought in the biggest buck. Jeff took his buck over and let them measure it for the contest. Sunset awarded the Bronco to Jeff, one of the last ones they gave away, because Wildlife Resources decided such contests gave incentive to poachers to take illegal bucks, and they were probably right.

Jeff and I never went hunting together again. We did go on one more scouting trip, however. One August afternoon we were climbing a steep, west facing slope so we could peek into a basin where we thought a buck or two might be hanging out. The temperature was about ninety degrees; the sun was shining on us, and the mountain became so steep that we started losing our footing. We'd take three or four steps forward and slide back two or three. Our sweaty faces were covered with dirt. It wasn't much fun. At times like this you begin to wonder if what you are doing is worth so much effort and misery.

At one of those discouraging moments, after we had slid downhill a few feet again and were catching our breath, Jeff looked at me like he was Moses on Mt. Sinai and said,

"If you don't do it, pretty soon you can't."

Over the years, as I have gotten older, that statement has stuck with me, becoming kind of a motto as I look at other men my age who quit hunting and roping and doing any of the hard outdoor physical things that I think are so enriching to life. It seems the men and women who quit are soon unable to do those things anymore. As I continue vigorous outdoor activity into my sixties, I find that I get more tired, move slower, and need more time to recover, but I can still do it. When a colt bucks me off, it doesn't hurt any worse than when I was young. It just takes longer to get up and a lot longer for the aches and pains to go away.

Several years later, Russell and I were hunting the Wyoming Range between Afton and Big Piney, Wyoming, not far from South Pass, the sagebrush flat where early pioneers crossed the Continental Divide and started heading downhill toward the Pacific Ocean on their way to Utah, California, and Oregon. During a summer scouting trip, we had located a monster buck in one of the highest basins above the Gray's River. Now we were coming back to get him.

As we approached the basin from the east, before daylight on the first morning of the hunt, we heard what sounded like men talking on walkie-talkies. When we arrived at the head of the basin where we had seen the buck, four or five other hunters, the ones with the walkie-talkies, were spreading out through the loose rock on top of the ridge, their boots making crunching noises while they continued talking. Russell and I figured they were making more noise than a herd of elephants. Then we could hear talking and breaking limbs below us as another group of hunters were coming from the Gray's River up the bottom of the basin. We were so disappointed. By now the desired trophy would be miles away. We sat down on the edge of the rim and waited for daylight.

Finally, we walked back to camp, saddled the horses, and loaded the pack mule. On our maps we had located a spot that was many miles from our present location. The new location seemed remote, with no pack or jeep trails leading in or out. We had never been there, so there was a lot of uncertainty as we headed in that direction.

It took all day to get there, and with the weather being unseasonably warm, we consumed a lot of water and Gatorade during our afternoon ride, and a lot more as we climbed the steep mountainside, well above timberline, to our desired campsite in some wind-twisted brush.

There was still some daylight remaining, so we hurried to the top of the nearest ridge and started glassing. We were relieved to find no sign of other hunters; no camps, no horses tied to trees, and no orange shirts. Then we started seeing bucks leaving their afternoon beds for the evening feed; one here, three there, two on a far ridge.

Russell hurried down the hill to get closer. I stayed up high and continued to glass. Looking through my binoculars, I slowly moved my eyes from ridge to hillside and back again. Every few minutes I'd try to find Russell. The last time he looked back at me, I pointed to the biggest buck I had seen. Russell was working along the edge of a rugged ridge and could see a lot of country I couldn't see. He didn't go where I was pointing, so I figured he had seen a deer he thought might be bigger than the one I was pointing at.

It was almost dark when I heard the two shots. I hadn't seen Russell for some time. I knew that if he had killed a deer, by the time he dressed it out and returned, it would be a long time—at least several hours. I hunkered down and waited.

When he finally reached the top of the hill where I was waiting, I could see and smell the blood on his hands. He had been successful. In fact, he said he had killed his biggest buck ever. We hurried back to camp and gulped down several bottles of water.

The next morning, when we finished off the last packet of Capri Sun, we were still thirsty, and there was nothing else to drink. Russell had dressed out the buck in the bottom of a deep canyon where it would be difficult to take the horses, so we decided to put on our back packs and walk. We figured there would be a spring where we could drink, in the bottom of such a deep canyon. The sun came up, the beginning of another warm day. We were not wearing our coats.

While Russell was skinning the deer and filling our packs with meat, I searched for water around the bottom of the deep canyon. I found an elk wallow, but no spring. The water in the wallow was brown, with patches of green moss scum. Plenty of little brown balls of elk feces were floating in it. When I looked closely at the surface of the water, I could see little wiggly things moving about. I filled a Gatorade bottle with the ugly brown stuff and headed back to Russell, where I built a little fire and tried to boil some of the disgusting water in an old can left behind by a sheepherder. After boiling the water for a while, the only difference I could see was that the live wiggly things had changed to dead wiggly things, plus some ashes from the fire had found their way into the can. The taste was disgusting and nauseating, and we couldn't drink it.

After the deer meat was safely packed away and the cape and antlers were removed from the carcass, we settled under the shade of a nearby tree to discuss our alternatives. Russell said his body was shutting down, a result of dehydration. He didn't have the strength to climb up the steep canyon walls carrying a pack full of meat. I felt the same. We figured the elevation difference between our location and where the horses were tied was several thousand feet, and the daytime temperature was now in the eighties—very unusual for Wyoming this time of year.

We finally decided there was only one thing to do. We had to drink the wallow water to curb the dehydration process. If we contracted giardia or any other bacteria-related sickness, there were medications physicians could prescribe to clear up such sicknesses.

We headed down to the wallow, each of us with a one-liter empty Gatorade bottle in hand. Before drinking, Russell rummaged through the pockets in is pack and finally pulled out a disposable camera. The plan was to take pictures of each of us drinking the brown muck. If we were poisoned and died on the way back to the truck, our loved ones would discover what had killed us when they developed the film.

I tiptoed along a partially submerged log to the middle of the wallow where the water was less brown, filled my plastic bottle, and started drinking while Russell took a few pictures. Then he went out to the same spot where I took photos of him drinking.

When we put on our packs to begin the hike back to the horses, I asked him how he felt. He said he felt fine. I felt fine too.

We hadn't gone very far, working uphill away from the wallow, when Russell spotted a large boulder off to our left that had some green moss on it. He wanted to check it for water. I said I had been over there earlier while I was scouting for water, and that the ground in front of the boulder was dry. He wanted to check it again.

When he scraped out a little basin in front of the boulder, the ground was quite moist just a few inches down. Russell then scraped some moss off the face of the boulder, and almost immediately, little clear drops of water began dripping into the newly made basin at the base of the rock. In half an hour, enough water had accumulated to fill the cap of one of his water bottles. Nothing had ever tasted so good, and in the warm afternoon air we were surprised that the water tasted freezing cold. We made the basin a little larger and scraped away more moss. In fifteen minutes we enjoyed another capful of water, and then another. After about two hours our thirst was quenched. We hiked back to camp, saddled the horses, loaded the mule, and headed back to the truck.

About every fifteen minutes, while driving back to Utah, I'd ask Russell how he felt. He'd say he felt fine. Then he'd ask how I felt. Fine too.

CHAPTER XX

Energy and persistence conquer all things.

—BENJAMIN FRANKLIN

In 1986, I left the *Utah County Journal*, or I should say they fired me. I came in one morning and was asked to go up to Don Oldham's office, where he told me his mother felt that I should not work for them anymore. Don said his mother's inspirations had guided the company through many important business decisions, and he wasn't about to ignore her inspiration now. This whole thing surprised me. I thought I was doing an excellent job. I knew many thousands of people were reading the paper, but maybe the Oldhams didn't like the controversy and investigative reports. They wanted to print only the good news and maybe thought they needed someone else to do that. They gave back the rights to my best-selling *Storm Testament* books and sold me the remaining inventory. Their printing and computer business continued to do well from what I heard, but the *Journal* eventually died, perhaps because readers became weary of reading only good news.

Storm Testament V was the last of my stories serialized in the *Journal*. My next three books were biographical novels on Porter Rockwell, Ute Chief Walkara, and Butch Cassidy.

When my *Rockwell* book came out, I started getting calls and letters from Mormon women scolding me for using the Lord's name in vain in my story. They had read the part where Porter Rockwell rode his weary horse through the streets of Nauvoo early in the morning following the night Joseph and Hyrum Smith had been murdered at Carthage jail. As his horse trotted along, Rockwell was yelling loud enough for all to hear,

> Joseph [Smith] is killed—they have killed him! God damn them! They have killed him![1]

My callers couldn't believe that a writer of Mormon fiction could use such words in a book. After a couple of such calls I had a good answer worked out, if they would listen. Most would not.

I explained that I wrote historical fiction; that as I fictionalized and dramatized historical events, I tried very hard never to change known facts. Rockwell's words that morning were a matter of public record. The same words I put in his mouth were found in two places in the *Documentary History of the Church*. I didn't feel at liberty to change the truth, and I thought my readers deserved to hear what he actually said that morning. I wasn't about to have him say shucks or darn when I knew for sure he said something else.

Furthermore, Rockwell was not using the Lord's name in vain. He was not swearing. He really, and very sincerely, wanted God to damn the people who killed Joseph and Hyrum. He wanted God to damn the murderers straight to Hell. So that's what he said. I commend him for saying it, and I commend Willard Richards for writing it down in the official documentary history. I'm not aware of anyone ever contacting the Church and demanding it cease publishing Rockwell's words in its history, but those same people continue calling and getting after me, even fifteen years after my book was published.

Shortly after the Cassidy book came out, I received a call from the librarian at the Utah State Prison at Draper. He said Lee Nelson and Louis L'Amour were the two most-read authors in the Utah prison system, and since Louis had recently died, I was now the most-read living author in Utah prisons. He wanted to know if I would come up to Draper and speak to the inmates. I said I would.

Bobby was planning a career in law enforcement, so he went with me. After passing through several checkpoints where they took our wallets and pocketknives, we were ushered into a large hall. We took our seats as about three hundred inmates were ushered into the room. They were quiet and respectful, not like the typical junior high school assembly crowd.

As I looked around, waiting for the meeting to begin, I noticed there were no guards. I asked the librarian about this. He said not to worry. I asked if these were low-security inmates. He assured me there were some murderers and armed robbers in the audience.

When I got up to speak, I decided to warm up the audience with some humor, so I said, "It's a real pleasure for the first time in my life to be speaking to a truly captive audience."

I was the only one laughing at my joke. The inmates booed. I suppose they had heard that pun too many times before. It was nothing original or clever for this audience. Hoping to redeem myself, I then said, "Actually I feel quite at home here tonight, having spent the last five years of my life researching and writing about killers, horse thieves, and bank robbers."

They cheered. I was their hero. I talked for an hour and a half, and they didn't want me to stop. I have never spoken to a warmer, kinder, or more respectful audience. I still get asked to speak to prison groups from time to time.

NOTE

1. Harold Schindler, *Orrin Porter Rockwell: Man of God/Son of Thunder* (Salt Lake City: University of Utah Press, 1983), 142; see also Anson Call, "Life and Record" (Salt Lake City: Utah State Historical Society), 27.

Chapter XXI

The heights by great men reached and kept were not obtained by sudden flight, but they while their companions slept were toiling upward through the night.

—Henry Wadsworth Longfellow
US poet (1807–1882)

One fall, Ben Gardner and I were coming home from a deer hunt in Idaho's Salmon River country, one of those endurance trips where it had snowed on us about a foot every single night. As we were traveling down I-15 through Salt Lake City, I asked Ben a question. "What would happen if we rented the Salt Palace (at that time the largest convention facility in SLC) and put about three hundred monster bucks on display, like state records, Boone and Crockett record animals—that kind of thing. How many people would pay five bucks to look at them?" I didn't really have a purpose behind asking the question. I just knew there were a lot of deer hunters like us who liked to look at big bucks. I don't remember exactly how Ben responded, other than he seemed kind of excited about the idea.

He called me the next morning and told me it would cost twelve thousand dollars to rent the Salt Palace for one weekend. He had called the scheduling people. Ben called me again that afternoon informing me that we could sell 10 x 10 exhibit spaces to businesses who wanted to sell products to deer hunters for about four hundred dollars per space.

He called me again the next day to say he knew where he could get a list of vendors who paid to exhibit products at hunting and fishing shows. He called a little later to inform me he had located the world's greatest deer hunter, Kirt Darner, who had ten or twelve bucks in the *Boon and Crockett Record Book*. We could get him to come to our show, bring a bunch of his record bucks, and give lectures on his hunting techniques. The next day Ben told me he had found a guy in Montana who had hundreds of record book mule deer, mounted heads, and that the fellow would bring them to our show. Ben had also located the world's biggest trophy mule deer somewhere in Texas. Maybe we could get its owner to bring it up.

Ben wouldn't leave me alone, so I figured it was time for me to do something too. I wrote copy for a radio ad that went something like this: "The most trophy mule deer ever assembled at one time in one place in the history of the world, including the world's biggest buck, lectures from the world's greatest deer hunter, and . . ."

We couldn't stop now. We each put up a thousand dollars and opened a checking account under the name Rocky Mountain Mule Deer Expo. We lined up the items mentioned in the ad so I could write a brochure, which we printed and sent to two thousand potential exhibitors. We scheduled three days at the Salt Palace for the following July. They didn't make us pay anything in advance.

The checks for exhibit spaces started pouring in. By July, about 350 vendors paid $400 each for exhibit spaces. If they displayed a monster buck in their booth, we discounted the price one dollar for each inch of width on the antler spread of their big buck. Between the exhibitors and the head collectors, we had about seven hundred trophy bucks scheduled for our show. The exhibit money paid for the Salt Palace rental.

Then we received a phone call that started us worrying. Ed Rice, who owned a business called International Sportsman's Expo, a producer of fishing and hunting shows in major metropolitan markets like San Francisco and Seattle, said he would fly to Salt Lake and buy us both steak dinners if we could get more than four thousand people to a hunting show in July. He said he had been doing these kinds of shows for twenty years and had learned through sad experience that the only time one could draw a crowd was during the cabin fever months, January, February, and March, the months when hunters and fishermen didn't go into the mountains. July simply wouldn't work. Deer hunters wouldn't come, because they wanted to be in the mountains scouting for their next big buck. Insisting he was our mentor, he urged us to reschedule to a January through March date.

There was too much water under the bridge. Exhibitors had given us their money, and we had paid the Salt Palace. We hoped Mr. Rice was wrong, but we had never done this before. He had done it lots of times. We should have found a mentor like him before we started, to point out the land mines, but now it was too late. We plunged ahead.

We designed a coupon that looked like a dollar bill—a big buck in the middle instead of George Washington. Anybody with the coupon would receive a dollar off on an admission ticket. All the details of the show were printed on it. We printed a couple hundred thousand coupons and hired our children—at least those old enough to drive—to put a stack of them in every gas station from Reno to Grand Junction and from Boise to Flagstaff. Friday after school, we'd give the boys our credit cards and away they would go.

My initial question, the one I asked Ben on the way home from our hunt in Idaho, was finally answered. Twenty-two thousand people paid five dollars to enter our show. In addition to the exhibits, there were lectures and seminars and a wildlife benefit auction, where we auctioned off products donated by the exhibitors, with all proceeds going to mule deer benefit projects—building guzzlers in areas where water was scarce, seeding winter range, and even offering reward money for people turning in hunters guilty of poaching. We had taken in six thousand of the dollar-off coupons. The boys had done a good job getting them everywhere.

When the dust finally settled, after we had counted the gate, paid all the bills, and given all the auction money to wildlife causes, there was sixty thousand left over, which Ben and I divided between us. Not bad for three days' work. In actuality, it was a lot more than three days. We tried to be quiet about the money we made, but guys started calling us, criticizing us for cashing in on wildlife. We shrugged our shoulders and decided to do it again. In the meantime,

Ed Rice flew to Salt Lake and bought us steak dinners.

In an effort to learn as much as possible about this new business, I had flown up to Seattle that spring to attend one of the Ed Rice shows. His main competitor, a group called Torro, was holding another hunting and fishing show that same weekend, also in Seattle. They were butting heads and trying to put each other out of business. I arrived the day it all started. When I found Ed, he showed me a beautiful hardwood coffin with a bunch of roses on it that had just arrived at his office, compliments of Torro, a not-so-subtle hint that they intended to bury him. I didn't think Ben and I wanted to butt heads with these guys.

The second year we offered a monthly newsletter, held a bigger auction, raised the price one hundred dollars for each exhibit space, and had television advertising in addition to the coupons, billboards, and radio. Only eighteen thousand came this time, but they paid ten dollars at the gate instead of five. When it was all over, we each took home forty thousand dollars, plus the auction funded some more wildlife projects.

Of course, I was the one who got to write the newsletter each month. I remember Ben and I staying up most of the night at a hotel room in Reno, scribbling down notes for what we called The Deer Hunter's Manifesto, an article we published in our newsletter. We told wildlife officials that Utah deer hunters were sick and tired of being part of an orange-shirted mob, a hundred eighty thousand strong, marching into the woods on the third Saturday in October, the opening of the annual deer hunt, with little hope of ever seeing anything bigger than a forked horn or a two point. It was time to manage hunting pressure and game animals for a quality hunting experience. If the number of hunters had to be cut back to thirty or forty thousand a year, so be it. Utah used to be full of big, mature bucks, and hunters wanted that quality again. The article listed all the things that needed to be done to have quality hunting in Utah. Officials didn't seem very excited about our criticism, but in a few years, they adopted every one of our suggestions. Now the entire state is on a draw with about sixty thousand hunters in the field instead of the hundred eighty thousand they had when we wrote the article.

In another issue, we reported efforts by the Boone and Crockett organization to remove all of Kirt Darner's animals from the record book. I called them, and they told me they had evidence that Darner hadn't killed the bucks he had entered in the book. After interviewing Kirt, we published an article presenting both sides of the issue. Kirt called, accusing me of ruining his guide business. He said the article cost him a hundred thousand in guide fees. At first I felt bad, but later, when Colorado wildlife officials arrested him for about forty wildlife violations, I felt vindicated.

We didn't do another deer show. We felt that in order to be successful, the Expo needed to go on the road. Not in major metropolitan areas where there were already lots of sports shows and very few deer hunters, but in medium-sized cities in deer hunting areas like Grand Junction, Flagstaff, Boise, Billings, and Spokane—the middle markets where people don't see the big hunting shows.

The main problem was that Ben and I didn't want to take it on the road. He had a thriving dental practice, and my writing career was prospering too. The Deer Expo required too much time, and taking it out of state would be even more demanding. We decided to sell it, and it wasn't long until we found three guys associated with the Salt Palace and Utah Jazz who wanted to buy it. They knew how much money we had collected at the gate. They gave us a sizeable down payment, agreeing to pay the balance over several years, hoping it would come from show proceeds. We decided to take their money and go hunting.

To our surprise and horror, the new owners decided to take the Expo to Las Vegas. We tried to explain to them that there were hardly any deer hunters in Las Vegas and they couldn't get a crowd. They said their exhibitors wanted Vegas, so that's what they had to do.

The dollar-off coupons had brought six thousand people to our show each year, but they didn't even bother to print coupons. They were professional marketing and advertising guys who believed they could run circles around the writer and dentist from Mapleton, so they showed no interest in our counsel.

The Las Vegas deer show was a total flop, so they tried to do it the next year in Salt Lake as we had done. Again no coupons, and again they flopped, with attendance about 20 percent of what ours had been.

Then they dropped a lawsuit on us, claiming we had sold them a bill of goods, that the deer show wasn't what we claimed it to be, and that they were not going to pay the rest of the money owed.

We hired attorney David Nelson to respond to their suit against us. David was moving ahead with all the normal questions lawyers ask to earn their fees, when Ben and I got to thinking that these guys might have a tender spot. Two of them worked for Larry Miller's Utah Jazz organization. They loved their jobs. They had used their Jazz offices and positions to buy ads on credit, and some of those creditors had not been paid. So Ben and I came up with a bunch of questions concerning our buyers' relationship with Jazz owner Larry Miller. We asked for copies of their employment contracts, a list of unpaid advertising bills, whether or not Larry Miller knew they were using their Jazz positions and offices to conduct a Mule Deer Expo business. We even asked for Larry Miller's address and the name of his attorney. We told the lawyer we wanted about twenty questions containing Larry Miller's name.

When David presented them with the list of questions, the nature of the suit suddenly changed. They wanted to meet with us immediately to settle the dispute. Ben had a bunch of appointments that day, so he stayed in Springville. I told the opposition he didn't want to come, that Ben hoped we wouldn't settle so we could go to court to meet Larry Miller and call him to the witness stand.

Before we went into the meeting, David advised me to stand firm on what they owed us. David said all the signals from these guys indicated that they were wetting their pants and would pay the full amount owed. We did not need to negotiate anything. He was right. They dropped their suit. We agreed not to counter sue, and they gave us a cashier's check for all the money owed.

Ben and I added up what we had made at the two shows and how much we had sold the business for. We decided we could go hunting anywhere we wanted for the rest of our lives and would never be able to spend what the Rocky Mountain Mule Deer Expo had earned.

CHAPTER XXII

The yearnings of the heart assure us that miracles are possible, but natural law does not show us how to accomplish them. It is for us to uncover the spiritual keys which bring them to pass.

—LEE NELSON

By this time in my writing career, I was doing a lot of middle school and junior high school assemblies. I could always get a good laugh by telling the students about the time I woke up in the middle of the night with a great idea for a new book. I was very excited and decided I would start on the book the next morning. It was dark in my bedroom, and something told me I should write down the title of the book so I wouldn't forget, but I knew there was no way I could forget something so exciting. I had read a magazine article not long before, which claimed that many of our best ideas come in our sleep, and that we should keep a notepad and pen by the bed so we can avoid forgetting these good ideas by writing them down as soon as we wake up.

There was a notepad and pen on the little table by the bed, so without turning on the light, I scribbled down the name of the new book. With a big smile on my face, I went back to sleep.

The next morning as I started to get out of bed, I suddenly

remembered that I had had a great idea for a book during the night, but I couldn't remember what it was. I remembered thinking that I could never forget something so important, and yet I had forgotten it.

Then I remembered writing down the title on the notepad. It had been dark at the time, so my writing wasn't very easy to read, but as I studied the notepad, the words comprising the title of the book were very clear—*Tarzan goes to the Temple.*

I couldn't believe I had actually written down something that stupid. What scared me a little was knowing that in the middle of the night I had actually believed this was a great subject for a book. Sometimes when I was giving speeches I would tell this story to get a hearty laugh from the audience.

Then one day I was reading *The Seven Spiritual Laws of Success* by Deepak Chopra, an Indian doctor-philosopher, in which he said one should never ignore powerful dreams, the kind that wake us up with a jolt, or the kind that keep repeating themselves. Chopra believes that it is through these powerful dreams that the subconscious mind, even the combined intelligence of the universe—or God—tries to communicate, perhaps symbolically, with our conscious selves.

Chopra's words got me thinking and wondering about my *Tarzan Goes to the Temple* idea. I had read some of the Tarzan books to my older boys. Tarzan was the story of an English boy—a baby—whose parents died in a cabin on the West African coast. Female apes gathered up the abandoned baby, carried him to their home in the jungle, and raised him with the apes. I had never been to Africa at the time, and I didn't want to write another Tarzan story, plus I didn't know how the temple theme would fit in.

Then one day I was thumbing through a longtime file I had maintained that consisted of clippings and booklets about Old Ephraim, the huge and well-known grizzly bear that had been killed in Utah's Cache Mountains in the 1920s. Every good writer I know keeps files—lots of files on subjects to possibly write about some day. And because all good writers read a lot, there always seems to be a lot of things to file away.

As I was going through my Ephraim file, the idea came to me that I could write a Tarzan story about a boy being raised with the grizzly bears in the Utah mountains. Maybe that is what the dream was trying to tell me. As I continued to go through the file, I noticed a reference to Temple Mountain, Temple Spring, and Temple Fork. Temple Fork was a smaller canyon off Logan Canyon where the early Mormon pioneers had built a sawmill to produce lumber when they were building the Logan Temple. Therefore many of the landmarks in the area carried the temple name. These were the places where the famous bear had roamed. Finally, my *Tarzan goes to the Temple* dream made sense. I decided to write a Tarzan-like story, with a boy being raised by the grizzly bears in a setting near Temple Mountain. When I finally finished, it was called *The Ephraim Chronicles*. A lot of people enjoyed the story, especially middle-grade school children who bought about ten thousand books. It never became a bestseller like my dream indicated.

CHAPTER XXIII

Once we truly know that life is difficult then it is no longer difficult. Because once it is accepted, the fact that life is difficult no longer matters.

—M. Scott Peck

When my Cassidy story was getting ready to go to press for a second printing, probably because I was getting so many letters from teenage boys who were reading my books, I typed up an announcement to go on the back of the new book, inviting fans to come and ride the Outlaw Trail with me. I described a week-long trip that included daily horseback rides into wilderness backcountry once frequented by the Indians and outlaws in my books. The trip included Dutch oven dinners and storytelling around the campfire at night, with me telling about my books and research projects. The rides would take place only in the spring—the best time to visit the desert wilderness areas in my books.

The letters started pouring in, allowing me to put together seven weeks of trail rides that first season. I tried to limit the number of people in each group to about ten. I gave people a discount if they brought their own horse or if they were under eighteen years of age.

No dogs or stallions. I lined up some extra horses and hired Carla Randolph, a cook, and Ann Dancliff, a wrangler. The next season Bryce Clayton replaced Ann to become my wrangler for many years.

About half the people came from Utah and Idaho, but there were also guests from Oregon, California, Chicago, and even Texas. Ages ranged from eight to eighty-two. That first year, six people fell off their horses, two had runaways, four horses floundered in quicksand, and one woman got splattered with the contents of an exploding Porta Potty.

About halfway through the first season, I bought the potty to keep in one of the trailers, because some of the women were nervous about wandering off in the bushes and rocks to find private places to relieve themselves. Female guests sometimes wanted to know if there were cougars and bears that might present a danger if they wandered too far, so I bought the Porta Potty for their benefit.

The very first trip we used it, a little thing called the pressure relief valve got stuck. When a woman from Arizona pulled the trigger to make it flush, the contents of the holding tank exploded upward. I didn't know things like that happened with portable toilets, but I knew something was seriously wrong when she started screaming. When she finally stepped from the trailer there were brown stains everywhere, even on her brand new Stetson. Fortunately, we were camped by a stream—the Muddy River. She and her friend disappeared into the willows, returning an hour or two later spotlessly clean. The potty didn't get used much after that.

From this camping location, we'd ride up the Muddy River, see some amazing geological formations, and cross the river about a dozen times, which was exciting for the riders and good experience for the horses. After about five miles of this, we'd work our way up onto the benches above the river, where we'd find mustangs. Those who wanted could take pictures. Then we'd take a refreshment break at a place where lots of Indians used to camp, a sandy place with abundant shelter among white slick rock formations. There were literally piles of flint chips and some pottery shards left behind by primitive peoples.

I'd give a little lecture about how exciting it is to find a piece of pottery or a broken spearhead at the exact spot where an Indian lost or discarded it. But if you took any of these things home, perhaps placing them in a dish on a fireplace mantle, much of the former magic is lost. A spouse might think the dish contains merely clutter to be thrown out with the trash. Besides, taking artifacts home is against the law. A BLM officer might stop us on the way out and ask you to empty your pockets. If you have artifacts, even broken ones, he will arrest you. You'll have to go before a judge, and then there might be an article in the newspaper about how they arrested you to prevent you from selling priceless artifacts on the black market. "So please, leave the artifacts where you find them."

One year as we were getting ready to go on this ride, a man who had been with us the year before nodded for me to come over to his horse. He showed me a can containing pottery shards and some broken arrow and spear points, items he had picked up the year before. He said I was right—the items didn't seem nearly as precious when he looked at them at home. He said he felt so bad about what he had done that he arranged to come on another ride so he could return them. He hoped we would ride to the same place so he could do that. I told him we would. Later in the day, I watched from a distance as he sauntered around, dropping artifacts at the appropriate places.

At that same camping spot on the Muddy, on a hot June afternoon a few years later, a bunch of us rode into camp after a long and thirsty ride. That morning we had ridden up the Muddy River and onto the Perry Miller benches where we saw a band of mustangs. We followed them around an hour or two and then spent the middle part of the day looking for artifacts, mainly arrow and broken spear points. We had stayed longer than we should have in such hot weather, so as we approached camp, from the benches where there was no water for the thirsty horses, everyone was hot and very thirsty.

As we approached camp, I stopped my horse and asked everyone to come in close to hear what I wanted to say. I expressed the idea that the *natural* thing to do, upon reaching camp, is to jump off your horse and run to the cooler for a cold drink. But the *decent* thing to do is to unsaddle your horse first, let him roll, and take him down to the stream for a drink of cold water. Then, and only then, should you run to the cooler to fetch a cold drink for yourself. I explained that in my officer training in the Marine Corps it was an officer's duty to make sure his men were watered and fed before his own needs were met. Good horsemen behave the same way toward their horses.

No one chose to follow my advice or my example. While I was unsaddling my horse to let him roll, everyone else was crowded around the cooler. While they collapsed into folding chairs to guzzle down their drinks, I was by myself leading two horses through the willows and tamarisk to the stream.

As I led the thirsty horses out of the bushes onto the bank of the river, I forgot all about my negligent companions. About ten feet in front of me, standing in about a foot of water, was a naked woman who was not wearing a stitch of clothing. She had bright blue eyes and shoulder-length blond hair, which reminded me of Eve in the Garden of Eden. She was maybe twenty years old.

My first reaction was to turn and leave, but my thirsty horses were pulling me toward the water and the girl. Sensing my reluctance, she smiled. She was facing me and did not turn away, nor did she reach for her swimsuit, which was resting on some smooth stones behind her. I turned sideways, determined not to stare, and quietly asked her what she was doing here. She said she was with a group preparing to kayak down the Muddy River to where it became the Dirty Devil at Hanksville. I told her I was taking a group of people on a horseback adventure.

I was glad my horses were so thirsty. They just kept drinking and drinking. When they were finally finished, I wished her good luck on her river trip and said good-bye.

When I arrived back at camp, I tied up the horses, threw them some hay, and sauntered over to the cooler to find a drink. I told my friends how lucky I'd been for taking care of my horses first, and how sorry I was that they had not done the same. They tumbled out of their chairs, ran to their horses, and hurried down to the river. But it was too late. The girl with the blue eyes had slipped back into her swimming suit and climbed up the opposite bank to join her companions.

The week-long trips were too long. By Friday I couldn't get people on their horses. It seemed by then that everyone wanted to stay in camp and help the cook. I probably pushed some of the older people too hard. One year I made the trips three days long, but that was too short. People didn't get to know each other in such a short time, and we couldn't do enough riding to get comfortable with it. I ended up doing the Outlaw Trail rides in four days, Wednesday through Saturday. I did it every spring for about twenty years.

We usually began with a ride to the Butch Cassidy hideout on the Badland Benches above Nine Mile Canyon, or sometimes a shorter ride to the biggest Fremont ruin ever found, or the still-usable mustang trap and outlaw cabin on Flat Iron Mesa. Then we'd head over to the Little Grand Canyon on the San Rafael River, probably the most scenic horseback ride in Utah, and stop to see the dinosaur footprint on the way. Sometimes we'd ride the Jackass Benches or Cliff Dweller Flat and then head over to the Perry Miller Benches above the Muddy River to see mustangs.

One March, on a day that was cold and windy, we decided to ride through the Little Grand Canyon. We hauled the horses to the upstream end of the fifteen-mile canyon at a place called Fuller Bottom. The plan was to ride downstream to the corrals above what was called the Swinging Bridge at the mouth of Buckhorn Draw.

The group consisted of twenty-two riders from the Ogden area, more than I liked to have on a trip like this. As we were preparing to start, I told everyone there were pockets of quicksand in the river where your horse could sink to its belly real fast. Over the years I found that if I used the *quicksand* word to describe soft mud, people listened more carefully. I told them the only way to be sure to avoid it was to follow my mule through the river crossings. I had ridden this trail many times and knew where to cross. So to be safe, all they had to do was follow me. If they wanted to be more adventurous and find their own crossings, that was okay too, but they might get stuck in the mud. I warned them also of deep holes in the river where in a blink their horse could be in over its head and need to swim. Because the water was murky with the spring runoff, they wouldn't be able to see the deep holes, so the safe thing was to follow me when we crossed the river. Swift water indicated a hard bottom. Still water indicated a soft or deep bottom.

So with my little safety talk out of the way, down the river we headed, into the deep canyon, fenced in by sheer and majestic red, white, and brown thousand-foot cliffs on both sides. A cold wind was blowing, and all the coats and jackets were buttoned up tight.

At the very first crossing, after I had reached the far bank, I turned to see how my companions were handling the swift brown water, which was about two feet deep at the crossing. To my amazement, one of the women was holding onto the saddle horn with both hands as her horse turned away from the others and headed down the middle of the stream toward some very calm water that I guessed might be very deep.

Just as I started to yell at her to turn back, her horse disappeared from sight. The next thing I knew, the woman was trying to swim in her heavy, waterlogged coat. Almost before she knew it, the current carried her to the shallow end of the hole where she regained her footing and waded to shore. By this time her horse was on the bank too.

We were four or five miles from the trucks if we turned back, and ten miles from camp if we kept going. One of our riders was soaking wet. A cold March wind was blowing. Her teeth had already begun to chatter. No one had brought a dry change of clothing. In a matter of minutes this poor woman would be suffering from severe hypothermia. I had seen it before and knew the danger. She insisted she was fine, but I knew better.

I told the lady she would have to take off all her clothes, including her underwear, while we got a fire going. At first she protested, but I stood firm. Several of the other women led her behind some sagebrush, where they held up their slickers to give her some privacy as she stripped down. Then they bundled her up in their coats and slickers so she could wait out the drying process in relative modesty near the roaring fire.

I picked up a piece of dripping underwear, hung it on the end of stick, and pointed it toward the fire. The rest of the men did the same with other pieces of clothing. In an hour her clothes were dry, though very smoky. She put them back on, and we continued down the canyon. The woman smelled like a campfire the remainder of the trip. I liked to remind her from time to time that she smelled just like a real Indian.

One year I sponsored a writing contest involving ten middle and junior high schools. Students had to write essays or stories related in theme and content to my *Storm Testament* books which were in all the school libraries. The winner from each of the ten schools got to go on an Outlaw Trail ride with me. I picked three or four teachers from the schools to come along as wranglers and chaperones.

The week before the trip, one of the mothers called several times. She seemed terrified at the thought of sending her helpless little girl on a four-day horseback ride in the desert with a total stranger. Nothing I said made her feel better, so I invited her to come along. I said I didn't have a horse for her, but she could stay in camp, help the cook, and sleep with her daughter in the same tent at night.

The mother turned out to be a nice person, but not a happy camper. Swatting insects, breathing dust and smoke, smelling horse sweat, and sleeping on the ground didn't agree with her. When she asked me about restroom facilities, I pointed toward a nearby canyon, saying the restroom was anywhere she wanted it to be. After one night, the woman stopped worrying about her daughter, packed up, and headed home.

What she didn't know was that I was worried about her daughter too. I was worried about all the students. I was responsible for ten children who were not mine. Putting them on ten horses and turning them loose in a dangerous and rugged wilderness gave me plenty of things to worry about. I worried about the girl falling off her horse and hitting her head on a rock. I worried about her catching a foot in the stirrup and being dragged. I worried about trails along the edges of steep cliffs, rattlesnakes, and the three rivers we intended to cross that were filled with raging brown water from melting snow.

The worst thing that happened involved my daughter, Kristin, a fearless and experienced rider who was also a junior high school student. She came along to help with the horses and coach the students who didn't know how to ride. At our first campsite, her horse, Joe, somehow caught a hind foot in a long strand of barbed wire. When Kristin attempted to pick up the foot to remove the wire, the horse pulled away, spinning around, tangling his other feet and Kristin in the wire too. Then he tried to run away, dragging my daughter with him. Fortunately, we got the horse under control before any serious damage was done. Kristin ended up with some bloody lines across her arm and neck. She seemed pretty proud of those wounds, until the scabs dried up and went away. When students asked about the cuts on the horse's legs, I said I wasn't worried because they were a long way from the heart.

Some of my fondest memories of the Outlaw Trail rides involve my black mule, Ingersoll. I named him after a famous Butch Cassidy mule. We know about the mule from a letter Butch wrote to the owner of the Concordia Tin mine in the mountains above La Paz, Bolivia. Butch said he didn't come to a certain celebration because of a misunderstanding with Ingersoll, resulting in a broken jaw for the mule. That part of the letter showed Butch knew how to be forceful with animals. Then Butch explained how he had to spoon-feed mush into Ingersoll's mouth while the jaw was healing, because the mule couldn't graze with a broken jaw. This part of the letter showed how Butch could be compassionate to an animal. Butch ended the letter saying he would come to visit as soon as the jaw healed and Ingersoll could graze again.

Butch had switched from riding horses to mules not long after arriving in South America. A mule cannot run as fast as a horse but has a lot more stamina for long rides day after day. A mule is more sure-footed in rugged mountain country, and mules have harder feet, which don't need near as much care as horses' feet. A mule will live a lot longer than most horses. But a mule is also smarter than a horse, a condition that has its advantages and disadvantages. Old timers have told me you shouldn't own a mule unless you are smarter than the mule.

Ingersoll provided entertainment for my guests. One of my favorite things was to turn him loose immediately following the ride to the Butch Cassidy hideout at the head of Devil's Canyon. It is a long ride with little to drink along the way, so the horses are always thirsty when the ride is over.

We couldn't see it from camp, but the Nine Mile Canyon River was about a quarter mile away through some sagebrush and down a steep bank. As soon as I turned Ingersoll loose, he would head for the river lickety split, sometimes taking one or two horses with him. People would start yelling at me, "Lee, your mule is running away. Do you need help catching him?"

By this time the mule would be out of sight. In such wild and rugged country, I'm sure some of my guests were wondering if we would ever see him again.

"If he's not back in five minutes," I'd say, "we'll put together a search party."

In a few minutes we'd see Ingersoll coming back, usually at a full gallop.

What amazed me about this animal was his ability to remember things on the trail. One time we had a camera crew from Channel 4 tagging along, shooting some film for a story on the Outlaw Trail. We decided to take them to the hidden remains of an old cabin up

Chimney Canyon, a remote, rugged, and very scenic spot in lower Nine Mile Canyon. I hoped to show them the remains of a mustang trap not far from the cabin, made of juniper and pinyon trees and in nearly usable condition. It was likely a hundred years ago when horse thieves or cowboys last used it.

The trail up Chimney Canyon is difficult to follow because it hardly ever gets any use, and there's a fork or two where it is easy to go the wrong way if you are not familiar with the area. Bryce and I hadn't been up Chimney Canyon for several years, but we were certain we could find the way.

At a fork in the canyon it appeared the main trail continued straight ahead along what appeared to be the main part of the canyon, but Ingersoll was trying to turn right into a little side canyon that was blocked by a lot of brush and some fallen trees.

I stopped and asked Bryce if he thought we should continue in the main canyon. He said the main canyon did not look familiar to him, but he was absolutely sure the trail did not go up the brushy draw to our right. So I pulled Ingersoll's head around and made him go the way we had decided to go.

Fifteen minutes later there was no sign of a trail at all as we were pushing further and further into some steep and dangerous country. We finally had to admit that we had made a mistake. We worked our way back to the brush-filled draw where Ingersoll had wanted to turn right. Almost immediately, as we passed through the brush, we found ourselves on the main trail that took us to the old cabin.

People talk about dumb animals. Bryce and I, both college graduates, had been up Chimney Canyon to the old cabin at least twice. Ingersoll had been there once. The combined memory and intelligence of Bryce and me was no match for that of an ugly black mule.

A better example of the superiority of animal intelligence occurred on the slick rock Angel Trail, the route outlaws used to take from Hanksville to Robbers' Roost. Using one of the Michael Kelsey trail guides, we found the trail and scouted it out in March that year just before the trail rides began. It was spectacular, winding down some red slick-rock cliffs and looking a lot scarier than it actually was. It eventually crossed the Dirty Devil River at a beautiful spot with grassy meadows, sandy beaches, and Indian writings under the ledges. At one point coming up the trail, if the horses didn't learn to strike the front of their shod hooves against the smooth rock to make toe holds, they would slip and slide and rub the skin off their knees.

There were three or four older women in the first group that year, and when they saw how steep the trail was where it dropped off the sandy bench onto the slick rock cliffs, they said they were not going with us. They thought it was too dangerous to walk on the trail, but taking their horses would be certain suicide.

I tied Ingersoll's reins over his neck and then patted him on the rump, the signal for him to go ahead on his own. I told my two wranglers, Bryce and Wally, who had been with me on the scouting trip in March, to lead the way. I told them I was staying behind to help the women with their ponies. The women finally agreed to come, if I promised to stay with them and continue helping with their horses. Instead of riding, we were leading our horses along this steep and possibly dangerous portion of the trail.

We were moving along just fine when all of a sudden I noticed that the immediate surroundings were not familiar. I didn't remember the trail being this steep at this approximate location. It appeared we were going off the edge of a gently rounded cliff. The trail was getting steeper and steeper, and soon we would not be able to turn back. Wally and Bryce finally stopped, no longer sure which way to go. They yelled back at me, wanting me to tell them what to do.

I looked around. Ingersoll was no longer with the group, but off to the right, a hundred yards or so, standing by a little pile of rocks, looking back at us, as if wondering why we were not staying on the trial with him. I told Bryce and Wally to take everybody over by the mule, that that's where the trail was. Soon we were going the right way again. I was still in the rear with the three women.

It wasn't long until we were headed over another gentle sand rock cliff that was getting steeper and steeper and nothing looked familiar. Wally and Bryce stopped for a second time, once again not sure they were on the trail. Again, Ingersoll was not with the group, but off to the right, looking back at us and wondering why we insisted on going the wrong way. That's when I gathered everyone around, telling them that if they wanted to reach the bottom of the canyon in safety, they should follow the mule and not the men, so that's what we did. Ingersoll, his reins tied over his neck, led the group down the Angel Trail to the Dirty Devil River.

On another trip, Ingersoll exhibited a different kind of intelligence. Some friends and I had purchased 160 acres in Nine Mile Canyon, a spot centrally located to the Butch Cassidy hideout ride and Flat Iron Mesa. One year I invited the people who wanted to come on trail rides to come to the new ranch property and help us build trails and clear brush. Of course, there would be no charge, just lots of good food to accompany the hard work.

A group from Ogden brought a handicapped boy named Steve. He was about forty years old but acted and talked like a four-year-old. He had a big teddy bear, and he sucked his thumb. He loved the horses, and while the rest of us were setting up camp, he hung around the horses, petting one whenever he got the chance.

Our plan for the next day was to build a trail up the steep rocky ridge leading to the Chimney Canyon hideout and mustang trap. With this new trail in place, the ride up to the mustang trap and cabin could become an all-day scenic loop.

Steve's friends were concerned for his safety. They feared he wouldn't be able to stay on the steep trail and that he would fall. They didn't dare leave him behind by himself in camp either. Everyone wanted to work, so no one wanted to babysit Steve. When we headed up the mountain the next morning, we took Steve with us and agreed that we would take turns keeping a close eye on him.

I put the sawbuck saddle on Ingersoll that morning, along with the canvas panniers so he could carry the picks, shovels, sharpening tools, first aid kit, water, and lunches. As we worked our way to the steep part of the mountain, I noticed that Steve kept coming over by me so he could pet Ingersoll.

At a steep place in the trail I handed the brand new soft cotton lead rope to Steve, telling him to hold onto Ingersoll while I pushed a rock out of the trail. When I finished and looked around, Steve had lost his footing and was sliding off the trail. He wouldn't let go of the lead rope, however, and was trying to pull Ingersoll with him. The mule had other ideas. He wasn't about to step off the trail, no matter how hard Steve pulled on the rope. By hanging onto the lead rope, Steve was able to pull himself back to the trail. I commended him for his effort and informed him that his job for the rest of the day was to hold Ingersoll's lead rope. That's how he could help. I told him to never let go of the rope.

Three or four times Steve slipped and fell, and each time he was able to pull himself back to the trail using the lead rope. The reader should understand here that Ingersoll is a well-broken mule. I can lead him off ledges into rivers, through brush too thick to see where you are going, up and down ledges where horses refuse to go, and through places where people have to crawl. Ingersoll does all that. He goes where he is supposed to go. But he knew enough not to let Steve pull him off the trail. In addition to carrying all our stuff and tools, Ingersoll was the babysitter that day, and he did a mighty fine job of it.

One of the most memorable Outlaw Trail rides involved five or six old men from Moses Lake, Washington. They had been doing trips like this on their own for some time. They had their own mules, tents, and everything else they might need for such an adventure. Five of them were within a year or two of eighty, so I expressed concern about their ability to endure such an adventure. They assured me everything would be fine.

The oldest member of the group was Lloyd Jackson, who was eighty-two years old. He rode a white mule, one of the best mules I have ever met. To know he was good, all you had to do was stand in front of his face and look into his steady and kind eyes. I remember that a couple of days into the trip I tried to talk Lloyd out of the ride to the Butch Cassidy hideout. Lloyd had bad knees and hips, which made it necessary for us to help him on and off his mule. I told him about a portion of the trail in some very steep and dangerous country in lower Daddy Canyon where it was necessary to get off and lead your mount under a ledge or overhang. I didn't think he would be able to do this because the trail was so narrow, and a steep drop-off to the canyon bottom would make it very difficult for us to help him on and off the mule.

Lloyd let me say everything I wanted to say, and then he looked me straight in the eye and said the following:

> Lee, I am eighty-two years old. In a year or two they will put me in a rest home. If I die on this ride, I will do it with a smile. I'd rather die on a horseback adventure with my favorite author than waste away in a rest home with a gum-chewing teenager changing my diapers.

Lloyd went on every ride, confident in his white mule, no fear of cliffs or quicksand, and never complaining.

One of his buddies did complain, however. We were galloping across some sand dunes to intercept a band of mustangs when I noticed by the look on his face that something was terribly wrong. I stopped my mule and asked him what was the matter.

"I swallowed my false teeth," he said.

"Do we need to take you to a hospital?" I asked.

"I don't know."

A minute later he found his teeth in his coat pocket. He had put them there before the romp through the sand dunes.

Dusty and dirty, those five old guys went skinny-dipping in the San Rafael River one night. I'll never forget them, especially Lloyd Jackson on his white mule.

The potential for injury on the trail rides was huge. Every year people fell off their horses. One time, as ten of us mounted up for a single-file journey into the Little Grand Canyon, the last rider, an overweight middle-aged man, lost his balance while climbing into the saddle and fell off the far side of his horse. His foot caught in the stirrup on the near side, which left him hanging upside down, his head nearly touching the ground. The gentle disposition of his horse was the only thing that saved him from serious injury. Rather than buck or stampede, the old buckskin just plodded up the trail, following the horse in front.

The proud victim, not wanting the rest of us to see his awkward and embarrassing plight, refused to yell for help. Instead he kept whispering the name of the friend directly in front, hoping to quietly be helped out of his predicament. When the friend finally turned around, the rest of us saw him too, and everyone raced to the rescue. Fortunately, the old horse remained calm.

After ten years of trail rides, I let this sideline to my writing get smaller and smaller until I was usually taking only one or two groups a year. It was a lot of work, but lots of fun too, and I made many friends. It gave me an excuse to do lots of backcountry horseback riding.

CHAPTER XXIV

My posterity cannot fully benefit from the life I have lived unless I write it down. Likewise, I cannot fully understand the life I have lived unless I write it down.

—LEE NELSON

When I was doing research on the early cowboy life of Butch Cassidy, I joined the Hobble Creek Riding Club so I could learn to rope. Derk Palfreyman, Dean Bryan, and Jim Anderson were my mentors. The club kept some cattle at the city arena west of Springville where we roped two evenings a week.

I got the roping bug like a disease, and before I knew it, I had built my own arena at home. I bought ten roping steers and started roping four or five times a week. Jim and Derk weren't nearly as enthusiastic about it as I was, so I found a new partner, Brad Mangum. He lived in Mapleton too and was willing to come down nearly every night. He heeled, and I headed. It seemed our lives revolved around team roping, a hobby that continued long after I finished the Cassidy book.

One weekend we went to a jackpot-roping competition in Farmington, Utah. As Brad and I were paying our entry fees, I ran into Jan Price from McCammon, Idaho, the husband of my cousin, Karen. Jan had been roping for years and was a heeler, so we entered up. Jan and I caught all four steers and won over twelve hundred dollars. We were so excited that you'd think we'd won twelve million.

About this time Ben Gardner started calling me again. We didn't have a deer show to do anymore, so he thought we ought to find something else. I shudder when I remember borrowing over half a million dollars to make a down payment on a ranch on the Nevada-Utah border and stocking it with nearly four hundred cows that we trucked down from Wyoming. We turned them out on hundreds of square miles of desert wilderness with hardly any fences.

It was the Wild West, a desolate and remote land with rattlesnake dens, Indians who hated white men, cougars, eagles, cattle rustlers, bands of wild horses, and rebellious polygamist cults avoiding the law.

Our grazing area bordered the Hill Air Force Base bombing range, and the night sky often became like day as pilots trained and experimented with new armaments and explosives. On the other side of the Deep Creek Mountains was the land the Goshute Indians wanted to turn into the nation's nuclear waste dumping ground.

The closest rancher to the west was an Oklahoma Indian named Hank Vogler. He ran huge herds of sheep and about six hundred cows. One afternoon when I was helping him brand calves, he put his hand on my shoulder and warned me that this new place I had come to was still the Wild West. He said there were people who would steal my calves if I didn't brand them better. He told me that I should also cut their ears and attach ear tags and cut waddles, which are dangling strips of flesh on their necks. That fall when we rounded up our cattle, sixteen calves were missing. I believed they were rustled by a certain polygamist, but I couldn't prove it.

Three hired hands had worked for us, but the one that warrants mention here is Birdie Jolly from Baggs, Wyoming, who at the time was a divorced cowgirl with two little boys. When she came to us, her claim to fame was hauling an illegally rounded up band of mustangs to Texas and selling them on the open market without getting caught. A hundred years ago she would have been riding with Butch Cassidy's Wild Bunch. She liked a horse that would show some spunk and buck a little when you first mounted up on a cold morning. One day she told me that when she was a little girl she watched her father and brother get so mad at a horse that they stabbed it to death with a pitchfork.

One spring day when we were checking our cows for new calves, we found a cow with a swollen milk bag who had lost her calf. Not very far from her we found an orphan calf, all gaunted up from lack of milk, standing beside its dead mother, bawling.

I had been ranching long enough to know the mother with the swollen bag, the one who had lost her calf, would not let the orphan calf from the other cow drink her milk. She knew that it wasn't her baby, so she wouldn't let it nurse. All the little calves might look the same to someone from the city, but the mother cows knew their own, not so much from sight, but mostly from smell it seemed.

Birdie said she knew what to do. She pulled out her pocketknife and went to work skinning the dead calf. I helped as much as I could. While she was finishing, she had me fetch a few pieces of orange bailing twine. Once the skin was removed, she cut holes around the edges.

We then caught the live calf, the one whose mother had died, and tied the slippery, bloody skin from the dead calf over its back, hair side up. We drove the mother with the swollen bag into a corral by the ranch house and put the double-skinned calf in with her. When the calf tried to suck, the cow reached around and sniffed the tied-on skin from her dead calf. Recognizing her dead baby's scent, she relaxed and let down her milk for the orphan so it could finally have some breakfast. We left the cow and calf in the pen for about a week to make sure the bonding was complete before we removed the skin and turned them out on the open range.

One day Birdie and Bryce Clayton accompanied me to Ibapah to look for some cows that had strayed onto Indian land from a section of summer range we had high in the Deep Creek Mountains.

We stopped for fuel at the only store in Ibapah. It was a bunkhouse-like structure behind a ranch house. A Budweiser truck stopped in front of the building. While we were talking to the clerk and eating candy bars, the driver brought in cases of beer, using a two-wheeled hand truck to roll them through the open door. We continued to talk as the driver made his delivery.

Ibapah has a population of about two hundred, all Goshute Indians, including women, children, and old people, so I was surprised when the driver brought in two five-foot stacks of beer cases and was returning to his truck for more—a lot more. Ten minutes later, the entire middle of the store was crammed with more than seventy cases of beer. I asked the clerk what was going on.

She said this was the Thanksgiving order. If we wanted to see something truly amazing we ought to come back when the Christmas order arrived, which would be more than twice as big as this one. She explained that the Indians received food commodities and housing from the government. Those who wanted to could spend their entire monthly cash allowance on beer, and it seemed that Budweiser was the only brand they liked.

She said each Indian, except for children, received a monthly cash allowance from the government, usually three or four hundred dollars. The payments to the children were held in interest-bearing accounts, released to the child in a lump sum on his or her eighteenth birthday, which usually totaled fifty or sixty thousand dollars. She said the boys would buy a new pickup, spend the rest on booze and drugs, and usually be broke in six months to a year. The girls often used their money to go away to college or trade school.

As we rode up Johnson Canyon toward our summer range, we couldn't find the cows we were looking for, but we did find one of Hank Vogler's bulls, which having caught the scent of some Indian cows in heat, had wandered away from his home herd. It was dark by the time we herded the bull into a corral so we could load him in the trailer and take him back to Hank's grazing area.

The only problem was the bull didn't like being separated from the cows. He was mad at us. "On the fight" was the cowboy term to describe his attitude. We loaded our horses in the front part of the trailer and then backed up to the end of an alley where we hoped to run the bull into the back of the trailer. The only problem was that whenever one of us got into the pen with the bull to drive him into the alley, he would charge after us, forcing whoever it was in the pen to jump up on the fence.

We simply couldn't get him into the alley. I was about to give up trying to take him home, when Birdie removed her horse from the trailer. She told Bryce and me to be ready to slam the trailer door when she gave the signal.

Whereas the bull wouldn't let us near him when we were on foot, he allowed Birdie to ride right up to him on her horse and haze him into the alley. It was so dark we could not see what was happening, but we could hear the bull and Birdie's horse galloping up the alley toward the trailer.

The bull led the way and leapt into the trailer. At the same time, Birdie reached above her head with both hands and grabbed a support pole across the top of the alley.

"Now," she yelled as her horse leaped out from under her into the back of the trailer with the bull. We slammed and locked the door as Birdie dropped to the ground. Then she sauntered to the dark area in front of the truck, dropped her trousers, and took a whiz. Wow, what a cowgirl.

We summered about sixty cows at a place called Stone Cabin in Spring Valley, about forty miles to the west of the main ranch. The cattle did well there, but when we sold the calves in the fall, there were no corrals and chutes to load them into the big cattle trucks. So one snowy morning, my son Russell and I hauled our horses over there so we could drive the cattle nineteen miles to the Reed Robison ranch where there was a nice loading facility.

We started the drive about seven in the morning and were in the saddle until after dark. It snowed off and on throughout the day, and by midafternoon the cows and smaller calves didn't want to go any further. Neither did I, but we had no choice but to keep yelling and pushing. Of course, Russell was happy the entire time. He never complained at times like this.

In the early part of the day, when the cows were moving more easily, Russell spotted what looked like a little mustang off in the sagebrush. There were a lot of wild horses in this country, but it was unusual to see a young one all by itself. Russell rode over to check it out, and in a few minutes, he was galloping behind it. He pushed it into the middle of our herd of cows. It was a very skinny, pot-bellied mustang foal, apparently separated from its mother for some time. Perhaps the mother had died. It stayed with the cows all day, and when we finally pushed the cows into the Robison pasture that night, the little horse went with them.

Our main cowherd was grazing in an area of a hundred or so square miles with few fences and corrals. When stock needed doctoring and care, we did not have modern stock handling conveniences like calf tables and squeeze chutes. If we wanted to catch a calf, we usually roped it by the hind feet. If we caught two feet at the same time, the calf was quickly and easily immobilized so we could work on it.

If we wanted to catch a cow or a bull, one roper would usually catch a front foot to slow it down, while the second roper scooped up the hind feet. It was suicide to throw a loop around a bull's neck, especially on a rocky hillside. Our huge Chiangus bulls could pull a horse over in a second.

So we roped feet, and it was frustrating when you went to all the trouble to get your horse into position for a good catch and then missed because you didn't handle a rope very well.

As a result, I was constantly playing with my ropes, trying to improve my skill at roping feet. A friend, Jeff Wolf, welded two pipes to look like legs on the back end of a barrel that simulated a cow body. He propped it up in the yard by the house, and I would spend hours roping those pipe feet.

I had been team roping since doing the research for my Cassidy book, but I had mostly roped the heads and horns. With the necessity of roping feet to manage our cattle, I decided to become a heeler.

To occupy the time and keep myself from going to sleep at the wheel as I drove back and forth between Mapleton and the ranch, I started trying to figure out how I might build a better practice device; one with hind feet that hopped like those of a loping or hopping cow so I could learn the timing necessary to be more successful at roping feet.

At first I just wanted to build something that would help me rope better, but in time I decided that as much time as I was investing, I might as well go a step farther and build something that could be sold commercially to team ropers. Because I liked math and physics so much, when I first entered college I thought I would eventually become a civil or mechanical engineer. And whenever I took an aptitude test, I always scored highest in math and science subjects. Here was a chance to apply that aptitude. I was surprised how much my creative aptitude was challenged in trying to build what had not been built before. There were already roping practice machines where legs swung back and forth like pendulums, but no one had ever built one with an up and down hopping motion similar to that of a real cow.

I started dropping by a welding shop in Spanish Fork to get them to make the frame and some parts for me, but they never seemed to get around to doing anything. Jim Brown, who had helped me get started roping, could weld, so I explained my idea to him, but he thought I was nuts thinking I could make something ropers would want to buy. Finally, I ended up going over to Marion Manwill's home in Payson.

He had a welder, a cutting torch, grinders, and everything needed to build the metal parts. He roped too.

Marion would come over to rope. I called this our research on studying the movement of hind feet, and then we would fool around with the roping machine.

When we needed legs, I took a chain saw down to the fairgrounds where one of Paul Carnesecca's roping steers had died. It was frozen solid when I cut off one of its legs. A local vet put a plaster cast on the leg so we had a mold when we took off the cast. Eventually we had a fiberglass set of legs that looked pretty good.

For the body, we gave a big chunk of Styrofoam to Jeff Wolf. He came over and took some measurements on one of my live steers in the chute and carved the back half of a cow body out of the big piece of foam. Soon we had a fiberglass body.

We experimented with lots of different motors, sled designs, and mechanical workings. I noticed a tendency to add parts and complexity. It took a conscious effort to work toward simplicity. We built six or seven prototypes before we finally had one that worked well, and the final version was simpler, had fewer parts, and would be less expensive to build than the earlier prototypes. Albert Einstein said everything should be made as simple as possible, but not one bit simpler.

We mounted the roping machine on a sled with runners, and one of us would drag it around the arena behind a horse, pickup, or four-wheeler, while the other followed it on a horse, trying to rope the feet.

I took the prototype to attorney Dave Nelson and asked him to start the patent application process. By this time I think I had spent about fifteen thousand dollars, and I was getting really nervous. I finally had a machine I could practice on, which was my original intent, but it had cost too much. I figured we needed to sell a bunch of them to get my money back. There were legs and bodies with holes in the wrong places, steel parts cut too short, and underpowered and overpowered motors scattered around my barn.

One day I was talking to Rick Evans, author of the highly successful book *The Christmas Box*. He was an advertising executive, and before his book was published, he had helped get Bob Bennett elected to the United States Senate. I explained my roping machine idea, fishing for his expert advice. He said I needed to find a world champion team roper, one everyone knew about, and get him to endorse my machine. He said this was the single most important thing I could do. I made a video in which I showed the machine and explained how it worked and sent copies to three or four of the top ropers in the world.

About a month later, Allen Bach's wife called. Allen had been world champion three times. I had been to a school he put on with Jake Barnes. Allen was a great teacher, and everyone in team roping knew and respected him. In a few weeks, Allen was endorsing the Heel-O-Matic. I paid him one hundred dollars for each unit sold. He came to my house and helped produce a twenty-minute video in which I explained how the machine worked. Allen explained the fundamentals of heeling and how one could use the Heel-O-Matic to develop those fundamentals.

I started running ads in *SuperLooper*, the largest roping magazine at the time. The sole object of the ads was to get ropers to call and order the free video. It was the video that sold the machine. We had a toll-free number.

The first time the ad ran, I think we sold four machines in about a month, and then six or seven the next month. We rented shop space across from the fairgrounds and set up a little assembly line to build frames for a hundred machines at a time. The Pecks in Payson, who built boats, did the fiberglass work.

We started taking the machine to ropings and roping schools, and even to the big United States Team Roping Championships in Oklahoma City. By then we were selling a dozen or so units a month. We sold the Heel-O-Matic for $1,500. Later we raised the price to $1,695, since I started doing more advertising. That first year I believe I went to ten of Allen's roping schools; places like Portland, Sacramento, Phoenix, Billings, and a lot of places in Texas.

While the business was growing, I didn't have a lot of cash in the bank. I paid Marion a salary and tried to make my house and truck payments. Marion got mad one day and quit. He said I had paid him a fair wage for everything he had done, so we could call it even, no hard feelings, and he walked out the door.

I moved to a commercial building owned by Jim Brown, which was located west of the freeway, and hired Jim to build and ship the machines. I paid him one hundred dollars a unit on each machine sold. He could answer the phone when I wasn't around and make sales. He worked hard and did a good job. By now we were up to about twenty units a month.

Then I had a great promotional idea. I announced the Heel-O-Matic Challenge. I invited ten heelers to come to Allen's arena near Phoenix to be guinea pigs in an experiment. On the day the ropers arrived with their horses, we would turn ten cows for each man and write down their scores. We'd record how many they caught by two feet, one foot, and how many misses. For three days the participants would do nothing but rope the Heel-O-Matic. They would rope stationary machines from platforms and moving ones from horseback. They would have a thousand practice opportunities on the Heel-O-Matic every day. Then, after the third day, we would turn another ten live cows for each participant and write down the results. We promised to publish the results, good or bad, in *SuperLooper*. We charged each participant three hundred dollars and were filled up a week after the ad came out.

It was a lot of work, but when the dust settled and we evaluated the results, the participants caught twice as many feet the last day, essentially doubling their ability to rope feet with only three days of practice on the Heel-O-Matic. These results became the focus of our ads in the months to come.

The following December we sold sixty-two machines, and Allen introduced me to Dennis Carroll, who wanted to buy the business. I agreed to sell it for an amount I thought would scare him off. When he agreed to pay it, I felt a little sick, thinking I could have gotten more, but I went ahead with the deal. After giving some of the proceeds to Allen and Marion, I paid off a line of credit and covered losses on cattle in Nevada. It was time to write some more books. I was pleasantly surprised a few years later when a Chevy truck ad on the Super Bowl showed a new truck dragging my Heel-O-Matic in front of a mounted teenage boy learning to rope.

While all this was going on, my book distributor in Salt Lake City called to announce he was going out of business. I'd been so busy with the roping machines and ranching challenges that I hadn't noticed their troubles. I took the inventory down to Lyle Mortimer at Cedar Fort, Inc. Instead of paying me for the books, he made me a partner. We were located in a building Lyle owned at the north end of Springville.

Lyle and I had gotten to know each other through the *Beyond the Veil* series. After Raymond Moody's book *Life After Life* had become an international bestseller, Lyle decided to publish a book similar in content and theme for the LDS market. He had several false starts with writers who couldn't seem to get it done, so one day he approached me and asked me to interview about twenty people who had out-of-body or near death experiences. I would write up their stories, and he would publish them in a book called *Beyond the Veil*. I asked him where I would find the people to interview. He said he didn't know, that I was the writer and ought to be able to figure that out. I told him I'd think about it a day or two and get back to him. He said he'd be willing to pay an advance.

That afternoon I attended one of my son's soccer games at Springville High School. While visiting with parents and friends along the sidelines, I mentioned the project Lyle was trying to get me to write, and people started making suggestions.

"Call my sister in Lehi. Her neighbor was electrocuted in an industrial accident. He was dead for half an hour and can tell you about it."

"My mother in Seattle has a good friend who died during childbirth. She was pronounced dead, but she returned and has an amazing story . . ."

Such were the comments. By the end of the soccer match, I had written down the phone numbers of four people I could call who would help set up interviews with individuals who had died and returned to tell about it.

In my research, I discovered that Gallup did a poll in which they estimated that as many as six million Americans have had some kind of out-of-body experience, and that the number of individuals experiencing this phenomenon was much larger than anyone ever thought before Moody's book was published.

I started interviewing people in earnest, eventually soliciting the help of my son, Richard, who by this time was a student at BYU. In time, four books were published, selling hundreds of thousands of copies. Every month I received a royalty check from Lyle. Sometimes when we'd meet, he'd suggest that I bring in my *Storm Testament* books and let Cedar Fort be my publisher. So when my distributor went broke, that's what I did. I trusted Lyle.

He had become a good friend. It was the right thing to do.

My responsibility at Cedar Fort was to go through the manuscript submissions to find ones we could publish. At that time we were receiving about five hundred submissions a year. A lot of the manuscripts were obviously not good enough to publish, making them easy to reject and send back. Also, once in a while we found one that we knew would be successful, so we'd send the author a contract and publish it. Sometimes we were wrong and the book would not sell. The biggest frustration was all the submissions in between; the ones we thought might sell, but then again, might not. You could spend so much time and energy discussing the merits, and in the end, you were still just guessing.

While working in acquisitions, I wrote and published *Black Hawk Journey, Ephraim Chronicles, Thousand Souls*, and *Born to Rope*.

In the spring of 2002, I remembered an unfinished story by Mark Twain that had been published in *Life Magazine* in January 1968. I remembered reading the story in the BYU barbershop at the time, how Huck, Tom, and Jim were heading west to have adventures with the Indians. After about fifteen thousand words, while Huck and Tom were following some Indians in a daring attempt to rescue two white girls who had been kidnapped, Twain suddenly stopped writing in the middle of a sentence, never to go back and finish the story. His working title was *Huck Finn and Tom Sawyer Among the Indians*.

The thought occurred to me that I could finish Twain's story. I certainly had done plenty of research on the Indians of the 1800s. A little research on the Internet revealed that the Mark Twain Foundation and the University of California Press still owned the rights, the copyright period beginning in 1968 when it was published in *Life Magazine*.

My e-mails to the foundation were passed back and forth and forwarded, until I ended up communicating with the UC Press lawyer, Dan Dixon, who was extremely accommodating. In short order we had a simple agreement wherein I could finish the story. The foundation received a percentage of the royalties equal to the percentage of words in the final work written by Mark Twain. Their percentage turned out to be about 20 percent. I didn't have to pay any money up front. I went ahead and finished the story before the end of the year.

CHAPTER XXV

Writing a personal history is the process of using words to paint a self-portrait. Some say a picture is worth a thousand words, but I say a thousand words can be worth ten thousand pictures.

—LEE NELSON

Sometimes people ask if I'm ever afraid to get on a horse after all the close calls. I like to think I have become more cautious over time, but I don't have a fear of getting in the saddle, especially if the horse or mule is an old friend I have learned to trust.

Sometimes at the end of a ride, when we are about to jump the horses into the trailer to return home, I'll mention to Russell or my good friend Gary Fulton that we're about to begin the most dangerous portion of our journey. They know what I mean. Pulling a trailer full of horses down a busy highway at sixty miles per hour is more dangerous than riding a horse down a trail at six miles per hour. On the highway we're at the mercy of other drivers who may be as tired as we are, or talking on cell phones or drinking.

There was one time, however, when I was so afraid I felt physically sick, not from anything a horse did, but something I did with my horse trailer.

The upper portion of my aluminum four-horse trailer extends

over the pickup box so the hitch can attach to a ball mounted in the center of the box directly over the axle. This type of hookup gives the truck and trailer excellent stability when moving down the highway at high speeds.

I don't remember where I was going or how many horses I was hauling when I backed under the front of the trailer on this particular day. My youngest son, Benjamin, probably seven or eight at the time, climbed into the back of the truck to secure the hitch to the ball, something he often did because I could not reach it from the ground where I stood.

A minute later I was driving slowly out of the barnyard, over a berm or mound where an irrigation ditch passed under the driveway. Ben didn't respond to something I said, so I wondered if he had stayed in the box. I glanced in the rearview mirror. Apparently he had moved to the back of the box to look over the closed tailgate at the ground moving beneath the truck, perhaps looking for the dog. His little hands were frantically pushing, pulling, and slapping at the tailgate. It appeared his head was stuck between the top edge of the tailgate and the steel beam supporting the front portion of the trailer. As the front axle of the truck moved down the far side of the berm, the rear axle was still moving to the top of the berm, causing the tailgate to move closer to the steel bottom of the trailer. If I kept moving, the gap might narrow even more—perhaps several more inches—and in the process, partially crush my little boy's head.

I braked to a stop, wondering if I had seriously injured or even killed my son already. I couldn't be absolutely sure where the rear wheels were in relation to the top of the berm, so instead of backing up, I shifted into park and set the emergency brake. Jumping out of the cab, I said, "Benjamin, are you all right?" I feared he was already too badly injured to be able to answer.

"My head is caught," he said. He was not crying.

"Hold still."

I ran to the back of the truck, carefully unlatched the tailgate, and slowly pulled it open. His head was free. There was a guilty look on his face, like he had done something wrong. Instead of scolding him, I wanted to hug and kiss him, but I turned around and stepped toward the ditch instead. I was physically sick, thinking

I was going to throw up in the next instant.

I felt a little better in a minute and we went into the house. I sat down in the family room and told Sharon what had happened. It was a half hour before my legs felt strong enough to go back outside. By that time we had a new rule; nobody ever again would be allowed in the pickup box when the ball was hitched to a trailer—not ever. As far as I know, that rule has never been broken.

I never felt this way when my own life was at risk. A close call never made me sick. Sometimes, after looking death in the eye, I talk to myself. *Sooner or later I'm going to find out what's on the other side of the veil. Might as well be sooner,* or, *I'd rather go like this than in a rest home while a gum-chewing teenager is changing my diaper.*

But with your children, the feelings are different—more intense. I remember all my children as beautiful, happy, and smart, but one time I remember looking at Sarah when she was three or four years old as she played hopscotch in her snow boots in July. I thought to myself, *I think my little Sarah is the most beautiful child on this planet. I can't imagine any child anywhere being more beautiful than this one.*

I think I'm a pretty normal parent having feelings like this for a child. But sometimes that love can take a sinister turn.

When my oldest daughter, Virginia, was sixteen, she was one of the top players on the Springville High School tennis team. She was trim and beautiful, with long blond hair. Strange cars started cruising up our long driveway, with boys wanting to see Virginia. I didn't know how to behave around them. Should I be openly friendly and swap silly jokes with them, hoping to make them feel comfortable at our home? Or should I remain distant and mysterious in the hope they might treat my daughter better if they were afraid of me?

That year I had bought ten yearling longhorn bulls for our roping practice. They seemed a little rowdy at times and not as agreeable to the team roping routine as steers usually are, so I decided to castrate them—not all at once, but one or two each night as it fit into our usual practice routine. When the header caught two horns instead of a neck so the bull wouldn't choke when stretched out on the ground, and when the heeler scooped up two feet, which prevented the animal from thrashing about too much, those two ropers would hold the bull stretched out on the ground while someone else jumped off his horse and performed the necessary procedure to turn that bull into a steer.

That's when the boy who seemed to be coming up our driveway the most cruised into the barnyard to ask if Virginia was around. When I told him we needed a hand doctoring one of the bulls, he agreed to help.

Right away two of us caught a bull by the horns and both hind feet. I told the boy how to sit on the front shoulder and hold up a front leg, further immobilizing the little bull. Then, one of the ropers on the ground pulled out his pocketknife, bent over the bull, grabbed the scrotum, and sliced away the bottom portion. He squeezed the testicles until they popped into view and then slowly cut the connecting tissue.

I told the boy not to look so surprised. Cowboys did this kind of thing all the time. I had probably done it a hundred times. It was easy—no big deal. Then I said what I had been wanting to say all along.

"If anyone ever hurts one of my daughters in a sexual way . . . I think you know what I mean . . . this is what I would want to do to him before calling the police."

He laughed like I had told a joke, but it was a nervous laugh. The boy hurried to his car and left. I'm not sure how much he avoided me after that, but I can say he was the most polite and respectful high school senior I have ever known.

I'm a storyteller. I love to listen to stories, read stories, tell stories, and write stories. When I meet a person who can't tell a good story around the campfire but wants to write fiction, I seriously doubt that person will ever succeed as a novelist.

I find stories I like to tell about everything I do. I have horse stories, hunting stories, children stories, gardening stories, sports stories, love stories, dog stories, fishing stories, and even business stories. If I can't find the right story for a situation or interest, I make one up. Some stories have profound meaning; others are downright stupid and silly, but I love them anyway.

Shortly after my hip replacement surgery, when it was no longer painful to get on a horse, I went on a day ride with Jason Parkinson up Kirkham Hollow in the right-hand fork of Hobble Creek Canyon. Jason had been active in high school rodeo before fulfilling a mission to Oregon and was going to college. He was helping me start a bay mare.

We were riding up a fairly decent cattle trail. At a fork, where the canyon was narrow with steep hillsides on both sides, Jason said that if he were an Indian, he would pick this spot as a perfect place to ambush white men. Noticing the many big rocks on the steep hillsides where an ambushing Indian might hide, I agreed with him. Then he said, "Lee, you make a living using the English language. Tell me where the word ambush comes from."

"I can do that," I said.

"Illegal immigration from Mexico is nothing new. Ever since the Mexican-American war in the mid-eighteen hundreds, illegal aliens from Mexico have been entering the United States.

"Two of the first ones were Juan and Pedro. As they were coming up through Arizona, though they had plenty of water, they had run out of food and were beginning to fear that they might starve.

" 'Have no fear,' Juan yells. 'We will not starve after all. I see a bacon tree.'

" 'What is a bacon tree?' Pedro asks.

" 'In America, many kinds of foods grow on trees; not just apples, peaches, and cherries, but smoked meats too. I see a bacon tree. Let's hurry.'

"They get to the tree and begin pulling down pieces of bacon, slices of ham, and sausages. After filling their bellies, they start filling their pockets.

"A shot rings out. Juan gets hit in the leg. They dive behind a fallen log. Another shot rings out. Pedro gets hit in the shoulder.

" 'I am so sorry,' Juan cries. 'I made a terrible mistake.'

" 'What do you mean?' Pedro asks.

" 'This is not a bacon tree. It's a ham bush.' "

After we finished laughing over my little story, Jason expressed surprise that I would give such a silly answer to his serious question. I explained that since I didn't know the nonfiction answer to his question, I gave him a fiction answer. As a writer of fiction, that's what I like to do, and sometimes fiction answers are better than nonfiction answers.

As part owner of the Cedar Fort book publishing company, there's a story I love to tell when I am asked to speak to company gatherings. I think some of the long-term employees get tired of me telling it, but the message to book publishers is profound, and so well expressed in this little story that I just keep telling it.

The sales people for a major dog food manufacturer are gathered in a banquet room at the annual sales meeting. The sales people are seated at dinner tables while the sales manager is speaking. From his red and scowling face, it is obvious he is bothered about something.

He asks, "Which dog food has the best advertisements?"

"Ours does," the sales people respond in unison.

"Which dog food has the most attractive label, the best design?"

"Ours does."

"Which dog food has the best pricing and easiest payment terms for the retailers?"

"Ours does."

"Which dog food has the most vitamins and minerals?"

"Ours does."

The sales manager pauses for a minute, his face more crimson than ever. His voice louder now, he demands, "Then why don't we sell more dog food?"

The room is quiet. Nobody wants to answer his question. He asks a second time, his voice now a whisper.

"Why don't we sell more dog food?"

Again the room is quiet, but people notice that a man in the back row has raised his hand. The sales manager motions for him to speak.

"The dogs don't like it."

If I am in my garden in May and June when a visitor shows up, I walk him through the garden showing him the asparagus, strawberries, grapes, rhubarb, horseradish, corn, tomatoes, spinach, radishes, onions, potatoes, beets, beans, cucumbers, squash, melons, herbs, and anything else I might be trying to grow that season.

Sometimes visitors to my garden want to ask a question when we shake hands and they feel the blisters on my hand. Why would the author of so many books and a publisher involved in serious book ventures want to spend so much time gardening, shoeing horses, and cleaning irrigation ditches when it would be easier to hire teenagers to do such work?

That's when I tell the story about the southern farmer whose prize pig won the blue ribbon at the county fair every year. The other farmers visited him one day, wanting to know why his pig always got the blue ribbon while theirs were winning red, white, and yellow ribbons. All the pigs shared the same bloodlines and were fed the same kinds of feed. Why did his pigs always win the blue ribbons?

The farmer agrees to share his secret with his friends. He points to a little pig in the barnyard and says that this is the one he is confident will win the blue ribbon at the next fair. He picks up the little pig and places it on his shoulders. Then he walks toward the nearest oak tree and stops under one of the low-hanging branches. The little pig reaches up with his mouth and picks some of the best acorns.

"You see," the farmer says. "I do this with my show pigs, making it possible for them to reach the biggest and best acorns without having to compete with the deer and cows and other pigs for the acorns on the ground. This is why my show pigs are bigger and healthier when I enter them in the fair."

"But isn't it awful time consuming?" asks one of the visitors.

"What's time to a pig?" the farmer responded.

Sometimes when I tell this story, I'm not sure my visitor understands what I'm trying to say. As I get older, I find myself less interested in activities driven by time and money. Planting a seed in rich soil and expecting it to become a beautiful, healthy plant is an activity that makes me feel good. Slipping into the saddle and feeling a thousand pounds of muscle, blood, bone, a little brain, and a lot of energy, ready to take you any place you want to go, is every bit as exciting for me as climbing into the cockpit of an airplane. Hoeing and shoveling up weeds in my garden or irrigation ditch is as much fun as shooting down monsters in a video game. Sometimes it was hard convincing my children of this. As a young man, I learned to do hard physical work, something I continue to enjoy as I get older, though I am no longer able to do as much. I like the feel of sore muscles and sweat on my brow, blisters on my hands and dirt under my fingernails.

As a young man I set a goal to write books, and then, when asked to give speeches about my books, be able to do it without anguish. I wanted to live in a rural setting, surrounded by children and grandchildren, growing things in the soil, and working with cattle and horses. I have done that.

While enjoying my hobbies and rural lifestyle, I am determined to be seated before my computer each morning before 6:00 a.m., working on my next book. Unless a person is sick or handicapped in some way, I think it's a bad idea to start your day with your head on the same level as your gut. When you wake up, get up. If I can start the day with three or four hours of writing, I have a good day. Sometimes I will spend eight hours in reading and study that I call research.

It annoys me when someone reads one of my books or hears me give a speech and then says something about how easy they think it is for me to speak and write, as if it isn't fair that what is so hard for almost everyone else is so easy for me. They don't understand. Everything is hard before it is easy. After setting goals as a young man, I worked very hard for many years to achieve those goals. None of it was easy, though I think I was very lucky at times.

I know a lot of people who would prefer to just pass quietly into the night, leaving no written account behind at all. As good as that may sound at times, many of us have the same problem I have. If we don't do it ourselves, a well-meaning relative or biographer might step in and do it for us. The problem is that when loved ones write about us, there's a temptation to make us better or worse than we really are, or create a picture of our life that isn't very accurate or truthful, even though they think it is.

I write novels, believing that while nonfiction is about fact, fiction is about truth. I feel sorry for people who don't read fiction, who say they don't want to waste their time reading something that is not true, that didn't really happen, and that someone just made up. Some of the greatest learning experiences of my life occurred while reading someone else's novel.

I honestly believe those who come after, if they really want to get to know me, may discover more in my novels than in this personal history. Sure, there are more biographical facts here, but a more important side of my life, the lessons learned through living, reading, suffering and pondering; the deep feelings, the convictions that comprise my physical and spiritual self tend to permeate the fiction perhaps more than the nonfiction.

So I keep writing even in my retirement years. I have six or eight new works in the research and outline stage. I hope to finish them before I die, if good health and good fortune remain on my side and my four-legged guardian angel, Ingersoll, continues to look out for me.

I spent about ten years working on this personal history. I cringe to think how my posterity would see my life had I not undertaken this work. I wonder how some will react when they realize I am not who they thought I am. I'm hoping that my readers, along with being entertained, amused, and surprised, will be able to share with me, at least in part, some of the lessons learned.

Sometimes early in the quiet of the morning, when I am sitting at the computer while the world around me is still sleeping, I can feel hoof beats in my heart, whispering words to my soul. Sometimes they make sense and seem to be saying something like this:

> As offspring of the great God, and as beneficiaries of the Atonement, we hold in our DNA the power to control matter and energy and to heal the sick. We can obtain knowledge from God, see and talk with angels, communicate without words—even to animals and rocks—and travel with our minds through time and space and beyond. These gifts are dormant in each of us until awakened by the light, a potential that staggers the imagination, limited only by selfishness, human frailty, lack of vision, and laziness. Each of us has a place in the grand kingdom of heaven, which is waiting for us to discover it, perhaps just a little piece at a time, as the glorious panorama opens before us.

INDEX

Books by Lee Nelson

Available in some bookstores and online, and at
Cedarfort.com. Call 801-489-4084 for more information.

The Storm Testament

Dan Storm and escaped slave Ike flee Missouri mobs to face a fiercer destiny in the Rocky Mountains. The Storm Testament series is Nelson's best-selling fiction work, with nearly half a million books in print.

The Storm Testament II

Hired by a Philadelphia publisher to write the inside story on polygamy, Caroline Logan finds herself in a whirlwind of adventure, conflict, and romance as the Mormons flee westward to the Rocky Mountains.

The Storm Testament III

Sam Storm finds a profitable trade in firewater and stolen horses as he seeks the hand of the most beautiful woman in Great Salt Lake City, until a bizarre chain of events drags him and the women he loves into one of the most ruthless and deadly business schemes of the nineteenth century.

The Storm Testament IV

Dan Storm joins Porter Rockwell in the 1857 war against Johnston's Army, but he soon finds himself with Ike, the black Goshute war chief, trailing killer Dick Boggs and the Fancher wagon train south to Mountain Meadows.

Storm Testament V

Ben Storm declares war on the anti-Mormon forces of the 1880s, gunning for U.S. marshals and establishing a sanctuary for pregnant plural wives.

Rockwell, Storm Testament VI

In this biographical novel, a timid farm boy from New York becomes the greatest gun fighter in the history of the American West.

Walkara, Storm Testament VII

A biographical novel about a Ute savage from Spanish Fork Canyon who became the greatest horse thief in the history of the American West.

Cassidy, Storm Testament VIII

A biographical novel about the Mormon farm boy from Southern Utah Territory, who put together the longest string of successful bank and train robberies in the history of the American West.

Storm Gold, Storm Testament IX

A rich historical novel set in the Spanish history of Utah before the Mormon pioneers came, an era ending in a massacre bigger than the one at Little Big Horn, one that didn't get in the history books because the Indians, who didn't keep written records, were the winners.

The Blackhawk Journey, Storm Testament X

Half-breed Silas Hastings seeks forbidden love as Ute warriors sweep across Central Utah leaving death and destruction in their path.

The Ephraim Chronicles

Learn the true story of the great bear of the Cache Mountains through the fictional eyes of Danny Evans, the boy who lived with the grizzlies.

Huck Finn and Tom Sawyer among the Indians

Sequel to *The Adventures of Huckleberry Finn*, began by Mark Twain in 1885 and finished by Lee Nelson in 2003.

Born to Rope

"In *Born to Rope* I found something I didn't know I'd lost. Not since I was a child reading *King of the Wind* did I find myself caring like this about a horse."

—Warren Hatch, Salt Press

The Wasatch Savage

A white bull running free with the wild buffalo on Antelope Island brings the lives of four people onto a common path as the powerful story of *The Wasatch Savage* unfolds.

The Moriah Confession

In the heart of Utah's west desert wilderness, they call the wind and the mountain Moriah.

A Thousand Souls

Elder Nelson's autobiographical novel about heading off to Southern Germany in 1961 to convert a thousand souls.

Beyond the Veil (four volumes)

Each volume contains about twenty true near-death experiences, the stories of people who died, went beyond the veil, and returned to tell about it. Nearly half a million copies sold. These are Nelson's best-selling nonfiction books.

The Last Great Secret of the Third Reich

Coauthored with Arthur Naujoks, this is the true story of a Nazi submarine captain and a Luftwaffe general who defied Nazi orders and delivered their nuclear payload to the Americans instead of the Japanese—a course of action that very well may have changed the outcome of the war in the Pacific, saved millions of lives, and altered the course of modern history; a story lost in top secret files and documents until now.

Contact Lee at

authorleenelson@gmail.com